OXFORD EARLY CHRISTIAN STUDIES

General Editors

Gillian Clark   Andrew Louth

THE OXFORD EARLY CHRISTIAN STUDIES series includes scholarly volumes on the thought and history of the early Christian centuries. Covering a wide range of Greek, Latin, and Oriental sources, the books are of interest to theologians, ancient historians, and specialists in the classical and Jewish worlds.

Titles in the series include:

Hilary of Poitiers on the Trinity
From *De Fide* to *De Trinitate*
Carl L. Beckwith (2008)

The Easter Computus and the
Origins of the Christian Era
Alden A. Mosshammer (2008)

The Letters of Jerome
Asceticism, Biblical Exegesis, and the
Construction of Christian Authority in Late Antiquity
Andrew Cain (2009)

Basil of Caesarea, Gregory of Nyssa, and the
Transformation of Divine Simplicity
Andrew Radde-Gallwitz (2009)

The Asceticism of Isaac of Nineveh
Patrik Hagman (2010)

Palladius of Helenopolis
The Origenist Advocate
Demetrios S. Katos (2011)

Origen and Scripture
The Contours of the Exegetical Life
Peter Martens (2012)

Activity and Participation in Late Antique and Early Christian Thought
Torstein Theodor Tollefsen (2012)

Irenaeus of Lyons and the Theology of the Holy Spirit
Anthony Briggman (2012)

Apophasis and Pseudonymity in Dionysius the Areopagite
'No Longer I'
Charles M. Stang (2012)

Memory in Augustine's Theological Anthropology
Paige E. Hochschild (2012)

Orosius and the Rhetoric of History

PETER VAN NUFFELEN

OXFORD
UNIVERSITY PRESS

OXFORD
UNIVERSITY PRESS

Great Clarendon Street, Oxford, OX2 6DP,
United Kingdom

Oxford University Press is a department of the University of Oxford.
It furthers the University's objective of excellence in research, scholarship,
and education by publishing worldwide. Oxford is a registered trade mark of
Oxford University Press in the UK and in certain other countries

First published 2012
Impression: 1

British Library Cataloguing in Publication Data
Data available

Library of Congress Cataloging in Publication Data
Data available

ISBN 978-0-19-965527-4

Printed in Great Britain by
MPG Books Group, Bodmin and King's Lynn

Table of Contents

Preface

This monograph argues that close study of the rhetorical features and intentions of Orosius' *Historiae adversus paganos* permits a fundamental reassessment of the work. Often read as a theology of history in disguise rather than a proper history, Orosius' *Histories* can in fact be shown to deploy the breadth of rhetorical tools that classical historians used, with the ultimate aim of undermining the traditional, glorious view of the Roman past. This book constitutes, as it were, a digression from another monograph on late antique historiography. Because Orosius has often been depicted as the paradigm of how Christians wrote history, it hopes nevertheless to contribute to our general understanding of the writing of history in late Antiquity.

Research for this book was largely done at Oxford, where I was a Visiting Member of the Corpus Christi Classics Centre in 2009–10. I wish to thank Neil McLynn for hosting me and the Flemish Research Fund for funding the stay. He and Bryan Ward-Perkins invited me to give a paper on Orosius in their research seminar and I thank all present for their useful comments—not least Matthew Kempshall, who suggested the cover illustration. Parts of the book were presented to audiences in Brussels and Seville. A first draft was written during a stay in the Fondation Hardt (Geneva) in May and June 2010. Thanks to its dedicated staff, it is one of the few institutions in the world where one can write up a monograph in two months.

My sincerest thanks go to the series editors for accepting the book and offering much good advice. The comments of the external reader encouraged me to rethink my argument and to rewrite parts of the book. I also wish to thank the editorial staff of Oxford University Press for their efficient work. I thank Duckworth Publishers for allowing me to use material first published in Van Nuffelen (2010).

As ever, my most stringent critic was my wife, Lieve Van Hoof, who once again commented thoroughly on the entire manuscript. Having exhausted my ways of saying thanks in previous publications, I shall now have recourse to a most sincere *praeteritio*.

Note on Abbreviations

Abbreviations of journal titles follow the list of *L'Année philologique* (www.annee-philologique.com/aph/). Other abbreviations used in this book are:

ANRW	= Haase, W., e.a. (1972–) *Aufstieg und Niedergang der römischen Welt. Geschichte und Kultur Roms im Spiegel der neueren Forschung*. Berlin and New York, Walter de Gruyter.
FGrHist	= Jacoby, F., e.a. (1922–) *Die Fragmente der griechischen Historiker*. Berlin and Leiden, Weidmannsche Buchhandlung and Brill.
LCL	= (1912–) *Loeb Classical Library*. London and Cambridge (Mass.), Heinemann and Harvard University Press.
PL	= Migne, J.P. (1844–55, 1862–6) *Patrologia Latina*. Paris, Petit-Montrouge.

References to Orosius are to the *Historiae*, unless specified otherwise.

Introduction

The Spanish presbyter Orosius wrote his *Historiae adversus paganos* in 416/7, at the behest of Augustine.[1] Intended as a companion to the *City of God*, it has a similar apologetic aim, that is, demonstrating that the pagan perception of the classical Roman past as a time of glory and triumph is mistaken. The concomitant view that Christianity is responsible for the decline of Rome, as evidenced in Alaric's sack of Rome in AD 410, is turned upside down: in fact, Orosius argues, one is now better off than in the times of old. The *Historiae* tend to have a rather negative press in scholarship and are often seen as a superficial and ideologically charged compilation of earlier histories. This judgment has been extended to their author, whose intellectual qualities have been doubted. The present book puts forward a different view of Orosius and situates the *Historiae* in the context of the writing of history in the fourth and fifth centuries AD and in that of the rhetorical education of the period—two contexts that are, in fact, intimately linked. The more literary approach espoused here will, I hope, not only lead to a revaluation of the *Historiae*, but also generate a better understanding of the way history was written in the Latin West in late Antiquity.

I. OPTIMISM IN THE FACE OF ADVERSITY

A much maligned historian, Orosius seems to be in constant need of revisionism. Indeed, one of the first book-length studies of the

[1] Martínez Cavero 2002a: 52–4.

Historiae, A. Lippold's 1952 dissertation, presented itself as revisionist, emphasizing the need to study Orosius as a historian in contrast with more theological readings.[2] The present monograph, albeit very different in scope, approach, and outcome from Lippold's, has a similar aim. Hence, before I detail my own approach, it may be important to explain why, sixty years later, it still is necessary to make a similar argument. Apart from an intuitive dislike of apologetic in history among contemporary scholars, which seems to go against the duties of the modern historian, two specific reasons are, in my view, crucial.

The first is the fact that the optimism of the *Historiae* jars with our view of the fifth century in the Roman West as one prolonged agony. Although he does not deny the numerous problems that faced the empire in the first decades of the century, Orosius narrates them in a series of panegyrical chapters that conclude the work. Notwithstanding the efforts of recent scholarship,[3] the battle of Adrianople (378), the invasion of Radagaisus (405/6), and the sack of Rome (410) are still often seen as steps towards the inexorable fall of the Western empire.[4] Whereas Orosius sees conditions improving, even in the West after a series of invasions and usurpations, we see a tottering empire. It is the tragedy of Orosius that the green shoots of the stabilization of Roman power, which lend his vision some credibility, were soon swept away, leaving his optimism destitute. It does not help much that many shared his optimism in the years around 417/8[5]—even pagans such as Rutilius Namatianus and Olympiodorus of Thebes:[6] the collapse of the Western empire stigmatizes the *Historiae* as an inadequate assessment of their own age. The challenge of a study of Orosius is therefore to blend out our foreknowledge of what was to follow and to understand his history as the product of a very specific moment in time when optimism still seemed permitted. This is not to suggest that Orosius' optimism is merely the result of historical circumstances: it obviously is also driven by the apologetic intentions of the *Historiae*, being written at the demand of Augustine to supplement the argument of the *City of God*.

[2] Lippold 1952: 1, 66.
[3] See the overview of Pohl 2008.
[4] See most recently Ward-Perkins 2005 and Heather 2009.
[5] Courcelle 1964: 102–14.
[6] Rutilius Namatianus, *De reditu* 1.141–4. For Olympiodorus, see Van Nuffelen (forthcoming).

II. THE SHADOW OF AUGUSTINE

The second reason is, indeed, the special relationship that Orosius entertains with Augustine, a relationship that is even closer than the mere fact that the latter is the dedicatee of the *Historiae*. Indeed, Orosius is the paradigm of how an individual can come into the spotlight of history through association with a more famous person and how he can virtually disappear from our sight once that relationship has ended. Orosius arrived in Hippo in 414, from Braga in Galicia,[7] to see Augustine, and left Africa in 418. He made a voyage to Jerome in Bethlehem in between and intervened there unsuccessfully in the pelagian controversy. The only important testimony to his life besides his acquaintance with the two most famous Latin fathers of his age is in the Letter of Severus of Minorca, describing the arrival of the relics of Saint Stephen on the island (418). The presbyter said in the letter to be accompanying the relics of Saint Stephen to Minorca is probably Orosius. He is depicted as planning to return to Spain but forced to go to Africa.[8] What Orosius did before 414 and after 418 is a matter of speculation.[9] Although he also visited Jerome, it is mainly Augustine with whom Orosius was involved. Indeed, Orosius deliberately sought to establish a link with Augustine and, as I shall argue in this book, consciously tried to cash in on the latter's fame. He gained his place in history through advertising his intimacy with the most famous Latin Church father.

Whether the intimacy with Augustine is historical or not is of less importance than its consequences for how the *Historiae* have been read. Indeed, Augustine casts a long shadow on Orosius. Commanded by, and dedicated to, the bishop of Hippo, the *Historiae* are usually read in the light of Augustine's theology and thus as a theology of history rather than a proper history. The traditional

[7] *Epistula Aviti ad Palchonium* PL 41.805–7. The most likely origin, but not the only one proposed: see Martínez Cavero 2002a: 22–5; Fear 2010a: 3.

[8] Severus, *Epistula* 4.1–2.

[9] That Orosius died soon after 418 in a shipwreck (Arnaud-Lindet 1990–1: i.ix) is an example of such speculation. I follow the traditional chronology, as set out in Vilella 2000. The chronology proposed in Bradbury 1996: 24–5 and Fear 2010a: 5 situates the transfer of the relics and visit to Minorca before the writing of the *Historiae*.

On Orosius' life, see also Lippold 1976: i.xi–xxii; Torres Rodríguez 1985: 16–45; Arnaud-Lindet 1990–1: i.ix–xx; Martínez Cavero 2002a; Fear 2010a: 3–7.

approach is well summed up in the title of a classic article by Hans-Werner Goetz: *Orosius und die Barbaren: Zu den umstrittenen Vorstellungen eines spätantiken Geschichtstheologen* (1980b). Goetz defines Orosius as a theologian of history, not as a historian, who is supposed to have systematic views that can be reconstructed and assessed.

This approach to Orosius has deep roots in scholarship on historiography of late Antiquity: it is commonly assumed that in Christian historiography, theology trumps history. Because Christianity is a historical religion and sees time evolving from Creation through Incarnation to the Second Coming, so it is argued, all Christian histories aim at tracing God's plan of salvation.[10] There is therefore no meaningful distinction between exegesis, theology, and historiography in the Christian mind. In such a view, Christian historiography does not have an identity of its own, but is a subcontractor for theology. As a consequence, a Church history and Augustine's *City of God* can be depicted as identical undertakings.[11] Unsurprisingly, then, studies of Christian historiography have often seen literary and historiographical characteristics as merely preparatory for the real questions on the divinely inspired evolution of history. To quote again H.-W. Goetz, in his monograph on Orosius' theology of history: 'Das Anliegen des christlichen Geschichtschreibers ist notwendigerweise die Geschichtsdeutung.'[12] Recently, one scholar has equated intertextuality, secular historiography, Hellenism, and paganism.[13] Secular works of history are thus complex, allusive, and artful; Christian histories are simple, unelaborated, and theologies in disguise.

As we shall see in more detail below, scholars have started to explore the importance of genre and literary art in Christian histories, thus questioning the false divide between Christian and 'classicizing' histories in late Antiquity. This is, I would suggest, also the route to be taken by scholarship on Orosius: we can only gain new insights in the *Historiae* on condition that we take its self-description and self-understanding as a history seriously. Whilst not denying that Orosius

[10] Dawson 1977: 30–7; Latourelle 1977: 75–7; Luiselli 1980; Goetz 1991: 247; Winkelmann 2002; Wallraff 2004 and 2005: 4. A strong influence was exercised by Löwith 1953.

[11] Luiselli 1980: 518; Press 1982: 123–6; Zakai and Mali 1992–3; Allan 2003: 24–5; Alonso-Nuñez 2005.

[12] Goetz 1980a: 44.

[13] Kaldellis 2004.

had some ideas, this book argues that we cannot try to deduct views from a work of history without understanding it on its own terms. As a profoundly rhetorical work (as any history from Antiquity), opinions that are aired need to be situated in their narrative and argumentative context, and cannot be isolated to construct the fragile edifice of Orosius' theology of history.

III. THE MASTER MISUNDERSTOOD

The most important shift in scholarship on Orosius happened in the middle of the twentieth century and regards his intellectual relationship with Augustine. For a long time the *Historiae* had been interpreted as an illustration of some of the themes of the *City of God*, as Orosius' preface itself suggests. Little difference was noticed between Augustine's view of history and that of Orosius. This view changed slowly in the *interbellum* and radically in the early fifties.[14] Scholars started to notice in the *City of God* the depreciation of human history in favour of personal salvation, and the opposition between ephemeral felicity of this world and the eternal beatitude of the world to come. The optimistic view of the *Historiae*, where Christianity is depicted as improving the world and spreading peace, was, scholars realized, difficult to reconcile with that of Augustine as expressed in the *City of God*. Hence scholarship started to focus even more on the particularities of Orosius' 'theology of history', always in comparison with Augustine. The titles of some fundamental studies on Orosius of the past half a century are eloquent in this respect: *Paul Orose et sa conception de l'histoire* (Fainck 1951); *Die Geschichtstheologie des Orosius* (Schöndorf 1952; Goetz 1980a); *Orose et ses idées* (Lacroix 1965). The conclusion usually was that, in comparison with Augustine, Orosius had few ideas of limited value. Indeed, the paradox that a pupil could so fundamentally misunderstand his master was explained by increasingly dismissive judgments on Orosius' intelligence and culture: that his was a small mind with barely a proper education is a polite

[14] Particularly important are Kamlah 1951; Schöndorf 1952; Maier 1955; Mommsen 1959b. See the earlier studies of Fuchs 1938 and Straub 1972c, originally published in 1939.

summary of some of the judgments.[15] Unsurprisingly, such a largely negative judgment has been countered by a minority of scholars who lapse into the opposite vice of excessive praise and consider Orosius' thought profound and daring.[16] The following judgment expressed in a recent survey illustrates well the traditional assessment of Orosius: 'While his recounting of the facts is often unimpressive, his complex systematizing reveals his bold and original mind.'[17] Here Orosius' work as a historian is explicitly devaluated at the expense of supposed originality in the field of theology.

A series of first-rate editions and translations has continued to draw attention to Orosius as a historian,[18] but even they have been influenced by the persistent value judgments. Given the role played by the heavily charged opposition between Orosius and Augustine in generating these judgments, it is useful to take a closer look at the precise scholarly context in which that contrast developed. To do so, I shall briefly discuss two dominant figures in twentieth-century patristic studies, Erik Peterson (1890–1960) and Henri-Irénée Marrou (1904–77). Whilst Orosius never was central to their work, Augustine was, and their interpretation of Augustine was crucially shaped by the social and political changes of the 1930s in Europe.

Erik Peterson was a theologian and Church historian who had to abandon his chair at the University of Bonn when he converted from Lutheranism to Catholicism in 1930. In the 1930s his theology developed a clearly political character: against the fascination for a secular eschatology, evidenced in the Nazi claim to a Third Reich and the exaltation of the historical achievements of the German race, he re-emphasized the spiritual nature of Christian eschatology, which could not and should not serve a secular state. This argument was directed in the first place against the alliance that had developed between Protestant Churches and the Reich and the attraction that Nazi

[15] Paschoud 1967: 277, 291; Corsini 1968: 50–1; Markus 1970: 162; Marrou 1970: 83; Straub 1972a: 266; Martelli 1982; Arnaud-Lindet 1990–1: i.xxi; Alonso-Núñez 1993: 208; Inglebert 1996: 582; Spät 1998: 359; Marcone 2002: 864; Cesa 2003: 30; Kany 2006: 576. Exceptions are Fainck 1951: 10; Lippold 1976: i.xxxv; Fabbrini 1979: 77–81.

[16] Fabbrini 1979: 46 ('la profondità dei concetti espressi'); Polichetti 2000: 99 ('un coraggioso pioniere nella storia della cultura occidentale'); Zecchini 2003: 320 ('a masterpiece').

[17] Rohrbacher 2002: 138.

[18] Deferrari 1964; Lippold 1976; Arnaud-Lindet 1990–1; Fear 2010a.

ideology started to have on some Catholic theologians.[19] The problem of the relationship between Church and state and the theological justification of state power lie at the heart of the famous tract *Der Monotheismus als politisches Problem*, published in 1935.[20] Peterson challenged 'political theology', particularly of the Eusebian kind, in order to show that a proper Nicaean, Trinitarian theology was not open to the temptation of becoming subservient to imperial power. Eusebius had used theological arguments to justify the empire of Constantine, but this had, according to Peterson, been facilitated by his unorthodox, subordinationist Christology. Ostensibly an argument about patristics, the work was as much a scholarly treatise as a political statement. For the theologian Peterson, the religious justification of tyrannical power was based on an erroneous theology. He singled out Orosius as the culmination of the *Augustustheologie*, which theologically justified the role the Roman Empire had to play in the history of salvation, and suggested that his lack of theological insight had turned him into an apprentice-sorcerer playing dangerous games. In this he was the heir to Eusebius, but whereas the dazzle of Constantine's sudden conversion could count as an excuse, no pardon was forthcoming for Orosius, still exalting a tottering Christian empire. Nazi Germany had, Peterson suggests, too many Orosii: possibly well-meaning but dangerously flawed well-wishers of the regime. Significantly, Peterson puts forward Augustine as the counterpoint of Orosius and the *Augustustheologie*: the *City of God*, which turns mankind's mind away from the worries and entanglements of earthly life, refocuses attention on the eschatological essence of Christianity, and warns against the dangers of identifying an earthly state (or Church) as the fulfilment of God's plans. Orosius and Augustine thus occupy opposite sides of a heavily charged theological spectrum.

Marrou's interest in Augustine was kindled by the parallels he noticed between late Antiquity and Europe in the 1930s, namely the sense of cultural crisis and decline.[21] He later revised his negative assessment of the age of Augustine to develop a much more positive view of the period, becoming, through his influence on Peter Brown,

[19] Maier 2001.

[20] Nichtweiss 1992: 470–97, 763–830; Dückers 1999: 254–5 and 264–7; Maier 2001: 246.

[21] Riché 2003: 40–1. See Marrou 1938.

the grandfather of the contemporary field of late Antiquity.[22] In one damning paper, published in 1970, he drew a stark contrast between Orosius' view on history and that of his master Augustine.[23] Relying on earlier Orosian scholarship,[24] Marrou's central argument was that, whereas Augustine takes a critical distance from human history, pagan and Christian, and downplays its importance in favour of the salvation of the individual, Orosius exalts history since the Incarnation and sees the Christian empire as the culmination of history. The latter position is deemed naive and ill-advised. The explanation for this stark contrast and the curt dismissal of Orosius lies in Marrou's own view of history, which can be termed Augustinian. Although he never developed these ideas explicitly in his historical works, Marrou too reacted against the desire to see history achieve its end in historical time and re-emphasized the eschatological dimension of a Christian understanding of history. The achievement of history, for a Christian, cannot lie in the temptations of temporal power, but must be the ultimate return to God.[25] This position probably was influenced by the events of the 1930s, but there is also a specifically French context. Orosius' perspective was, implicitly, deemed irreconcilable with the view of a secular French society, as it had developed at the end of the nineteenth century, in which religion was essentially a private affair. After the initial resistance of the Church to the creation of the public *laicité*, French Catholics espoused this model of Church-state relations as opening up the possibility of living a truly Christian life: liberated from the dangers of serving temporal power, as the established Church in, for example, Belgium illustrated, Catholics were free to challenge the state and, where possible, to improve it. The vision of society and human history that transpires in the *City of God* suited this perspective well: Augustine's sense for the imperfection of all that is earthly, both Church and state, was not seen as pessimistic but as opening up the chance to strive for improvement by taking the ideal, heavenly city as a model for one's actions. In abandoning the ideological identification of Church and state and the naive belief in the perfection of the former, the *City of God*

22 Vessey 1998.
23 Marrou 1970.
24 In particular Corsini 1968. See the critique of Firpo 1983 on this work.
25 Mandouze 1999.

allowed Christians to play a role in modern society without falling into the trap of exalting, or even needing, a particular state.

As one scholar put it, Augustine's view on history and society seems 'modern' to us,[26] and underpins, for example, Robert Markus's *Saeculum*,[27] but also a series of pre- and post-war studies by Johannes Straub about the way Christians dealt with the crises of the fourth and fifth centuries.[28] It is not my intention to suggest that this understanding of Augustine is flawed because it has roots in European history. I am rather interested in its consequences for the study of Orosius. In order to construct Orosius as the contrast of Augustine, attention was shifted to his theology of history, whilst his place in ancient historiography remained obscure. Because Augustine became a beacon for modern Christians, showing the way out of the shifting sands of politics, Orosius, understood as Augustine's opposite, became almost necessarily an example not to follow.

IV. HISTORY AND RHETORIC

The present book proposes an alternative approach, which, in contrast with the traditional, theological one, can be termed rhetorical. This label, in turn, covers two different, but interrelated aspects. First, my approach to the *Historiae* is literary, that is, we need first to understand the form of the *Historiae* before we can grasp its content. Orosius deploys a full panoply of literary techniques, ranging from allusions over metaphors to panegyric, in order to suggest a specific interpretation of the past. A correct understanding of these techniques, rarely studied in their own right, will, I suggest, show that Orosius' intention is not so much the exposition of a Christian theology of history as an attempt to destabilize the traditional Roman view of the past as glorious and praiseworthy—a view that makes it hard for elite Romans to see the present in its true colours. The traditional view was inculcated in the school of rhetoric, where

[26] Paschoud 1967: 274.

[27] Markus sees, for example, Augustine as identifying and accepting 'pluralism' in society—a profoundly modern concept.

[28] Straub 1972a, 1972b, and 1972c, originally published in, respectively, 1950, 1954, and 1939.

the study of great poets, the exempla of the forefathers, and traditional accounts of Roman history not only shaped the words but also the minds of the late Roman elite. There is, thus, also a social aspect to the rhetorical approach espoused in this book. Orosius informs us in more than one way about the type of training received in the school of rhetoric. Not only does he offer some amusing vignettes of the rhetorically 'over-determined' elite individual, but his own *Historiae* are also the product of the school of rhetoric: the histories he used as sources are mainly the ones read there, and he uses different rhetorical techniques in order to undermine the traditional view of the past. Thus, rather than being a paradigm of a late antique theology of history, this book argues that the *Historiae* are exemplary of the close intertwining of history and rhetoric in this period.

In choosing this approach, I am indebted to several recent tendencies in scholarship. Mainly German scholars have increasingly drawn attention to the *Sitz im Leben* of ancient works of history in the school of rhetoric. History was obviously a common topic of declamations and other exercises. But it has been argued that late ancient breviaries, and also earlier works such as those by Justin and Florus, found their main readership in students and teachers of rhetoric.[29] These works aimed at conveying a standard, idealized image of the Roman past. As has been shown by U. Eigler, the educational system privileged as its historical focus the period from Troy to Augustus. Knowledge of this period was transmitted and maintained through a variety of texts—not in the least Vergil—and a good command of the history of this period was a sign of education. It thus permitted to display or to maintain social status. Eigler argues that, as long as the educational system continued to shape the late antique elite, the canonical understanding of Roman history remained in place, even against Christian attempts to put the Bible at the heart of society.[30] Eigler's socio-literary perspective provides a crucial context for Orosius: the historian challenges the canonical understanding of the past and the mindset it produces, but from within the education that underpins it. Orosius deploys all the sources and resources of the education, but to show that the idealization of the past, and concomitant rejection of the present, is mistaken.

[29] Schmidt 1968, 1988, and 1989; Fugmann 1990–2003; Hose 1994; Felmy 2001; Eigler 2003; Sehlmeyer 2009.

[30] Eigler 2003.

In taking this stance, Orosius is probably indebted to Augustine, who, as has been shown by C. Tornau, suspected the education of his age to produce amoral individuals who only aimed at glory.[31] At the same time, Augustine continued to use the rhetorical conventions of his age. A firm grasp of these conventions and their use, in Tornau's case in the *City of God*, is thus crucial to an understanding of the argument of Augustine. Rather than seeing it as mere decoration, the form may actually shape the content. In studies on late antique literature particular attention has been devoted to one such formal aspect: literary allusions. In a recent monograph on Ammianus Marcellinus, G. Kelly sees allusions as the key to understanding that historian. He stresses in particular that an allusion is never passive, but often involves the conscious adaptation of the original passage to a new context. In fact, he argues in particular that we should see Ammianus as part of the mainstream of Latin literature in this respect.[32] Claiming a similar place for Orosius in the history of literature may seem hazardous. Yet the principle that allusions create meaning is applicable to Orosius too: whilst his use of Vergilian verses is well known, they are often seen as mere decoration, a few stray flower-pots in front of a drab house. However, the verses drawn from Vergil are rarely accidentally inserted, but rather carefully selected, and if the reader is capable of recalling the Vergilian context of the verses quoted, he is rewarded with additional insight in to the message of the *Historiae*. Given Vergil's central role in Roman education, Orosius' allusions to mainly the *Aeneid* often subtly invert the meaning they had in the original context, much like Augustine's complex and subtle engagement with Vergil as traced by S. MacCormack.[33] All these scholars apply frameworks and approaches long reserved for the 'real' classics, and in this way contribute to a revolution in our understanding of late antique literature, much like the boom in studies on the Second Sophistic, now considered one of the most fascinating periods in Antiquity, was prompted by the choice not to consider its literature as second-rate.[34] Together with many other recent contributions,[35] this book hopes to contribute to the further

[31] Tornau 2006.

[32] Kelly 2008: 161–221 offers a good introduction to the issues involved.

[33] MacCormack 1998.

[34] e.g. Swain 1996; Goldhill 2001; Whitmarsh 2001; Van Hoof 2010a.

[35] e.g. S.F. Johnson 2006; Scourfield 2007; Cain 2009; Van Hoof 2010b.

refutation (if need be) of the view that late ancient literature was merely derivative, or, in the case of Christian texts, mainly interested in content and not in form.

The role of rhetoric in ancient historiography is currently a central issue in the study of ancient historiography. How did rhetoric impact on the representation of the facts and how was the relationship between both conceptualized by practitioners of the genre are some of the central questions today.[36] In modern literary criticism, the starting point is usually Hayden White's *The content of the form* (1978), who argued that we should understand different styles of historiography as rhetorical tropes, but the issue has deeper roots in the study of ancient historiography, in which the impact of rhetoric is obvious from the start—just think of Thucydides' comments on the orations he inserted in his history.[37] The increased attention for the literary form of historiography has spurred a long and impressive series of works on dramatization, tragedy, and rhetoric in classical works of history,[38] and has made clear that one should understand first their literary form before one can assess their content. Discussions of the role of rhetoric in ancient historiography have often centred on the role of fiction in historiography. Indeed, in the book that constitutes the point of reference in the debate among ancient historians, *Rhetoric in Classical Historiography* (1988), Tony Woodman argued that scholars had long tended to see ancient and modern historiography as fundamentally identical undertakings, both aiming at establishing the truth. In his view, however, the ancients consciously allowed the use of rhetorical *inventio* in history not only to embellish the narrative, but also, if necessary, to invent facts. Understanding *inventio* as introducing fiction in history, Woodman's book has had the result that discussions of the relationship between rhetoric and historiography have focused on the presence of fiction in historiography. In fact, as has been argued recently, this is too narrow a conception of *inventio*, which, moreover, still relies on the assumption that rhetoric and historiography represent respectively the realm of fiction and the realm of facts. But for orators, rhetorical techniques, such as dramatization, do not serve the invention of fictive facts,

[36] e.g. Fox 2001; Laird 1999 and 2009; Lendon 2009.

[37] Thucydides 1.21–2. See already Peter 1911.

[38] e.g. Cameron 1989; Fox 1996; Shumate 1997; Feldherr 1998; Chaplin 2000; Dué 2000; Foucher 2000a and 2000b; Marincola 2003.

but rather tools that help to display facts to an audience in such a way that they almost feel present themselves. Depending on their perspective, historians could chide rhetoric as dangerous for the veracity of the narrative or praise it as contributing to its verisimilitude.[39]

I shall argue that Orosius implicitly belongs to the latter category: his often pathetic descriptions of the suffering of the past render his mode of writing similar to that of the so-called tragic history of the Hellenistic period, that is, of a group of historians who consciously used rhetorical techniques to display dramatic events to their audience and conjure up their pity and passion.[40] In drawing, directly or indirectly, on rhetorical handbooks, he can be understood as suggesting that his rhetoric does not replace fiction with truth, but rather displays true events to his audience. The repeated rhetorical interjections and elaborations have made scholars doubt if the *Historiae* really are a history at all: its apologetic intention, calling forth polemic and rhetoric, seems to impinge on the value of objectivity that one expects of a historian.[41] Many readers today would agree with a possible 'pagan' criticism of his argument as *artificiose*.[42] As I hope to show, such views betray the assumption that a text must be objective and neutral in content and form alike to count as a work of history. In that case, much ancient historiography would disqualify. Having an agenda does not disqualify someone from being a historian: most ancient historians were highly partisan and not a few of their modern colleagues fail to live up to the lofty ideal of objectivity.[43]

The foregoing brief discussion of the scholarly tendencies that shape this book demonstrates sufficiently that it is my intention to situate Orosius in the context of ancient literature and historiography, that is, in the tradition that shaped him. This is, in fact, the direction taken in many a work on late antique historiography. Most attention has, understandably, gone to Ammianus,[44] but Christian historians

[39] Fox 2001; Laird 2009. See also Kempshall 2011: 4–5.

[40] Walbank 1960 and 2002a.

[41] Schöndorf 1952: 70–1; Lacroix 1965: 70; Koch-Peters 1984: 23; Lippold 1976: i.xxix; Herzog 2002: 304.

[42] Orosius 7.27.2.

[43] One is justified to ask whether the Orosian mode of writing history is totally absent in modern historiography. Howard Zinn's *A people's history of the United States* (London, 1980) shares with Orosius the reliance on other works of history, an emphasis on the suffering of ordinary people, and an appeal to emotions.

[44] Rosen 1970 and 1982; Matthews 1989; Barnes 1998; Wittchow 2001; Kelly 2008.

have received their share of attention too.[45] This implies that I will disregard his influence on medieval historiography, a tradition that he helped to shape. As is well known, Orosius enjoyed huge success in the Middle Ages: in the Latin West he soon developed into a model for the writing of history.[46] Medievalists have looked at Orosius as the origin of medieval historiography, and even the founder of the genre of 'historia' in the Middle Ages.[47] As a consequence, the elements in Orosius that announce future developments, in particular the providential interpretation of the past, have been emphasized at the expense of what ties him to Antiquity, and the classical is obscured in favour of the Christian. I do not wish to dispute that Orosius has come to define history in the eyes of later readers, but that later perspective may not do justice to the *Historiae* in their own day and age. This book will thus strictly confine itself to interpreting Orosius in the light of what preceded and accompanied him.

Even if I am of the view that earlier scholarship of Orosius has too much tended to understand Orosius as a theologian and failed to situate him back in the classical tradition, I remain obviously heavily indebted to my predecessors, who have provided many of the building blocks for my argument and who have taken many a stride in the direction that I consider the right one.[48] A.H. Merrills has, for example, contextualized Orosius' geographical introduction in the development of ancient geographical writings and has shown how Orosius became a model for later historians in this respect.[49] The recent translation by A. Fear, as did the earlier editions of Arnaud-Lindet and Lippold, provides a wealth of information on sources and parallels, and his introduction many a pointer on Orosius' rhetoric and views. In several papers he has sought to reassess Orosius' historical views.[50] In a brilliant paper that provides a tableau of the

[45] See the overviews of Rohrbacher 2002 and Marasco 2003.

[46] Cf. Goetz 1980a: 148–65; Schmale 1985; Kempshall 2011: 64–80.

[47] Werner 1987: 9; Heinzelmann 2001: 105–6 with references to earlier literature. Heinzelmann wrongly states that Orosius wrote the first 'church history'.

[48] Useful general assessments are Fabbrini 1979, Goetz 1980a, Firpo 1983, and Torres Rodríguez 1985. For style and rhetoric, see Svennung 1922 and Bartalucci 1976. For Orosius as a historian, see in particular Lippold 1952, Koch-Peters 1984: 17–38, and Arnaud-Lindet 1990–1991. Important work on the sources is done by Hingst 1973.

Traditional assessments of Orosius' theology of history are Schöndorf 1952, Goetz 1980a, Inglebert 1996, and Martínez Cavero 2002.

[49] Merrills 2005.

[50] Fear 2005 and 2010b.

literary landscape of the fourth and fifth centuries, R. Herzog has argued that Orosius developed a highly optimistic concept of historical progress out of the experience of decline of his own age.[51] In his recent *Rhetoric and the Writing of History 400–1500*, M. Kempshall has briefly offered some important reassessments of Orosius, in particular drawing attention to the rhetorical aspects of the *Historiae* and the way in which he set the standard, together with Eusebius, for the writing of history in the Middle Ages.[52]

V. BIOGRAPHY, AUDIENCE, AND REDACTION

The approach espoused in this book has an immediate impact on three traditional issues of Orosian scholarship: his personal biography, his audience, and the supposed multiple redactions of the *Historiae*. I wish to clarify these before I set out the argument of this book.

Above I have given a traditional chronology of known facts about Orosius. Remarks about himself are spread across the *Historiae* and in the so-called *Commonitorium*, a brief tract with which Orosius drew the attention of Augustine to the spread of priscillianism in Spain. The preface of the *Historiae* is densely self-referential. Scholars have been tempted to fill in the canvas of Orosius' life, even going so far as to draw a psychological portrait of Orosius based on certain passages, in particular the preface.[53] In fact, as I shall argue in the first chapter, the expression of certain states of mind in a text, such as deference and subservience towards Augustine in the case of Orosius, or references to personal experiences, fulfil in the first place a function within the text. Construing a biography out of such self-presentation may be misleading, as they often are contradictory. The awareness of the rhetoric of the text limits the possibility of biographical reconstruction.[54] In other words, whereas previous scholarship sometimes has tended to see the text as a way of getting at Orosius' state of mind

[51] Herzog 2002.

[52] Kempshall 2011.

[53] Corsini 1968: 41–51; Marrou 1970: 67; Arnaud-Lindet 1990–1: i.xix; Merrills 2005: 40.

[54] See Kelly 2008, Part I: 'the limits of biography'. For self-presentation, see Oliensis 1998 and Van Hoof 2010a.

and his theory of history, this book inverts the relationship: expressions of psychology and emotions and the use of theoretical statements serve a purpose within the text in order to draw the reader into the narrative and convince him of the correctness of Orosius' depiction of past and present.

I have suggested that we should understand the *Historiae* as stemming from and reacting against the view of the past generated by the elite education of the school of rhetoric. This has important consequences for our identification of the audience of the work. The title *Historiae adversus paganos* indicates whom the work is directed against, namely the pagans, and this has sometimes been taken as the real audience too.[55] Most scholars, however, propose a different intended audience: given the widespread view that Orosius represents a 'lower' type of literature, the uneducated masses have been repeatedly proposed.[56] In the light of the highly rhetorical character of the *Historiae* and, more generally, the nature of literature as an elite undertaking in Antiquity, such a suggestion is a priori unlikely. In fact, the intended readership of the *Historiae* probably was similar to that of Augustine's *City of God.* As is well known, the latter wrote in the first place to rebut criticism of Christianity among the elite that had fled Rome after 410 and had settled in Africa and Sicily.[57] *De civitate dei* addresses itself to Christians or to those who sympathize with Christianity and might be on their way to conversion.[58] This contrasts with the explicit target of the work, which directs itself against die-hard pagans. As shown by C. Tornau, Augustine consciously constructs the work as a 'three-way dialogue': he argues against the pagans to convince his intended audience, who, as it were, have to judge the rhetorical debate between Augustine and the pagans.[59] The intended audience is thus not necessarily pagan; rather it is still open to arguments from both sides and needs to be persuaded to choose for Christianity and against paganism. The close connection between the *City of God* and the *Historiae*, the latter being

[55] Orosius 1.pr.9, 2.11.10, 7.1.5. Lippold 1952: 4 accepts this at face value, but he is more nuanced on page 67. Orosius himself states explicitly that only a few people criticize Christianity (1.6.3), thus suggesting that his audience is not limited to these.

[56] Lacroix 1965: 45; Lippold 1976: i.xxxiii; Martelli 1982: 238.

[57] Courcelle 1964: 56–8; McLynn 1999; O'Daly 1999a: 36.

[58] Augustine, *Epistula* 135, 137, 2*.3.

[59] Tornau 2006: 113. On Augustine's audience, see also Cameron 2011: 792–3. A parallel for Orosius and Augustine would be Prosper Tiro *De providentia dei.*

presented as a supplement of the former, makes it likely that both target a similar audience.

There are further indications in favour of this suggestion. The fall of Rome obviously plays a key role in the work, and is repeatedly referred to.[60] Orosius has a particular interest in Africa and Sicily: he repeatedly contrasts the peace that Africa and Sicily enjoy today with the troubles they experienced in the past. Today Africa is hospitable, but in the past it used to reject strangers. Its ancient hate for foreigners is underscored by a quotation of Vergil, in which Africa turns away Aeneas and his companions.[61] Sicily is often expressly and exaggeratedly depicted as a hotbed of tyranny, wars of all sorts, and natural disasters in the past: indeed, Orosius emphasizes the remarkable sympathy between the eruptions of Mount Etna and the political troubles. At the moment of his writing, however, nature nor mankind disturb the peace on the island.[62] The high frequency of such comments suggests that Orosius is demonstrating to his target audience that they must praise themselves lucky: indeed, they had to flee, but thanks to the combined efforts of the Roman Empire and Christianity, no differences of customs or religion mar the unity of the Mediterranean. There may be some troubles today, but in contrast to the past, there is always a hospitable place to flee to.[63] At the very end of the *Historiae* Orosius makes it explicitly clear that Christianity has turned Africa and Sicily into safe havens: in his depiction, the Gothic leader Vallia decided to conclude a peace agreement with the emperor Honorius because he rightly interpreted the disaster of the Gothic attempt to cross over to Africa in 415 and that of the earlier failed attack of Alaric on Sicily (410) as divine disapproval.[64] These references to Africa and Sicily are too ubiquitous and too often strategically placed to be accidental and should be interpreted as direct appeals to his audience. Like the first ten books of the *De civitate Dei*, then, the *Historiae* are an attempt to convince the wavering on the basis of the inconsistency and incoherence of the arguments of the

[60] See chapter 2.

[61] Orosius 5.2.1–4; Vergil, *Aeneis* 1.540–1. See also Orosius 5.11, dependent on Augustine, *De civitate Dei* 3.31.

[62] Orosius 1.17.3, 1.20.1, 1.20.6, 2.14.1, 2.14.4, 2.18.6, 4.6.33, 4.9.12–13, 4.10, 4.18.2, 5.6, 5.10.11, 5.11, 5.13.3, 6.3.5, 6.18.30–2, 7.5.4, 7.43.12. Salvo 2008: 237–40 lists these passages.

[63] The argument is explicitly made in Orosius 5.1 and 7.41.

[64] Orosius 7.43.11–12.

others. Hence Orosius explicitly wishes not to rely on biblical authority to show that the pagan idealization of the past is untrue, but remains within the methodological limits of classical historiography.[65] He positions himself consciously in the playing field of the others.

The rhetorical approach espoused in this book argues that we should understand the various statements and literary techniques within the overall narrative. This presupposes that one should read the *Historiae* as a whole. In fact, it has been argued that the redaction of the *Historiae* falls into two stages, before and after his trip to Palestine (415/6). The argument goes back to T. von Mörner, who proposed that the first five books were composed before Orosius' departure.[66] The hypothesis was picked up by G. Fink, who argued that Orosius first worked as an assistant for Augustine to gather historical data, and after his return developed these into a work of his own.[67] Endorsed by H.-I. Marrou, this hypothesis now seems orthodoxy in French scholarship.[68] The idea has been criticized repeatedly, on the combined grounds that there is no evidence and no need for such a hypothesis.[69] There are no signs of interruptions in the work, and the dependency of Augustine and Orosius on roughly the same set of sources is most logically explained by the obvious fact that both used the same library, and wrote for similar audiences and about the same themes. The idea of a unitary redaction presupposes that the work was completed in little over a year after Orosius' return from Palestine. This is not unlikely, as the *Historiae* rely heavily on easily accessible sources: the double redaction thesis should therefore be laid to rest.

VI. FROM VERGIL TO AUGUSTINE

The various chapters of this book explore different aspects of the *Historiae* and deploy literary analysis, not only to improve our

[65] See Orosius 1.1 and 7.1.
[66] Mörner 1844: 21.
[67] Fink-Ferrera 1954.
[68] Marrou 1970; Arnaud-Lindet 1990–1: i.xxii–iv; Inglebert 1996: 508–9.
[69] Paschoud 1967: 277; Corsini 1968: 20–5; Vilella 2000: 99; Martínez Cavero 2002a: 54–6.

understanding of the message of the work, but also to situate it in the social and cultural context that shaped it. Together they propose an interpretation of Orosius that is substantially different from the traditional one. The contention of this book is that the literary and historiographical approach it espouses is not just a complement to the theological reading of Orosius. In fact, it questions many of the results of such an approach. Indeed, a traditional way of reading the *Historiae* has been to focus on apparently theoretical passages, such as the prefaces and the 'four empire theory' at the beginning of book 2, and construct his views out of these. Large tracts of the *Historiae* are hardly ever read, or make no impact on the overall interpretation of the work. In fact, I argue, the message of the *Historiae* is to be found in the construction of the narrative in which apparently theoretical statements serve specific purposes. I shall suggest in particular that what has been construed as theological statements are often literary tools drawn from classical historiography. The more literary approach ventured in this book will thus also have an impact on what we think the *Historiae* are about.

Chapter 1 sets the scene for the rest of the book by exploring the prefaces to the *Historiae* and to another, smaller work of Orosius, namely the 'consultation or reminder to Augustine about the errors of the Priscillianists and Origenists' (*consultatio sive commonitorium Orosii ad Augustinum de errore priscillianistarum et origenistarum*). Both strategically deploy Vergilian allusions as part of a literary self-presentation that seeks to enhance Orosius' standing as an author. Contrary to dismissive views of his literary qualities, the chapter argues that we should take ancient references to Orosius' learning seriously: his literary practice, as well as the kind of sources he uses, points to a good rhetorical training.

The following three chapters discuss the three forms of intertextuality that Gavin Kelly has recently put at the heart of his study of Ammianus Marcellinus: allusions to earlier literature, the use of exempla, and the rewriting of sources for the events.[70] In understanding all of these as instances of intertextuality, Kelly has sought to remove the label of passivity that is sometimes attached to the way late ancient historians deal with earlier texts. According to an old-fashioned view of late ancient historiography, allusions to Vergil are

[70] Kelly 2008.

just the perfunctory display of learning, exempla are used according to the rhetorical training and merely copied from handbooks, and sources are slavishly copied. As Kelly shows for Ammianus, an understanding of these three techniques improves our grasp of the message the historian wishes to convey. Chapters 2 to 4 of this book argue that the same holds for Orosius. More than Kelly, I emphasize the social context in which we have to understand these techniques, precisely because they also serve Orosius to criticize the cultural habits of the elite.

Chapter 2 argues that Vergil is the key *intertext* in book 2. Often only the introductory chapters, where the 'four empire theory' is propounded, receive attention, but in fact the entire book explores the theme of the fall of Rome against the background of the events of 410. Contrary to traditional readings, which see the 'four empire theory' as celebrating the eternity of Rome, I suggest that it consciously evokes the possibility of Rome's fall and reminds the reader that it is only because of God's intervention that Rome has not yet fallen. Judicious references to Vergil's description of the sack of Troy throughout the book reinforce the suggestion of the opening chapters. Rather than setting out a coherent theology of history, Orosius deploys traditional rhetorical and historiographical tools, such as synchronism and allusion, to underscore the paradoxical survival of Rome.

Chapter 3 starts out from a ubiquitous feature of the *Historiae*, the comparison between past and present. This is obviously part of an apologetic attempt to show the superiority of the Christian present. But much more is going on. Focusing on book 4, the chapter argues that Orosius pretends to have identified why his contemporaries fail to see the present in its true colours: their rhetorical education has inculcated them a mistaken, majestic view of the past. He hence argues that the great exempla of the past are in fact far less glorious than they seem, and that he is the only historian who puts forward the facts. He thus suggests that he is the only one who lives up to what classical historiography had set as its task, namely to tell the truth. Undermining the traditional, glorious view of the past by omitting traditional good exempla, Orosius highlights and reinterprets negative exempla so as to show what the past really looked like.

The fourth chapter emphasizes Orosius' active engagement with his sources. It is still often alleged that he copied a single source, whilst it can be demonstrated that he contaminated various sources, amplified, and rewrote them. The chapter argues in particular that Orosius used the exempla collection of Valerius Maximus, a work specifically aimed at orators, thus demonstrating once again the close relationship with rhetorical education that the previous chapters have detected. In addition, Orosius repeatedly used the technique of amplification to expand brief notices from *breviaria* and chronicles into a fully fledged narrative, especially towards the end of the *Historiae*. This suggests he did not have access to a continuous narrative of his own times.

Already chapter 3 has shown how Orosius challenges the rhetorical mindset of his contemporaries with rhetorical arguments and tools: rather than presenting a totally different, Christian alternative to traditional culture, he situates himself in the tradition he is combating. This is the result of his conscious decision to challenge the pagans with their own tools, but also because he was himself rhetorically trained. This becomes fully clear in chapter 5. Orosius' professed aim to show the facts as they are does not result in a terse narrative. On the contrary, because he wishes to depict the suffering of the past in its full, gruesome reality, he frequently has recourse to pathetic modes of writing, in particular *enargeia*: as an analysis of book 5 shows, he consciously seeks to conjure up the emotions of his readers to ensure that they can feel the misery of the past and cannot indulge anymore in the naive, rosy view of the classical past. The recourse to emotional writing was not new in ancient historiography and Orosius' highly rhetorical mode of writing is as much indebted to pre-existing historiographical traditions as to Christian apologetic.

Chapter 6 turns the attention to two of the features that have been used to relegate the *Historiae* from the realm of historiography: the various metaphors and models for historical development throughout the work, and the panegyrical passages at the end of book 7. Both should be seen, in fact, as tools that were not uncommon in ancient historiography. Models such as the 'four empire theory' and the metaphor of a human life span for a state, recur regularly in ancient historiography, where they serve the purpose to make a point about the present. Similarly, as chapter 2 shows, the 'four empire theory' draws attention to the paradoxical survival of Rome after 410. Orosius also describes Rome as being in her old age, again to emphasize the same point. The panegyrical passages at the end of book 7 have often been read as an exaltation of the Christian Roman Empire. I wish to suggest a different reading on three levels. First, the agent being praised is in fact God: towards the end of the *Historiae*, God, responding to individual virtue and sin, appears as the only true actor in history, eclipsing emperors and generals. This is in line with Orosius' tendency elsewhere to identify the Church, the believer's morality, and God's response to the latter, as the engines of history. Second, Orosius is heavily dependent on Augustine and picks up the arguments of the conclusion of book 5 of the *De civitate Dei*, especially about the inanity of human virtue without divine grace. But for apologetic purposes, the success of Christianity in this world is much more emphasized. Finally, the last chapters of book 7 of the *Historiae* also remind the target audience of the safety and prosperity of Africa and Sicily, the safe havens that the Christian empire has created for those who had to flee the sack of Rome—and suggest that such an opportunity did not exist in the past when similar disasters struck Rome.

Chapter 7 discusses two traditional themes of Orosian scholarship: the suggestion that the *Historiae* are a universal history, and the issue of whether he had a positive or negative view of the barbarian invaders. The chapter argues that we should frame both questions differently. Whilst Orosius suggests that his *Historiae* cover the entire world—most obviously in the long geographical introduction in 1.2—this should in the first place be understood as another rhetorical technique that aims at undermining the traditional view of Roman history. Indeed, the suggestion of universal coverage does not result in a different selection of facts from traditional Roman histories. The pretension that he covers the history of the entire world helps, however, to suggest the vastness of the suffering in the past and to destabilize the romanocentric view of traditional education. In its second section, the chapter rejects attempts to determine the essence of Orosius' views of the barbarians. Rather, the barbarian functions in the *Historiae* as a figure of contrast, much as he did in earlier Roman histories. Depending on the context of his narrative, Orosius can hence efface the distinction between barbarians and Romans or stylize pagan barbarians as the archenemies of the day. This rhetorical play with the category of the barbarian again helps Orosius to question the traditional view of the past, in which the barbarians often served to highlight Roman virtue and prowess.

As noted above, the relationship with Augustine is central to any understanding of the *Historiae*. Augustine is the dedicatee, and Orosius depicts the work as a supplement to Augustine's *City of God*, which could not include all disasters of the past.[71] Earlier chapters have explored how Orosius consciously evokes Augustine and the *City of God* as part of his deft literary self-presentation: he can indeed be interpreted as capitalizing on the fame of his dedicatee. The appeal to Augustine, however, is more than lip-service. The *City of God* is used throughout as a source and provides inspiration for many a passage in the *Historiae*, and the last chapters of the work, highly panegyrical and often interpreted as the clearest evidence of Orosius' divergence from Augustine, draw, in fact, heavily on the concluding chapters of book 5 of the *De civitate Dei*. Notwithstanding these evident points of contact, the apparent gap that has been detected between the theologies of history of Orosius and Augustine have made scholars look for different sources of Orosius' ideas, in particular Eusebius of Caesarea, and they have tended to minimize the importance of the *City of God*. It has even been suggested that Orosius simply went his own way.[72] The pervasive influence of Augustine on the *Historiae* suggests otherwise. In the last chapter of the book, I argue that master and pupil were much closer to one another than often assumed, and the difference in perspective not as radical. Rather, both grapple with the same issue, namely what difference Christianity makes in this world. But the genres in which they frame their responses are different, the one writing history and the other apologetic. Moreover, Orosius did not have access to the fully developed thought of Augustine in all twenty-two books of the *City of God*: he only knew books 1–10 of that work, and the last pentad dealt with Roman religion and neo-platonist philosophy, obviously of less interest for a work of history. Orosius' repeated use of book 5 of the *City of God* is hence comprehensible and the views of Augustine expressed there have shaped the *Historiae*. Yet, Orosius and Augustine do differ on a fundamental issue: whilst Orosius is optimistic about the positive impact Church and Christianity have on society and history, Augustine is less so and, famously, sees the Church as part of the imperfect *civitas terrena*. Whereas traditionally it is stated that Augustine and Orosius part ways on the role of the empire, I wish to suggest that both differ actually in their appreciation of the historical role of the Church. It is not necessary to underline that my view, in a way, is

[71] See Augustine, *De civitate Dei* 4.2 on natural disasters.

[72] See, e.g. Arnaud-Lindet 1990–1: i.xx; Inglebert 1996: 514.

diametrically opposed to the traditional one that was put on the map by Marrou and Peterson and that sees the empire as the issue at stake.

To conclude this introduction, one last disclaimer. A revisionist book like the present one runs the risk of being interpreted as swinging the pendulum too much to the other side and preaching too optimistic a view of Orosius. To avoid being pressed into the camp of the naive admirers of Orosius, I wish to state just once that my argument does not aim at catapulting him among the stars of late antique literature. In the past such value judgments, negative and positive, have made scholars fail in the more important duty of contextualization. Hence, I do not wish to suggest more (but also no less) than that Orosius is a good example of how history was written in the fourth and fifth centuries AD and that this tradition is fully continuous with that of 'classical' Antiquity.

All translations are my own, except when mentioned otherwise. Orosius' style tends to be very florid, verging on the obscure. I have opted for literal translations that preserve as much as possible these features.

1

Unexpected Pearls: Prefaces and the Rhetoric of Deference

Subtlety and literary skill are qualities rarely ascribed to Orosius, whose intelligence and culture have generally been derided in scholarship for the past half a century. This judgment contrasts with the views of his late antique readers who emphasized his eloquence and rhetorical talent.[1] Indeed, an ability to write fluent, admittedly sometimes convoluted, rhetorical prose is obvious from every page of the *Historiae*. If that quality has not gone unnoticed among modern scholars, it is often assumed that Orosius manages to keep up a semblance of style without actually rising to the level of authors who had fully interiorized their literary education: his style is at best a collection of *topoi* and perfunctory references to the Latin canon.[2] On such an understanding, the *Historiae* are a limpid text: stripped of its embellishments, the narrative easily hands over its historical and autobiographical information. This book argues against such a reductive view of Orosius' rhetorical qualities and the apparent simplicity of his history. As a start, this chapter suggests, on the contrary, that Orosius combines Vergilian allusions and deft self-presentation in the prefaces to the *Commonitorium* and the *Historiae* so as to harness Augustine's authority for his own credit. Both resources can be detected in the works of many ancient and late antique writers:[3]

[1] Augustine, *Epistula* 166: promptus eloquio; Prosper Tiro, *Chronicon* a. 396: vir eloquens; Gennadius, *De viris illustribus* 39: vir eloquens. For modern stylistic analyses, see Svennung 1922; Mulder 1926: 174; Wotke 1939; Hingst 1972: 173–95, 236–54; Bartalucci 1976.

[2] See P.6, note 15, of the introduction.

[3] Felgentreu 1999; Trout 1999; Lühken 2002; Rees 2004; Kelly 2008; Mastrangelo 2008; Swain 2010.

Orosius was thus doing what reasonably could be expected of any aspiring author. As a consequence, the autobiographical comments interspersed in both works have first and foremost a rhetorical function, which we need to fully understand before we attempt to write Orosius' biography.[4]

I. SINNER AND SAINT

Orosius washed up on the shores of North Africa, probably in 414. The reasons for his arrival from Spain remain unknown. In the recommendation letter to Jerome that Orosius took with him to Bethlehem (415), Augustine attributed Orosius' choice of destination to his own reputation,[5] but a more violent cause has been construed from passages in the *Histories* which seem to indicate that their author once narrowly escaped a barbarian raid.[6] Neither explanation can be decisive. Whilst Augustine's reputation surely played a role, he immediately disowns it: he suggests he teaches his pupils only what he can and, since he is lacking in knowledge in certain fields, he has to send Orosius to his learned colleague Jerome. The relevant passages from the *Historiae*, as we shall see in chapter 5, are primarily aimed at arousing the sympathy of the reader and at displaying the sort of emotions the rest of the work wishes to provoke. Moreover, they do not link the escape from barbarians with the choice of Africa as a destination. Significantly, Orosius' first preserved work, the 'consultation or reminder to Augustine about the errors of the Priscillianists and Origenists' (*Consultatio sive commonitorium Orosii ad Augustinum de errore priscillianistarum et origenistarum*),[7] written probably in 414 shortly after his arrival, fails to give a precise reason for his coming, and its preface consciously plays on the bafflement that the

[4] See Kelly 2008, 104–58 for a similar argument about Ammianus.

[5] Augustine, *Epistula* 166: fama excitus, quod a me posset de his quae scire vellet quidquid vellet audire. Cf. Lacroix 1965: 34; Fabbrini 1979: 52–3; Martínez Cavero, Beltrán Corbalán, and González Fernández 1999: 68–70.

[6] Orosius 3.20.6 and 5.2.1–2. Cf. Corsini 1968: 10–12; Arnaud-Lindet 1990–1: ix–xii. Both positions are reconciled by Mörner 1844: 20; Lippold 1976: i.xx; Torres Rodríguez 1985: 33; Martínez Cavero 2002: 32–4.

[7] On Orosius and Priscillianism, see Sanchez 2009: 51–2.

sudden and unannounced debarkation of a young Spanish presbyter must have generated in Hippo.

The *Commonitorium* reminds Augustine of a demand Orosius had made orally before, namely, to provide him with arguments against heretics in Spain. Orosius places high hopes on the bishop of Hippo: only he will be able to root out the tree of heresy and plant new, healthy seeds. Augustine is depicted as a tool of God: 'Through you, saintly father, through you, I say, our Lord God will mend with the word the ways of those he has castigated with the sword.'[8] Divine providence, therefore, has sent Orosius to Augustine (ad te per deum missus sum). The unfathomable ways of God are then made explicit in the following confession:

> I do not know why I came. Without wish, without necessity, without permission I left my homeland, driven by some unknown force, and I then arrived on the shores of this land. At this point I finally have seen reason again in the fact that I was sent to you. You will not judge me impudent if you accept my confession. Make me return to my beloved homeland as a good merchant having found the pearl, and not as a fugitive slave after a reversal of fortune.

> agnosco cur venerim. sine voluntate, sine necessitate, sine consensu de patria egressus sum occulta quadam vi actus, donec in istius terrae litus allatus sum. Hic demum in eum resipui intellectum, quod ad te venire mandabar. Impudentem non iudices, si accipis confitentem. Fac me ad dilectam dominam meam idoneum negotiatorem inventa margarita, non fugitivum servum eversa substantia reverti.[9]

The passage suggests that Orosius' departure from Spain was not uncontroversial. By saying *sine voluntate* Orosius lays himself open to the charge of *akedia*, the accusation of spiritual lethargy; *sine necessitate* suggests that he absconded without there being a pressing cause, whereas *sine consensu* points to the fact that presbyters were not supposed to travel without permission. Orosius had clearly taken leave without asking. Only Augustine can redeem him. If he provides him with the advice asked for, the presbyter will be able to regain Spain as the good merchant in the parable in the Gospel of Matthew (13, 45–6): the Kingdom of Heavens resembles a merchant of pearls who sells all his possessions when he finds one pearl of immense

[8] Orosius, *Commonitorium* 1: per te dominus deus noster, per te, inquam, beate pater, quos castigavit in gladio, emendet in verbo.

[9] Orosius, *Commonitorium* 1.

value. But if Augustine refuses to grant advice, Orosius will go back like a fugitive slave who is forced back to his master by poverty and hunger. His departure from Spain was thus at least a breach of decorum and without proper justification. The reference to the parable suggests that Orosius left all he had (possessions? career prospects?) behind in order to travel to Africa. This does not lend much credence to the hypothesis that barbarian invaders chased Orosius.

Yet, it is dangerous to draw too many historical conclusions from what is, after all, a rhetorical self-presentation in the context of a preface. Orosius harnesses the clearly uncommon fact that he had arrived in Hippo on his own initiative to his personal advantage. He consciously styles himself as a sinner, not just in the anaphora *sine voluntate, sine necessitate, sine consensu*, but also in the reference to his own confession (si accipis confitentem). The last lines of the preface take this self-depiction as a sinner even further: through a shift from the singular to the plural, Orosius identifies himself with the sinful, because heretical, Spaniards (nos confitemur offensam, tu pervides plagam: 'we confess the offense, you see clearly the wound'). Conversely, Augustine is elevated above the mortal fray. Not only is he an instrument of divine providence, but Orosius assimilates the pearl, which in Matthew stands for the Kingdom of Heavens, with Augustine's teaching. The word of Augustine, Orosius suggests, is the word of God. The confessional tone of Orosius and the relationship of sinner and saint that he construes between himself and Augustine are reminiscent of how Augustine positions himself towards God in his *Confessions*.[10] The emphasis on a lack of self-knowledge and ignorance of one's own motifs also picks up one of the key themes of Augustine's most famous work, as well as the way in which providence ultimately guides one through sin towards a good purpose.[11] None of these themes would be outlandish in any Christian work, but their close occurrence in a dedication to Augustine is intriguing. It is therefore tempting to interpret Orosius' double use of *confitentem/confitemur* as a conscious reference to the *Confessiones*. Such covert

[10] See also Augustine, *Sermo* 67.2, where confession is defined as confessing one's sins and praising God. This is the double movement detectable in the preface of Orosius, with Augustine taking the place of God. See also *Sermo* 131.2, describing how one is drawn to God by love. Shared love is a central theme in the preface to the *Historiae* (pr. 8).

[11] Augustine, *Confessiones* 5.(8)14, 9.(10)23. See Crosson 2003; Clark 2005.

references to a work of an addressee are not uncommon[12] and Orosius did know Augustine's most famous work when he wrote his *Historiae*.[13]

In the *Commonitorium*, Orosius has, however, another trick up his sleeve to draw the attention of Augustine. His description of his wanderings through the Mediterranean is not as innocent as it looks: *de patria egressus sum occulta quadam vi actus, donec in istius terrae litus allatus sum* contains an allusion to the preface of the Aeneid (1–4: Arma virumque cano, Troiae qui primus ab oris/ Italiam, fato profugus, Laviniaque venit/litora, multum ille et terris iactatus et alto/vi superum saevae memorem Iunonis ob iram). The chance to associate one's travels through the Mediterranean with the fate of Aeneas was too great to resist for a cultured individual, who had learnt Vergil by heart, as Augustine himself illustrates in the *Confessions*, where his farewell to his mother Monica in Ostia is modelled on that of Aeneas to Dido.[14] The allusion is more than a flourish. It creates a sense of homecoming: just as Italy was to be Aeneas' new home, Hippo and Augustine will be for Orosius. Like the rhetoric of sinfulness, the statement invites Augustine to create a new home for Orosius. It also underscores the providential nature of his arrival in Hippo: just as Aeneas was guided by fate without knowing it, Orosius is directed by providence. How far one can press such subtle allusions is hard to tell: the assumption of the persona of Aeneas might, for example, support the idea that violence and upheaval caused Orosius to leave his hometown, although that seems to contradict the rest of the preface. Equally, Vergilian allusions during a disembarkation in Africa can hardly not conjure up the image of Dido.[15] Orosius might thus be alluding to the fact that he will have to leave at some point, whilst at the same time hoping for a relationship of friendship between himself and

[12] The *carmen* by Licentius, following his letter to Augustine (Augustine, *Epistula* 26), contains references to Augustine's Cassiacium dialogues: see Shanzer 1991: 127–33.

[13] Orosius 7.30.3 derives from Augustine, *Confessions* 8.(5.)10 (cf. Courcelle 1963: 204). The *Confessions* were a work that made an impact: Paulinus of Nola draws on it in his *Eucharisticos* (cf. Courcelle 1963: 206–22; Coskun 2006: 294–305).

[14] Augustine, *Confessiones* 5.(8)14, with Bennett 1988: 65. See also the correspondence with the pagan Maximus (Augustine, *Epistulae* 16–17) and with Volusianus (Augustine, *Epistulae* 135–7), as analysed by Tornau 2006: 40–3, 57–69.

[15] Cf. Augustine, *Confessiones* 1.(13)22.

the bishop. The preface of the *Commonitorium*, with its demand for advice to be brought back to Spain, indeed implies that Orosius' presence in Africa will be temporary (cf. *me . . . reverti*), which would support this interpretation. These last suggestions are obviously speculative, but they draw attention to the methodological point that intertextual allusions are by their very nature unlimited, in that they can generate meanings that go beyond what the author may have intended. What we as scholars wish to ascribe to Orosius' intentions can only be determined by showing that certain messages generated by the allusion engage with the other themes the text deals with.[16]

In this case, the Vergilian allusion, however suggestive, adds depth and meaning to Orosius' description of his wanderings. Moreover, it is complemented by the reference to the merchant of the Gospel of Matthew, which skilfully continues the theme of travelling, but also adds a new element: Orosius hopes to take something valuable back home and avoid the fate of a fugitive slave. Such twin references to Vergil and the Bible recur, as we shall see immediately, in the preface of the *Historiae*, and together they symbolize the two pillars of learning of the Christian Latin elite of late Antiquity.[17] Orosius' deployment of both may have appealed to Augustine, who was steeped in Vergil but also keen to correct and contrast him with the Gospel.[18] The preface of the *Commonitorium* is thus very precisely targeted: Orosius displays implicitly but clearly a shared culture with the addressee, but also admiration for his work. This literary skill, combined with the self-effacement of a sinner who faces a saint, betrays a desire to be drawn into the orbit of Augustine, fountain of learning and wisdom. The bishop of Hippo seems to have liked it and paid Orosius in kind. His reply compliments Orosius by picking up several of the expressions and metaphors of the preface to the *Commonitorium*,[19] and, as we have already seen, he praises the learning and eloquence of his new pupil in the letter to Jerome.[20]

[16] For methodological reflections on intertextuality in ancient literature, see Fowler 2000: 127–8; Kelly 2008: 161–222. The latter provides a useful overview of views among scholars of Latin literature.

[17] See the essays in Rees 2004.

[18] On Augustine's attitude to Vergil, see MacCormack 1998; Clark 2004.

[19] See the references in the apparatus of Augustine, *Ad Orosium* (Corpus Christianorum. Series Latina 49, 165–7).

[20] Augustine, *Epistula* 166: vigil ingenio, promptus eloquio, flagrans studio.

II. THE LORD'S DOG

The preface to the *Historiae* may look like an incongruous whole: it starts with setting out Augustine's *praeceptum* to Orosius (1–2), then elaborates a comparison of a dog and his master (3–7), often taken to symbolize the relationship between God and the Church, and finally returns to the *praeceptum* (8–16).[21] When read, however, in the light of Orosius' self-presentation and his use of Vergilian allusions as detected in the *Commonitorium*, the middle section fits perfectly in the preface, which aims at capitalizing on Augustine's fame as a theologian and author.

The preface falls into two parts, clearly delineated by Orosius. The first half, opening with *praeceptis tuis parui* ('I have obeyed your orders'), elaborates the relationship between the author and the dedicatee, Augustine (1.pr.1–8). Picking up twice the opening words of the preface (1.pr.9: *praeceperas mihi*; 1.pr.10: *praeceperas ergo*), the second part sets out the nature of the commandment, and reveals that additional encouragement for the work was given by a certain Julian of Carthage, who is further unknown (1.pr.12).[22] Given his position in the preface, Julian is completely subordinated to Augustine and he will play no further role in the *Historiae*. He is also absent from the postface, in which Augustine, on the contrary, gets pride of place (7.43.19–20).

A first approach to the *proemium* is to set it against the background of contemporary literary habits. It partakes in two general tendencies of later Latin prefaces, as analysed by T. Janson.[23] First, there is little in the preface that is specific for historical works: no praise for the usefulness of history, no justification through reference to the greatness of the deeds told, no claim of impartiality.[24] This should create no doubts as to the genre of the *Historiae*: apart from the title, the definition of their subject in 1.pr.10 as warfare, disease, and natural disasters is exactly that of earlier and later historians,[25] and one can

[21] For useful analyses of the preface, see Arnaud-Lindet 1990–91: i.3; Fear 2010a: 31.

[22] Mandouze, Marrou, and Palanque 1982: 616 speculate he might have been a monk.

[23] Janson 1964: 115–16.

[24] For these *topoi*, see Marincola 1997: 34–43, 158–73.

[25] Thucydides 1.23; Tacitus, *Historiae* 1.2–3; Herodian 1.4; Sidonius Apollinaris, *Epistula* 4.22.3; Agathias, *Historiae* pr.10, 1.1.2.

detect an avatar of the idea of the greatness of the subject in his contention that the events of the past were more cruel than those of the present. Even the admission that Orosius himself was first not convinced of the superiority of the present (1.pr.13) can be read as a claim for objectivity: Orosius presents himself as an originally sceptical historian who was convinced by his own research. Nevertheless, all in all, the preface well illustrates the tendency towards homogenization of the prefaces for different genres that Janson has detected. The second tendency is the reduced popularity of non-dedicatory prefaces: most late-antique works present themselves as having been written at the behest of an individual. The commandment of the dedicatee usually raises doubts in the mind of the author regarding the feasibility of the task and his own competence, but then the author adjusts his will to that of the dedicatee: he freely and sometimes eagerly fulfils the task set to him, in the expectation that the work will bring him intellectual, spiritual, or material rewards.[26] Unsurprisingly, much of the vocabulary and themes expressing these sentiments is shared by Orosius and contemporary authors, such as *labor*,[27] *libentia*,[28] and *voluntas*,[29] but also expressions of submission[30] and modesty.[31] Such a similarity in general outlook may point to a reliance on the same examples. A possible model is the preface of the *Rhetorica ad Herennium*, a late Republican work ascribed to Cicero, which enjoyed particular popularity in late fourth-century rhetorical education.[32] That preface is of the dedicatory type,

[26] See, e.g. Itinerarium Alexandri 1.2: vicem sciam in me etiam redundaturam.

[27] Orosius 1.pr.1: tu enim iam isto iudicio laborasti; *Itinerarium Alexandri* 1.1: libens sane et laboris cum amore succubui; Vegetius 1.pr.4: labor diligens ad fidelis; *Panegyrici latini* 5.1.1: labore ac diligentia; Sulpicius Severus, *Chronica* 1.1.1: quorum ego voluntatem secutus non peperci labori meo; cf. Orosius 1.pr.13: dedi operam.

[28] Orosius 1.pr.1: utinam efficaciter quam libenter, 1.pr.8: quod libens feci; *Itinerarium Alexandri* 1.1: libens sane et laboris cum amore succubui; Festus 1: parebo libens praecepto.

[29] Orosius 1.pr.2: voluntate conatuque decoravi; *Itinerarium Alexandri* 1.1: meum velle; Sulpicius Severus, *Chronica* 1.1.1: quorum ego voluntatem secutus non peperci labori meo; Eutropius, pr.: ex voluntate mansuetudinis.

[30] Orosius 1.pr.8: subiectio mea praecepto paternitatis tuae; *Itinerarium Alexandri* 1.1: libens sane et laboris cum amore succubui.

[31] Orosius 1.pr.12: levi opusculo; Vegetius 1.pr.4: in hoc opusculo, 1.pr.6: in hoc parvo libello.

[32] Jerome, *Apologia adversus libros Rufini* PL 23.409, *Commentarii in Abdiam* PL 25.1098; Rufinus, *De compositione et de metris oratorum* p. 577.29.

and has the adjustment of wills, as well as the typical vocabulary.[33] Its rebuttal of the inane arrogance of Greek rhetorical writers and their complex theories may have been the inspiration for Orosius' attack on the vain perversity of the pagans.[34]

The hallmark of a good preface, however, is that it cannot be reduced to a concatenation of commonplaces derived from a rhetorical education.[35] That of Orosius also merits closer attention, especially regarding the way he subtly creates a position of authority for himself out of the rhetoric of deference. Indeed, by their very nature, dedicatory prefaces establish an unequal relationship between the dedicatee and the author. Even if the dedicatee is not of a higher social status, the mere fact that he orders the work to be written gives him a position of power. As a consequence the author usually indulges in a rhetoric of subservience.[36] For Orosius, Augustine was obviously his social and intellectual superior, and the historian immediately emphasizes his obedience and humility: 'I have obeyed your orders, saintly father Augustine, and I hope I did it with as much good result as good will.' The hope of a good result is, however, subordinated to a more important matter, namely, obedience to Augustine's will:

> But I am, both positively and negatively, not really stirred by the question whether I have acted rightly or wrongly, for you have taken the effort to examine if I could do what you ordered me to. On my part I am content with the testimony of obedience alone, if at least I have embellished it with will and effort.[37]

[33] *Rhetorica ad Herrenium* 1.1: quod datur otii libentius in philosophia consumere consuevimus . . . tua nos voluntas commovit . . . ne aut tua causa noluisse aut fugisse nos laborem putasses.

[34] *Rhetorica ad Herrenium* 1.1: inanis adrogantiae causa; Orosius 1.pr.8: vaniloquem pravitatem.

[35] See the comments of Felgentreu 1999: 193 on Janson's rather reductive approach.

[36] Such a rhetoric is very manifest in works dedicated to the emperor, without him having asked for them: see, e.g. the preface of Vegetius and that of the *De rebus bellicis*.

[37] Orosius 1.pr.1–2. Praeceptis tuis parui, beatissime pater Augustine; atque utinam tam efficaciter quam libenter. quamquam ego in utramuis partem parum de explicito mouear, rectene an secus egerim: tu enim iam isto iudicio laborasti, utrumne hoc, quod praeciperes, possem; ego autem solius oboedientiae, si tamen eam uoluntate conatuque decoraui, testimonio contentus sum.

This is mirrored in the postface, where Orosius again stresses his obedience and asks Augustine, as his teacher, to judge the work.[38] The shift from uncertainty about the result to obedience to Augustine is in fact only apparent. Under the cover of humility and obedience, the first lines of Orosius' preface immediately signal to the reader that this work is not only written at the behest of Augustine, but also carries his approval: the insight of Augustine into Orosius' capacities guarantees the identity of the task set and the result executed. Obedience to Augustine thus ensures that the work lives up to his expectations. This suggests an uncommon closeness between both men, which is elaborated in the next five paragraphs, through a comparison of their relationship with that of a master and his dog.

The more ambitious of late Latin authors chose a striking image to run through their prefaces. Rufinus of Aquileia, a contemporary of Orosius, for example, had to write numerous *prooemia* for his translations from the Greek and often selected a specific theme for each of them.[39] The brief preface to Festus' *breviarium* in turn draws on the vocabulary of counting.[40] The convoluted Latin of the *Itinerarium Alexandri* aspires to more than it actually achieves, but the preface is strikingly replete with language of divination, possibly enhanced by a reference to the Delphic oracle from Statius' *Thebaid* in its very first line.[41] The comparison with a master and his dog can be seen as the Orosian equivalent of such literary games, and he packs a lot in it. The simile takes up most of the first half of the preface (1.pr.3–8). Already in Antiquity the dog was man's best friend: even in the houses of the great and worthy, Orosius notes, 'the care for dogs is not the least important' (cf. Vergil, *Georgica* 3.404). Of all animals, only dogs

[38] Orosius 7.43.20: ita iam ego certo et solo, quem concupiscere debui, oboedientiae meae fructu fruor; de qualitate autem opusculorum tu uideris qui praecepisti, tibi adiudicanda si edas, per te iudicata si deleas.

[39] e.g. Rufinus, *Historia ecclesiastica* pr. (medicine), *Explanatio Origenis super epistulam Pauli ad Romanos*, pr. (boats and sailing).

[40] Festus 1: ac morem secutus calculonum . . . quos breviter dictis brevius conputetur . . . numerare videaris.

[41] *Itinerarium Alexandri* 1.1: dextrum . . . et omine tibi et magisterio futurorum . . . regentium prospera, 1.3: obsecutam rationi fortunam . . . tu res martias auspicere . . . fortunae, 1.8: fatalem hanc belli lineam tangere, 1.10: fortuna. The first line of the preface (dextrum admodum sciens et omine tibi et magisterio futurorum) might contain an echo of Statius, *Thebais* 7.663–4 (. . . vociferans: prohibite manus, haec omine dextro/moenia Cirrhaea monstravit Apollo iuvenca). The preface is analysed by Tabacco 1990 and Callu 1992, but neither scholar notices the allusion.

voluntarily and eagerly do what they are trained for, and they are the only ones spontaneously held back by obedience until an order is given. 'For they have their own instincts, which elevate them as much above brutish animals as they approach them of rational beings, namely the capacity to distinguish, love, and serve.' Dogs distinguish their masters from strangers and are bound by a bond of love to the former. Their zeal against strangers is not an expression of hate for these but of love for their masters.[42] The comparison concludes with a reference to *Matthew* 15.27, where the woman from Canaan refers to the dogs eating the crumbs off the table, and to the prophet Tobias who had a dog,[43] showing that hounds have their usefulness in spreading the word of God.

Paragraphs 3–7 of the preface, where the comparison with a dog is made, open and close with an appeal to authority: at the end there is the explicit reference to the Gospel and to the Book of Tobias, and at the start the quotation of Vergil, *Georgics* 3.404 has often been noted, but there is more to it than usually thought.[44] The comparison has the same formal structure as the section of the *Commonitorium* which we analysed above, beginning with Vergil and closing with the Bible. Moreover, the reference to Vergil is not as innocent as it looks. *Georgics* 3.404–9 reads:

> Nor let the care of dogs be last in your thoughts, but feed swift Spartan whelps and fierce Molossians alike on fattening whey. Never, with them on guard, need you fear for your stalls a midnight thief, or onslaught of wolves, or restless Spaniards in your rear.

[42] Orosius 1.pr.3–5: nam et in magna magni patrisfamilias domo cum sint multa diuersi generis animalia adiumento rei familiaris commoda, non est tamen canum cura postrema; quibus solis natura insitum est, uoluntarie ad id quod praeparantur urgueri et per ingenitam quandam oboedientiae formulam sola disciplinati timoris exspectatione suspendi, donec ad peragendi licentiam nutu signoue mittantur. habent enim proprios appetitus, quantum brutis excellentiores tantum rationabilibus propinquantes, hoc est discernere amare seruire. nam discernentes inter dominos atque extraneos non eos quos insectantur oderunt sed iis quos amant zelant, et amantes dominum ac domum non quasi ex natura apti corporis uigilant sed ex conscientia solliciti amoris inuigilant.

[43] Orosius 1.pr.6–7: unde etiam mystico sacramento in Euangeliis, quod edant micas catelli sub mensa dominorum, et Chananaea non erubuit dicere et Dominus non fastidiuit audire. beatus etiam Tobias, ducem angelum sequens, canem comitem habere non spreuit; Matthew 15.27: At illa dixit: etiam Domine, nam et catelli edunt de micis quae cadunt de mensa dominorum suorum; *Tobias* 6.1: Profectus est autem Tobias, et canis secutus est eum.

[44] I am expanding on Lippold 1976: i.365 and Arnaud-Lindet 1990–91: i.191.

> nec tibi cura canum fuerit postrema sed una/velocis spartae catulos acremque Molossum/pasce sero pingui, numquam custodibus illis/nocturnum stabulis furem incursusque luporum/aut impacatos a tergo horrebis Hiberos.[45]

When read in conjunction with these Vergilian lines, the comparison starts to generate various interlacing meanings. First, Orosius' canine debasement is transformed into a strategy for literary authority. His capacity to appeal to literary models is an obvious display of literary skill and ambition. But even the comparison of himself to a dog is not just to the benefit of Augustine. At first sight, this may seem to be the case: Augustine is the master and Orosius the dog. Yet Orosius' rhetoric of deference also raises him through subservience. The dog was famously a symbol of intelligence and fidelity,[46] qualities specifically underlined by Orosius in the triad 'discerning, loving, and serving' (1.pr.4: discernere amare seruire). Comparing himself to Augustine's dog, Orosius therefore conflates his own *ingenium* and his submission to Augustine. Moreover, as the quotation from the *Georgics* makes clear, the dog is one of the most important animals in the *familia*. Orosius may be just the dog, but he stands close to the superior rational beings and way above the brutish animals:[47] there is an obvious distance between Augustine and Orosius, but there are still many lesser beings down the social ladder. The closeness thus suggested allows Orosius to claim that the present work is more Augustine's than his own. He did the work, but intellectually it belongs to his master.[48] As we shall see in chapter 8, Orosius is close to Augustine in many respects, but it would be mistaken to take this near identification of Augustine as the true author of the *Historiae* as a mere acknowledgment of intellectual debt on the part of Orosius. Rather, Orosius can be seen as trying to cash in on the status of Augustine. The latter is the intellectual father, but because Orosius was deemed worthy of the task, he cannot be a mean intellect either. Just as the dedication of the first books of Augustine's *City of God* to Marcellinus may have been a 'publishing coup', cashing in on the martyr-like reputation of this recently executed and consequently rehabilitated official,[49] Orosius, whose reputation was minimal and

[45] Tr. H. Rushton Fairclough (LCL).
[46] Hünemörder 1998.
[47] See Augustine, *Sermo* 77.10 and 113A.11.
[48] Orosius 1.pr.8, 1.pr.12.
[49] McLynn 1999.

whose association with Augustine had, all in all, been brief at the time of writing (at best 414–18, with the journey to Jerome in 415), tried to surf on the reputation of Augustine.[50]

So far, I have offered a surface reading of the comparison, based on what is explicitly said. But one can go further: a reader imbued with Vergil would know the context of the line quoted and he would grasp that the Vergilian hounds warding off wolves and thieves in the rest of the verses are an allusion to the apologetic nature of the work. Just as the Spartan and Molossian dogs defend the estate of the *familia*, Orosius and his *Histories* shall defend the Christian flock from the arguments of pagans. The apologetic purpose of the work is only made explicit six paragraphs later (1.pr.9), but a well-educated reader, having grasped the allusion, would be prepared for what is coming. It is thus likely that Orosius intended his readers to understand the deeper meaning of the allusion to Vergil.

Finally, the end of the Vergilian phrase designates the brigands that are warded off by the dog metonymically as 'Spaniards'. One can detect here an allusion to Orosius' demand in the *Commonitorium* to provide him with arguments against Spanish Priscillianists: Orosius the dog will continue Augustine's own battle against heresies in Spain. Yet one cannot fail to notice another and more ludic implication: Orosius himself was a Spaniard. Will he provide protection against himself? Will he stop pestering Augustine? It is not easy to make sense of this possible self-reference. One possibility is that, as Orosius left North Africa soon after the completion of his *Historiae*, it could be a covert and ironic allusion to the status of the work as a farewell present to Augustine: this work will see the Spaniards off, and in particular this Spaniard. Again, the admittedly speculative nature of this last reading should not detract from the fact that, just as in the *Commonitorium*, Orosius is capable of handling a Vergilian allusion to good effect and as a source of additional meaning.

The comparison is wound up with a paragraph that returns to the themes and vocabulary of the first two paragraphs:

[50] The preface has often been interpreted from a psychological perspective: Corsini 1968: 41–51 notes naive pride, followed by Marrou 1970: 67 ('un sentiment d'orgueilleusse et naive satisfaction'); Martelli 1982: 234 ('ipocrita umilità'); Merrills 2005: 40 finds anxiety in the preface. As shown by E. Oliensis 1998: 127–53 for Horace, in the presence of superiors, authors try to make the most of a rhetoric of deference.

> Being thus linked to universal love through your particular love, I voluntarily obey your wish. For, as my subjection owes its result to the command of your fatherhood and as the work is entirely yours, I return my work, which coming from you returns to you, with only this of mine in addition, that I did it willingly.[51]

These words are an obvious illustration of the theme of the adjustment of the will of the author on that of the dedicatee, which was already broached in the first two paragraphs of the preface. The nigh oxymoronic expression of the last paragraph makes this abundantly clear: 'I willingly obeyed your wish' (*voluntati tuae volens parui*). Yet we have moved on in one important respect, which was prepared for by the comparison with a dog: the insistence on mutual love creates a particularly close link between Augustine and Orosius, to the point that the former becomes the intellectual creator of the work. One could even say that Augustine is almost substituted for Orosius as the true author of the *Historiae* (1.pr.8: *totumque tuum sit*). In the second paragraph of the preface it was said that Augustine had set Orosius a task that was within his capacities; now the work is 'entirely' attributed to Augustine: it emanated from him and, through the dedication, it returns to its rightful owner and author. The striking use of repetitive vocabulary (*amori/amore*, *voluntati/volens*, *ex te/ad te*, *factum/feci*) suggests that the distinction between the author's work and the desires of the dedicatee have been completely overcome. Yet even though he can verbally efface the distinction between author and dedicatee, the very nature of the preface and the work make it impossible to forget that distinction and Orosius significantly ends the paragraph with an expression of his own authorship (*reddidi, quod libens feci*). Crucially, therefore, Orosius' rhetoric of deference and his apparent self-effacement in the face of Augustine do not make him disappear as an author: on the contrary, both are deployed as rhetorical tools to enhance the status of his own work as being of truly Augustinian standing.

The second part of the preface, which details Augustine's precept to Orosius and sets out the general argument, continues to raise the *Historiae* through rapprochement with Augustine. Most obviously, it inserts the present work in the grand apologetic enterprise of the *De*

[51] Orosius 1.pr.8: igitur generali amori tuo speciali amore conexus voluntati tuae volens parui. Nam cum subiectio mea praecepto paternitatis tuae factum debeat totumque tuum sit, quod ex te ad te redit, opus meum, hoc solo meo cumulatius reddidi, quod libens feci.

civitate Dei. Orosius explicitly notes that Augustine, who is now working on book 11, would not have the time to write the 'little book' that represents the *Historiae* (1.pr.12: *levi opusculo*). Yet the first sentence of the second part already alludes to the title and theme of the *City of God*, when defining his adversaries as 'those who are alien to the city of God and are called "pagans" for coming from the crossroads and villages of rural places or "gentiles" because of their earthly knowledge'.[52] This sub-clause is built on the contrast between a 'city of God' and earthly knowledge, just as Augustine developed the contrast between the *civitas dei* and the *civitas terrena*. Orosius then finally explains what Augustine had commanded him to do:

> You ordered that I collect, on the basis of all the records of histories and annals that are to be found at present, which were the grave deeds of war, the destruction of illness, the woes of famine, the terrible effects of earthquakes, the uncommonly grave floods, the fearful eruptions of fire, the cruelty of strikes of lightning and hailstorms, the miseries of murder and vice that were committed in past centuries and briefly set it all out in a well-ordered narrative.
>
> praeceperas ergo, ut ex omnibus qui haberi ad praesens possunt historiarum atque annalium fastis, quaecumque aut bellis grauia aut corrupta morbis aut fame tristia aut terrarum motibus terribilia aut inundationibus aquarum insolita aut eruptionibus ignium metuenda aut ictibus fulminum plagisque grandinum saeua uel etiam parricidiis flagitiisque misera per transacta retro saecula repperissem, ordinato breuiter uoluminis textu explicarem.[53]

As I have remarked earlier in this chapter, Orosius rhetorically elaborates, but still adheres to, a standard definition of the subject of history. In contrast to the traditional emphasis on the greatness of the past, Orosius is decidedly interested in the woes of the past: all topics are designated by a plural neuter adjective of emotion or pain (*gravia*, *corrupta*, *tristia*, *terribilia*, *insolita*, *metuenda*, *saeva*, *misera*). This announces a recurrent emphasis in the *Historiae*, where the sequence of time is seen as filled with misery.[54] This stress on the

[52] Orosius 1.pr.9: qui alieni a ciuitate Dei ex locorum agrestium conpitis et pagis pagani uocantur siue gentiles quia terrena sapiunt.

[53] Orosius 1.pr.10.

[54] See, e.g. Orosius 2.3.9: recolant sane mecum maiorum suorum tempora, bellis inquietissima, sceleribus exsecrabilia, dissensionibus foeda, miseriis continuatissima; 5.24.21: serie temporum et malis sequacibus cohaeserunt.

suffering again inserts Orosius into the apologetic enterprise of the *City of God*, where Augustine had already developed the same argument and emphasis on *mala* of the past, against the pagan critique that Christianity had caused the Roman Empire to slide downhill.[55] Just as the subservient near-identification with Augustine in the first part of the preface did not debase Orosius' status as an author, the assimilation of the *Historiae* with Augustine's project does not make the former superfluous: Orosius immediately admits that he himself first believed the pagan argument for the superiority of the past to be true, and that only his research convinced him of the contrary (1.pr.13). Not only does this allow Orosius to draw the pagan reader into his narrative by presenting himself as having shared their views, it also establishes the necessity of his own work: the history he is presenting to the reader is not just an expansion of what one could already read in Augustine and it proposes to challenge the intuitive perception of the present found among his audience.

The deft play of deference on which the preface to the *Historiae* is built, should not lead to scepticism about the reality of its statements. Assuming that rhetoric and reality cannot co-exist, some scholars have suggested that Orosius invented a *praeceptum* of Augustine or strongly modified it.[56] The presence of literary play does not preclude in any way the reality of such a commandment. Moreover, it is a priori unlikely that Orosius would dare, or be able, to publish a work in North Africa that would overstep the boundaries of what was acceptable by imputing to Augustine a fictitious commandment. More importantly, Orosius' rhetoric of deference and closeness stands out by its skilful appropriation of Augustine's intellectual authority. We cannot know if the *Historiae* would have had the same success had they been written in Spain without an Augustinian connection, but one strongly suspects the answer to be negative. Orosius' rhetoric of closeness has long influenced the interpretation of the Spanish presbyter as basically a subcontractor of Augustine. I hope the previous pages have shown that this rhetoric also serves another purpose,

[55] Augustine, *De civitate dei* 4.2: Promiseramus ergo quaedam nos esse dicturos aduersus eos, qui Romanae rei publicae clades in religionem nostram referunt, et commemoraturos quaecumque et quantacumque occurrere potuissent uel satis esse uiderentur mala, quae illa ciuitas pertulit uel ad eius imperium prouinciae pertinentes, antequam eorum sacrificia prohibita fuissent.

[56] Corsini 1968: 47; Paschoud 1980: 116; Martelli 1982: 234; Arnaud-Lindet 1990–1: i.xx; Martínez Cavero 2002: 144; Cesa 2003: 29.

namely to set Orosius apart and single out the uniqueness and importance of his work. Uncovering Orosius' hitherto neglected rhetorical qualities and exploring its consequences for the interpretation of the *Historiae* is what this book has set out to do.

III. PEARLS TO BE EXPECTED

Orosius is often thought incapable of intertextuality,[57] let alone of the rhetorical elaboration of the literary relationship between himself and his dedicatee Augustine. Yet the Vergilian allusions discussed in both prefaces are more than mere ornaments: as proper intertextual references, they generate new meanings and add further depth to the embedding text. Orosius' skill in the construction of the two prefaces suggests a degree of literary confidence that one would not expect from a clergyman with limited education, as some have depicted him. Ancient references to Orosius' training and culture confirm this. Augustine qualifies Orosius as *eloquio paratus* in his letter to Jerome, and later judgments follow suit.[58] This should be taken to mean that he had the power of *eloquentia*, i.e. that he had received a good rhetorical training—something Augustine, the former teacher of rhetoric, surely would have been able to appreciate.

On my reading, the allusions in the prefaces of Orosius play a double, interrelated role: they add additional layers of meaning to the surface text and they are part of a subtle rhetoric for authorial authority. I hence wish to emphasize their importance in fashioning the relationship between author and text and between text and audience. In discussions more in line with the orthodoxy of literary theory, authorial intent and audience hardly play a role and the focus is on the interaction between texts.[59] Besides such an approach, however, there is room for one that understands texts in their social

[57] P. Courcelle (1976 and 1984) was prepared to find Vergilian allusions in the oeuvre of such luminaries as Augustine and Claudian, but has little to say about Orosius. Work specifically on Orosius and Vergil tends to see the allusions to Vergil either as ornaments or as apologetic attacks on the pagan canon: Coffin 1936; Bartalucci 1976: 252; Rábade Navarro 1991; Martínez Camero 1994.

[58] Gennadius, *De viris illustribus* 39; Sidonius Apollinaris, *Epistula* 4.3; Venantius Fortunatus, *Carmen* 1.59.

[59] See, e.g. Kelly 2008: 182 on Ammianus.

context, as actors in a social network, an approach that has demonstrated its usefulness especially for the Second Sophistic.[60] As I have indicated above, I do not wish to claim that Orosius consciously pondered over every possible implication of every single allusion; rather, the allusions are part of a wider strategy for authorial authority and for the strengthening of his message. Such an approach is inspired, on the one hand, by the fact that the *Historiae* are a work that clearly wishes to engage its audience (not to say convert it) and repeatedly and explicitly addresses it, and on the other, by the current state of Orosius scholarship, which bases its interpretation of the work often on assumptions about the nature of his readership.[61] To conclude this chapter, I wish to discuss briefly the implications of the foregoing discussion for the latter aspect; the former will figure large in the following chapters.

The possibility that intertextual allusions can generate additional meaning is predicated on the fact that the reader knows the source text. Neither of the allusions to Vergil in the prefaces of the *Historiae* and the *Commonitorium* is made explicit, but the reader is obviously supposed to notice them. This is hardly surprising: Vergil was the shared cultural baggage of the educated elite of his age[62] and would remain the bedrock of education for a long time in the Christian West. Orosius thus writes for an audience that shared in this education. Most telling of this presupposition of learning among his readers are several *praeteritiones*: knowledge of Homer is presupposed, as well as the myth of Tantalus; the Catilinarian conspiracy is dealt with in a brief reference to the works of Cicero and Sallust 'which we all have read'.[63] That this is more than a polite nod to classical culture is shown by the preface to book 6 (6.1.1), where Orosius' opposition between *corpus* and *mens* recalls the classical contrast of Sallust's *Jugurtha* (1–2) between *anima* and *corpus*. Tellingly, in the light of my suggestion that the *Aeneid* is a key intertext for the *Historiae*, its twelve books are said to have been 'burned' into the reader's mind.[64] Contrary to some suggestions that the *Historiae* were addressed to the

[60] For work on these lines, see, e.g. Schmitz 1997 and Van Hoof 2010a.

[61] See the introduction.

[62] Hagendahl 1983: 75–7; Clark 2004: 84–5; Eigler 2003; Rees 2004; Cameron 2011: 567–626.

[63] Orosius 1.12.4–10, 1.17.2, 5.15.2, 6.6.6. On classical authors cited in Orosius, see Rábade Navarro 1991.

[64] Orosius 1.18.1: ludi litterarii disciplinae nostrae quoque memoriae inustum est.

uneducated masses,[65] one must accept that it was, like any work of literature in Antiquity, directed at an educated upper-class audience. Interestingly, although Orosius also refers to poets other than Vergil,[66] most of the authors he either relies on or mentions belong to the canon that was read in school: Sallust, Caesar, Cicero,[67] Livy, and Tacitus, supplemented by the *epitomae* of Justin and Florus, and the *breviarium* of Eutropius. It has been argued by P. Schmidt that the last three authors were primarily read and produced for use in rhetorical schools.[68] Chapter 4 argues that Orosius also drew on works specifically produced for orators, such as the exempla collection of Valerius Maximus. The present chapter has demonstrated that this is more than mere school learning: Orosius is capable of putting his literary knowledge to good use and presupposes that his audience is capable of picking up his allusions. The shared rhetorical education of the late antique elite, incorporated in their 'cultural habits and mindset',[69] thus forms the crucial background to the *Historiae*.

Disdainful judgments of Orosius' education are therefore unproductive: not only must they be dismissive of education in late Antiquity in general, but they fail to notice the historically most interesting, yet often neglected, grey zone of normality between genius and mediocrity.[70] More importantly, they neglect the contemporary rhetorical and literary culture as the key to understanding form and function of the *Historiae*.[71] Orosius is not a clergyman writing for other clerics, but a man with a rhetorical training targeting

[65] Lacroix 1965: 45; Lippold 1976: i.xxxiii; Martelli 1982: 238.

[66] Orosius 7.3.7: Lucan 1.337; Orosius 1.11.2: Claudian, *In Eutropium* 2.159–62; Orosius 1.20.1–4: Claudian, *In Eutropium* 2.163–6 (cf. Hingst 1972: 117, 170); Orosius 7.35.21: Claudian, *Panegyricus de tertio consulatu Honorii augusti* 96–8, quoted from Augustine, *De civitate Dei* 5.26. According to Hingst 1972: 162 Orosius 1.20.1–4 alludes to Ovid, *Tristia* 3.11.39–54. Orosius only seems to know Vergil's *Georgics* and the *Aeneid*, a fact that is common in this period (see Lühken 2002: 276 on Prudentius).

[67] Note the interesting argument of Hingst 1972: 236–54 that there is a strong stylistic influence from Cicero.

[68] Schmidt 1988. Florus was clearly read in later Antiquity, as Prudentius seems to be aware of his work: Florus 1.21 and Prudentius, *Contra Symmachum* 2.738–49 with Partoens 2000; Ammianus used Florus too: Kelly 2008: 178, 267.

[69] Cribiore 2001: 238.

[70] A sober assessment of the actual knowledge of earlier Latin literature in the fourth century can be found in Cameron 2011: 399–420. On rhetorical education in the fourth century, see Cribiore 2001: *passim*.

[71] See already Eigler 2003: 222–4.

others with the same background. If one looks at Orosius from this perspective, the small intertextual pearls fished above are hardly unexpected: they are the traces of a proper rhetorical education which is put to good use. They may not be the giant pearls of paradise Matthew's merchant abandoned his stocks for, but they are not to be despised either.

2

A Tale of Two Cities: Book 2 and the Fall of Rome

In the genesis of Augustine's *City of God*, the sack of Rome in 410 receives pride of place. As is well known, the work was conceived as a response to the queries of pagans and educated Christians about the ultimate responsibility for the events: did the decline of traditional worship rob Rome of divine protection? Logically, the *City of God* opens by addressing the looting of the city by Alaric and his Goths.[1] In Orosius the sack seems less prominent and submerged in an argument for the general superiority of the present over the past. We have seen that the preface focuses on the relationship with Augustine, and detailed discussion of the events of 410 is postponed until their proper place in the chronological narrative at the very end of the *Historiae*.[2] Yet the fall of Rome is much more present than such an impression suggests. Indirectly, mediated through Augustine's *praeceptum*, the *Historiae* are part of the same rebuttal of the critique on Christianity, and Orosius repeatedly draws comparisons between events of the past and the sack of 410.[3] This chapter argues that book 2 of the *Historiae* engages directly with arguments about the sack of Rome and explicitly explores the possibility that Rome would decline, fall, and disappear. The fall of Rome is the theme of book 2.

The book is often neglected. Readers hurry on to the last book, where the historian finally has things to say that cannot be found in another source, rather than simply rehashing the work of others. Only the first three chapters of book 2 are ranked among the key passages of

[1] Augustine, *De civitate Dei* 1.1–2.
[2] Orosius 7.39–40.
[3] Orosius 1.16–17, 2.19, 3.20.12, 3.22.15, 5.6.1.

the work. There, Orosius sets out his 'theory of the four empires', which is seen as a cornerstone of his theology of history.[4] Such readings usually lift these few chapters out of their narrative context in order to construct a theoretical edifice from them. I wish to suggest that a different interpretation, which takes into account the narrative construction of the entire book, is possible and more illuminating for the *Historiae* as a whole. Book 2 conveys to the reader the message that the threat of a decline and fall hangs like the sword of Damocles above Rome's head. The synchronism between Babylon and Rome is, together with intertextual references to Vergil, a narrative tool deployed to help the reader understand the meaning of the past. Such an interpretation not only makes better sense of the 'theory of the four empires', it also liberates Orosius from a systematizing theological reading, restores the whole of book 2 to the prominence in the *Historiae* it deserves, and makes Orosius engage in a much stronger way with the issue of the day, the fall of Rome. The argument has two parts: I offer first a new reading of the first chapters before demonstrating how a judicious and strategic use of Vergil's *Aeneid* keeps the theme of the fall of Rome prominent in the rest of book 2.

I. A GRAND THEORY TO BE DISCARDED

Book 2 occupies a key position in Orosius' *Historiae* by opening the large middle chunk of the *Historiae*. In the first chapter of book 1, Orosius operates a threefold division in his material: he will 'tell from the creation of the world until the foundation of the city, from there until the rule of Caesar and the birth of Christ, from when the world's empire was in the hands of Rome, and then until our own days'.[5] The history of Rome thus lies at the heart of the scheme: book 1, covering the period from Adam until the foundation of Rome, and book 7, describing the Roman Empire since Christ, stand guard next to books

[4] Goetz 1980a: 71–9; Alonso-Núñez 1993; Inglebert 1996: 574–5; Marcone 2002; Martínez Cavero 2002: 177–98.

[5] Orosius 1.1.14: dicturus igitur ab orbe condito usque ad urbem conditam, dehinc usque ad Caesaris principatum nativitatemque Christi, ex quo sub potestate urbis orbis mansit imperium, vel etiam usque ad dies nostros (. . .). Orosius engages here in one of his usual games of language (ab orbe condito usque ad urbem conditam): see Lippold 1976: i.367.

2–6.[6] With book 2 Orosius' focus thus shifts to his central interest: Rome.[7] While the importance of book 6, with the famous synchronism of the rise of Augustus and the Incarnation, has often been underscored,[8] that of book 2 remains underestimated.

The book opens with a logical argument towards the affirmation, drawn from *Romans* 13, that all powers are from God. God has created man, so he must have ordered the world for man. In such a providential order, all local powers fall under God's sway. If all the rulers do, so much more do the empires from which these local rulers derive their strength.[9] If empires are put in place by God, then surely He also did so for the four great empires that each consecutively have dominated world history: Babylonia, Macedonia, Carthage, and Rome. Reverting briefly to the claims of geographical universalism made in 1.2, Orosius situates each of these empires in the four corners of the earth: Babylonia in the East, Macedonia in the North, while Carthage represents the South and Rome the West. The two middling kingdoms are of minor importance: they are at best guardians and caretakers, but have no claim to the heritage of empire that is transferred from Babylon to Rome (2.1.4–6). The intimate link between the latter two is expressed in a series of synchronisms: Babylon falls to the Medes in the same year as Procas, the father of Amulius, starts to reign in what will become Rome (2.2.3); sixty-four years lie between the first Assyrian king (Ninus) and Semiramis, who refounds Babylon, and an equal amount separates Procas from the foundation of Rome (2.2.5);[10] Cyrus destroyed Babylon when the Tarquinii were chased from Rome (2.2.9); the length of the Assyrian empire was 1,164 years until its destruction by the Medes, equal in length to the duration of the Roman Empire from its foundation to its sack by Alaric in 410 (2.3.2–3); just as Babylon was destroyed by its general (*praefectus*) Arbatus, the imperial throne was briefly usurped by the prefect Attalus (2.3.4). This calculus is confirmed in book 7 (7.2.7), with the addition that Babylon lasted 1,400 years in total (7.2.12). This entire construction is obviously forced. It propels, for example, rather obscure individuals such as Arbatus and Procas to the

[6] Corsini 1968: 136–7 sees books 1–4 as discussing the first three empires and 5–7 the empire of Rome.

[7] Cf. Fear 2010a: 20.

[8] See, e.g. Corsini 1968: 137; Inglebert 1996; Rohrbacher 2002: 146.

[9] The argument may well be influenced by Augustine, *De civitate Dei* 5.11.

[10] This may have been picked up by Augustine, *De civitate Dei* 18.21.

forefront of history. In order to make the latter the founding father of Rome, Orosius claims that 'all Roman histories begin with Procas'. The improbability of such a starting point is explained away: during his reign, 'the seed of what will become Rome was sown, although no shoot appeared yet'.[11] As usual in such grand schemes, Orosius needs to elide huge differences between empires to create at least the limited number of building blocks requested. He admits, for example, to subordinating the Medes to Babylon, notwithstanding the fact that the former conquered the latter in 539 BC (2.1.6–7).

A lot is thus sacrificed for the beauty of the scheme. But what is its aim? The answer is not to be found in the antecedents of Orosius. Quite some energy has been spent in defining the sources of Orosius, without conclusive results. His main source, Justin, sees world rule passing from the Assyrians to the Medes, and then onto the Persians and Macedonians. That yields the number four, but the wrong empires.[12] Similarly, in the *City of God*, Augustine has the series Assyria, Persia, Macedonia, and Rome.[13] Orosius was sent to Bethlehem to study with Jerome, and a certain acquaintance with his writings is therefore not unlikely. In his commentary of the Book of Daniel, maybe written *ca.* 407,[14] Jerome identifies the various kingdoms in the visions of Nebucadnessar with Babylon, Persia, Macedonia, and Rome,[15] but the vision in *Daniel* 2 includes the fifth, eschatological empire of Christ which destroys all the others. This last one is prominent by its absence in Orosius. We now get more names right, but not the number. None of these antecedents can be the direct source for Orosius' sequence, but they do show that ordering world history into four or five empires was common in this period.[16]

[11] Orosius 1.2.4: omnes historiae Romanae a Proca exoriuntur; 1.2.5: ita regnante Proca futurae Romae sementis iacta est, etsi nondum germen apparet. The former statement is obviously exaggerated, but the anonymous fourth-century *De viris illustribus urbis romae* starts with Procas. Orosius may well have known this work: see p. 105.

[12] Corsini 1967: 166; Marrou 1970: 72; Alonso-Núñez 1993: 208; Sordi 2003.

[13] Augustine, *De civitate Dei* 4.7, see also 20.23.

[14] Glorie 1964: 751.

[15] Jerome, *In Danielem* I.ii.31–35, II.vii.1–7. A dependence on Jerome is argued by Lacroix 1965: 124. The same sequence is found in Sulpicius Severus, *Chronica* 2.3, alleged by Polichetti 2000: 309–10 to be the source of Orosius. That is unlikely in the light of the differences just noted.

[16] On the 'four empire theory', see Trieber 1892; Kocken 1935; Swain 1940; Sordi 2003.

In a Christian context, direct biblical inspiration is not to be precluded either. The parallel between Babylon the whore and Rome went back to *Revelation* 17.3, and the prophecies of Daniel were well known. Orosius' linking of the empires to the four corners of the world, for example, may derive from *Daniel* 7.[17] Orosius' 'theory of four empires' is thus an original concoction that is part of a long tradition and a contemporary vogue.

The differences between the various lists of empires demonstrate the malleability of the 'four empire theory'. Rather than reading Orosius' version as a systematic exposition of the course of history, we should place it back in its historiographical context and look at how earlier historians used synchronism and parallelism. In *Caesar's Calendar* Denis Feeney has shown how synchronisms were a traditional and important way in ancient historiography of creating meaning by linking various histories and regions together, whose separation was symbolized by the use of different calendars. A famous example is the argument put forward by West Greek historians that the battle of Himera between Sicilians and Carthaginians took place on the same day as that of Salamis (480 BC), with the aim of showing that the entire Greek world shared the same fate: while in the East one great enemy was defeated, the Greeks in the West accomplished a similar feat of arms. The Sicilian historian Timaeus even synchronized the Carthaginian defeat with Thermopylae (480), to argue that the Western Greeks were actually superior: on the day they defeated the Carthaginians, the Spartans were defeated by the Persians.[18] This example illustrates that synchronism can be used to establish parallels and contrasts, to show similarity and difference, and to argue for inferiority and superiority. As shown by Feeney, drawing on earlier scholarship, the early history of Rome has also been constructed with these tools: early historians of Rome made the foundation of Rome coincide with the presumed date of the fall of Assyria, thus suggesting a *translatio imperii*.[19] Synchronisms were thus a recognized narrative tool in ancient historiography to create meaning and were creatively deployed and redeployed to that end. In a Christian context, synchronism became a crucial aspect of

[17] Schöndorf 1952: 31; Arnaud-Lindet 1990–1: i.xlvi. Hingst 1972: 83 and Fear 2010a: 16 suggest, rightly, Orosius' independence.

[18] Polybius 12.26b.4–c.1, with Feeney 2007: 47–51.

[19] Trieber 1892: 336.

chronicle writing, permitting to demonstrate that the Judeo-Christian tradition was older than the pagan one.[20] It is in that context that Orosius' 'four empire theory' needs to be primarily understood: he is not so much importing alien considerations of theology into the writing of history[21] as, in a Christian context, drawing on a technique often used by classical authors before him.

Just as Timaeus' synchronism parallels and contrasts Sicilian Greeks and mainland Greeks, Orosius' parallelism between Babylon and Rome compares both empires in order to oppose them. It is obvious that Babylon and Rome are to be seen in parallel: they share the same lifespan and the same trajectory of rise and fall. Indeed, the sack of Babylon by the Medes, as the chronological endpoint of the power of Babylon, is mirrored in the sack of Rome by Alaric. In book 2, Orosius has little to say about the fate of Babylon afterwards and simply states that after 1,164 years Babylon had run its course and lost its empire.[22] Book 7, specifying a total of 1,400 years for Babylon, suggests that after the conquest by the Medes the city lingered on for a while. This later addition does not alter the fundamental conclusion: the sack of Babylon by the Medes signalled its definitive loss of power and its slide into insignificance. The parallelism between Babylon and Rome thus logically implies that, by 410, Rome had started the same decline and reached the endpoint of its world-historical lifetime. Orosius here concedes an important point to his pagan adversaries: the sack of 410 would have been, in the light of the course of history, the expected endpoint of Rome's empire. It should have started to lapse into oblivion, just as Babylon had. This concession is, however, only a springboard to draw attention more clearly to the difference in fate between Babylon and Rome. Although its fall would have been in line with laws of history, Rome is still standing and, Orosius suggests, in good health: God, who ordains everything, allows Rome to continue its existence because of its conversion to Christianity and its good, i.e. Christian, king. Orosius makes sure that this message is not lost on the reader:

[20] Pilhofer 1990; Burgess 2006; Grafton and Williams 2006.

[21] Some scholars have seen the chronological deformations of Orosius as typical for the Christian writing of history: Paschoud 1967: 281; Marrou 1970: 75.

[22] Orosius 2.2.10: tunc orientis occidit et ortum est occidentis imperium; 2.3.2: spoliata opibus et regno atque ipso rege privata est.

> Behold the similar birth of Babylon and Rome, similar power, similar extension, similar span of time, similar good things, similar evils. But not a similar decline, nor a similar end. For Babylon lost its empire, while Rome preserves it. The former was destroyed and its king killed, the latter is secure and its emperor unharmed.
>
> ecce similis Babyloniae ortus et Romae, similis potentia, similis magnitudo, similia tempora, similia bona, similia mala; tam en non similis exitus similisue defectus. illa enim regnum amisit, haec retinet; illa interfectione regis orbata, haec incolumi imperatore secura est (2.3.6).

Rome was delivered by its Christian inhabitants. Orosius concludes with a jibe at the pagans, probably inspired by Augustine: having been saved from absolute decline, they have profited from the Christians and should therefore convert rather than attack Christianity.[23]

Orosius' 'theory of four empires' thus highlights what the course of history should have been: the sack of Rome by Alaric should have meant the end of Rome, or at least the beginning of the end. But God effectively trumps the preordained course of history as expressed in the parallelism of Babylon and Rome because of the conversion of the Roman Empire to Christianity. Orosius emphasizes the historical necessity of the fall of Rome in the light of the 'theory of the four empires', in order to draw attention to its miraculous saving. The 'four empire theory' is therefore effectively a tool, used to show what one fails to see otherwise. It can be likened to Wittgenstein's view of his own description of the world with formal logic: as he states at the end of his *Tractatus logico-philosophicus*, his propositions are actually a ladder which the reader must throw away, after he has climbed up on it (6.54). In a similar way, the 'four empire theory' is an edifice constructed by Orosius to demonstrate that God is the ultimate arbiter of things and can go against the order of history, even if he has arranged that order himself.

God upsetting his own order is only superficially paradoxical: his miracles precisely overstep the order of nature which he has created himself. Indeed, Orosius probably read in Augustine that God, as the master of history, is not bound by his own providence.[24] God is even not bound by his own predictions, as Orosius illustrates later with an example taken from, again, Augustine. In 395 a terrible prophecy was announced to Constantinople: it would be destroyed in a few days'

[23] This is the argument with which Augustine opens *De civitate Dei* 1.1.
[24] Augustine, *De civitate Dei* 4.33.

time. An ominous cloud did indeed hover in the sky, but massive processions and a city-wide repentance averted the annihilation of the city. 'The events were predicted and happened as predicted, but they were not brought to completion': God threatens but he can be swayed by piety and morality. 'He wished to show that he alone is the preserver of the humble and the avenger of the wicked.'[25] What God does for Rome, not obeying his own predictions and providence, is therefore not exceptional, but it is worth reminding the pagans that he only does so for true Christians. Indeed, Orosius not only draws attention to what could have happened to Rome, but also to what ultimately matters in history: piety and worship of God. Rome is saved by Christianity, and this is interpreted in strong moral terms: the Babylonian turpitude of desires is contrasted with the moderation and continence of Christian Rome.[26] The moral undertone of comparing Rome to the biblical symbol of vice cannot be overlooked: on condition that it does not lapse into Babylonian vice, Rome shall outlive its predecessor. This moralism runs through the *Historiae* from beginning to end.[27] We will have to come back to this in chapter 8, but in the face of a tendency to emphasize how Orosius sees a divine plan at work in history, which is sometimes depicted as ineluctable and fixed, it is important to restore the moral dimension of history and the omnipotence of God to the prominence it deserves in Orosius' scheme of things.[28]

That Orosius affirms that Rome could and should have fallen, had it not been for Christianity, may come as a surprise to some Orosian scholarship, which has tended to argue that for Orosius, Rome was eternal and would last until the end of time.[29] But the position of

[25] Orosius 3.3.2: praedicta et facta sed non perfecta; 3.3.3: probans se solum esse et conseruatorem humilium et punitorem malorum. The source is Augustine, *De excidio urbis Romae* 7.

[26] Orosius 2.3.7: libidinum turpitudo, continentissima aequitas. The contrast is common in the later books of the *City of God* (16.17, 18.2, 18.20, 18.27, 19.26).

[27] See, e.g. Orosius 1.6.6, 5.22.11, 6.1.2, 6.22.11, 7.3.6, 7.37.17, with Goetz 1980a: 49–51.

[28] The emphasis on Christian morality is prominent in the books of the *City of God* (e.g. 5.15–19) that Orosius would have read.

[29] Paschoud 1967: 280–1; Lippold 1969; Goetz 1980a: 87; Klein 1985; Alonso-Núñez 1993; Martínez Cavero 2002: 248; Zecchini 2003: 324; Fear 2010a: 24. Straub 1972a: 266–8 argued that, for Orosius, the decline of the city of Rome was a real, if distant, possibility, but that Roman culture would survive. See Lippold 1969 for a review of earlier positions.

Orosius is hardly original. In assigning a limited lifespan to earthly empires, even Rome, he follows Augustine[30] and other Christian authors, such as his compatriots Juvencus[31] and Prudentius.[32] All human things come to an end, Orosius admits himself in 2.6.13, when comparing Rome and Babylon: 'whatever has been built up by the hand of man falls and comes to an end through the passage of time' (*quidquid enim est opere et manu factum, labi et consumi uetustate*).[33] Rome will not escape that fate and is not eternal. When it will happen, one cannot tell. As any Roman, Orosius might have hoped that Rome would last for a long time, but he was very much aware of the spectre of Babylon: Rome's survival is conditional on its morality. Christianity and morality have saved Rome: unlike Babylon, Rome is free, but only on parole. Rome has run most of its historical course and should be declining, but because it has become Christian, and as long as it remains so, God will allow it to survive—until his eternal wisdom decides otherwise.

II. VERGIL, TROY, AND ROME

The introduction of book 2 thus puts the fall of Rome at the heart of Orosius' argument. It is a significant choice to open a book that discusses Rome's foundation and rise in such a way. Throughout the book, the fall of Rome will function as the covert counterpoint to its rise. The reader is never allowed to indulge in the Vergilian illusion of an *imperium sine fine*, but is constantly reminded of the end of Rome.

After the three introductory chapters, chapter 4 opens with the foundation of Rome. Orosius notes that the city was founded on parricide and rape:

> Romulus at once ruined the reputation of his reign by murdering his brother and immediately followed this crime by another of equal cruelty. He gave as a dowry to the Sabine women, who had been seized

[30] O'Daly 1999b: 55.

[31] Juvencus, *Evangelia*, pr.1–2. See also Lactantius, *Institutiones* 7.15.12.

[32] Prudentius, *Contra Symmachum* 1.543 transfers the Vergilian *imperium sine fine* to eternal life, as does Augustine, *De civitate Dei* 2.29.

[33] A similar statement is in Eusebius, *Vita Constantini* 1.3.2.

contrary to custom and bound in shameless wedlock to the Romans, the blood of their husbands and parents.

cuius regnum continuo Romulus parricidio imbuit, parique successu crudelitatis sine more raptas Sabinas, inprobis nuptiis confoederatas maritorum et parentum cruore dotauit.[34]

The reference to the rape of the Sabine women is actually a quote of Vergil, *Aeneis* 8.635: *sine more raptas Sabinas.* Once again, there is more to this quotation than mere ornamental value. The line is drawn from Vergil's description of the shield of Aeneas, which gives, as is well known, a depiction of the glorious future (or history) of Rome. Already in classical Antiquity, Vergil was read as the poet of praise of Rome—in contrast with, for example, Horace, who, just as Orosius, had signalled that Rome was built on the blood of Remus.[35] Indeed, as Sabine MacCormack has stated: 'Vergil's authority was so great that his vision of early Italy and Rome did acquire a certain historiographical canonicity', as is exemplified, for example, in the *Origo gentis romanae* ascribed to Aurelius Victor and in Macrobius' *Saturnalia*.[36] The brief allusion to Vergil by Orosius draws attention to the fact that it is this glorious image of Rome that the historian wishes to counter. In line with what has been noticed for Augustine,[37] he will do so with arguments drawn from Vergil himself.

Indeed, Orosius does not restrict himself to a single allusion: although Florus' histories are his main source in this section,[38] the historian more than once refers to Vergil's description on the shield:[39]

Vergil, *Aeneid* 8.635–45: nec procul hinc Romam et raptas sine more Sabinas/consessu caueae, magnis Circensibus actis,/addiderat, subitoque nouum consurgere bellum/Romulidis Tatioque seni Curibusque

[34] Orosius 2.4.2. The idea is repeated at 5.16.23–4.

[35] Horace, *Epodon* 7.17–20. On these traditions, see Wiseman 1995. Vergil obviously does not hide the bloodshed that accompanied the settling of Aeneas in Latium (see, e.g. Aeneis 7.318–9). But it is embedded in a narrative that emphasizes future glory.

[36] MacCormack 1998: 180.

[37] Clark 2004; MacCormack 1998: 175–224.

[38] Florus is quoted at 2.4.7.

[39] None of these parallels can be traced to Florus, although he has been used. See, e.g. Florus 1.3.9 on the death of Mettus: Itaque hoste victo ruptorem foederis Mettum Fufetium religatum inter duos currus pernicibus equis distrahit. Lippold 1976: i.397 identifies Jerome, *Chronicon* a. Abr. 1264 as a source, but I fail to see correspondences. Lühken 2002: 277 notes the popularity of book 8 of the *Aeneid* in Orosius' Christian contemporary Prudentius.

seueris./post idem inter se posito certamine reges/armati Iouis ante aram paterasque tenentes/stabant et caesa iungebant foedera porca./ haud procul inde citae Mettum in diuersa quadrigae/distulerant (at tu dictis, Albane, maneres!),/raptabatque uiri mendacis uiscera Tullus/per siluam, et sparsi rorabant sanguine uepres.[40]

Orosius 2.4.2: cuius regnum continuo Romulus parricidio imbuit, parique successu crudelitatis sine more raptas Sabinas, inprobis nuptiis confoederatas maritorum et parentum cruore dotauit; 2.4.6: ducem eorum Titum Tatium, senem honestis pietatis causis insistentem, diu armis propulsatum, mox, ut in societatem regni adsumpsit, occidit; 2.4.10: rursus pace disrupta Mettum Fufetium Fidenate bello, meditata etiam proditione suspensum, curribus in diuersa raptantibus duplicis animi noxam poena diuisi corporis expendisse.[41]

The Vergilian flavour of the passage is further underscored by the allusion to two more verses from the *Aeneid* in the expression *egestas turpis atque obscena fama* (2.4.8, cf. Vergil, *Aeneis* 6.276, 3.367). To enhance the greatness of the suffering inflicted on mankind by Rome, one of them (*egestas turpis*) is drawn from the underworld scene in book 6.[42] In line with his habit of combining various sources,[43] Orosius also draws on Augustine's *City of God*, and in particular book 3,[44] but although Augustine also extensively

[40] Not far from here he had set Rome and the Sabine maidens, lawlessly carried off, when the great Circus Games were held, from the theatre's seated throng. Then the sudden uprising of a fresh war between the sons of Romulus and the aged Tatius and his stern Cures. Next, the same kings, the strife laid at rest, stood armed before Jove's altar, cup in hand, and made conventa with each other over sacrifice of swine. Not far from there, four-horse chariots, driven apart, had torn Mettus asunder (but you, Alban, should have stood by your words!) and Tullus dragged the liar's body through the woods and the brambles dripped with dew of blood. Tr. Rushton Fairclough (LCL).

[41] 2.4.2: Straightaway Romulus stained his rule with parricide and followed this with an equally cruel act by giving a dowry of their husbands' and fathers' blood to the Sabine women who had been seized contrary to custom and shamefully married off; 2.4.6: After a long period in which he had fought off by force of arms the Sabines' leader, Titus Tatius, an old man who walked in the noble ways of piety, he made him a partner in his rule, and then almost immediately killed him; 2.4.10: But the peace was broken again and Mettus Fufetius, who was caught while plotting treachery during the war against Fidenae, paid the price for his duplicity by having his body torn apart—it was pulled into pieces by chariots galloping in different directions. Tr. Fear (2010), 78–9.

[42] Coffin 1936: 237; Courcelle 1976: 255 and 1984: 538.

[43] See chapter 4.

[44] Augustine, *De civitate Dei* 3.13: *parentum sanguine dotarentur*; Orosius 2.4.2: *parentum cruore dotauit*. The term *parricidium* is also used by Augustine, *De civitate Dei* 3.6 for the murder of Remus. See also Orosius 2.5.5 and *De civitate Dei* 2.18 and 3.17.

uses Vergilian quotations, these cannot be matched with the selection made by Orosius. The Vergilian intertext is thus his own creation. The weaving of Vergil's glorified Roman past into Orosius' gory one sheds doubt on the two vectors of the poet's vision of Rome. The invalidation of Vergil's view of the past conjures up doubts about what the poet predicted of its future: Vergil famously claimed an *imperium sine fine* for Rome (*Aeneis* 1.278–9, 9.416–9). The glorious and eternal future of Rome as depicted on Aeneas' shield stands in marked opposition to Orosius' suggestion that Rome has more or less run its course, could have fallen in 410, and relies on Christianity to survive. The negative mirror image that Orosius sketches of the early history of Rome thus serves to invalidate the, in his eyes, naive view of an eternal and august Rome.

The references to Vergil also conjure up the memory of another city: Troy. In book 3 of the *City of God*, Augustine explicitly compares the events of the Trojan War with the foundation of Rome, with the aim of breaking up the ideological identification of both.[45] The events in Troy show that a city supposedly protected by its pagan gods could fall and hence demonstrate the inanity of those gods. Orosius does not follow in the footsteps of his master: he does not explicitly refer to Troy in book 2 and rather uses the traditional link between both cities to emphasize again the reality of the fall of Rome: the fall of Troy foreshadows the fall of Rome. He concludes chapter 5, which described the early years of the Republic until the defeat of the Fabii against the Veians (472 BC), with the following comment:

> Not only were these calamities taking place in Rome, but in addition each province was aflame with its own fires; and what the poet has particularly described in one city, I myself shall apply to the whole world: 'bitter mourning everywhere, everywhere fear, and many a shadow of death.'
>
> ad haec non Romae tantum talia gerebantur, sed quaeque prouincia suis ignibus aestuabat et, quod poeta praecipuus in una urbe descripsit, ego de toto orbe dixerim: crudelis ubique luctus, ubique pauor et plurima mortis imago (2.5.10).

[45] See also Augustine, *Sermo* 81.9.

The Vergilian lines (*Aeneis* 2.368–9) refer to the sack of Troy,[46] but Orosius extends their application to the entire world, whilst still maintaining the link with Rome. Troy itself could be a symbol of Rome,[47] and to quote these verses was therefore already a reminder of the fall of Rome. Orosius conspicuously fails to mention that the verses apply to Troy, preferring to note that he applies what Vergil said about *una urbe* to *toto orbe.* As is well known, *urbs* often is shorthand for Rome itself. Orosius' vagueness invites the reader to understand the quotation on three levels: as a general moral lesson drawn from Vergil about the horror of warfare, as an artful reference to the fall of Troy, and as a reminder of the fall of Rome. The third level is as intentional as the first two, which may seem the more obvious ones. Indeed, the quotation from Vergil is immediately followed by the narrative of how Cyrus took Babylon (539 BC): with both Troy and Babylon being ciphers for Rome, it is hardly accidental that Orosius juxtaposes a verse about the sack of Troy with a description of the taking of Babylon.

Orosius makes sure that his reader does not fail to grasp the message. He greatly amplifies the wealth and strength of Babylon,[48] so as to rhetorically enhance the drama of its demise. The obvious aim is to remind the reader of what could have befallen Rome. In addition, the final sentence of the section attributes a consciousness of decline and looming fall, without certainty about the cause, to his contemporaries:

> our contemporaries discuss with a careless anxiety, if the foundations of that once so great Roman Republic are now tottering more because of the weakness of its old age than because of external forces.
>
> et nostri incircumspecta anxietate causantur, si potentissimae illae quondam Romanae reipublicae moles nunc magis inbecillitate propriae senectutis quam alienis concussae uiribus contremescunt.[49]

[46] See Courcelle 1984: 179–82 on the popularity of these verses.

[47] Orosius himself explicitly compares Troy and present day Rome in 1.17.2.

[48] Orosius 2.6.2: gentem urbemque tunc cunctis opulentiorem; 2.6.6: quam vel humano opere exstrui potuisse vel humana virtute destrui posse utrumque paene incredibile apud mortales erat; 2.6.8–10 is a description of the incredible extent and greatness of the city; 2.6.11: magna illa Babylon; 2.6.13: primum imperium ac potentissimum.

[49] Orosius 2.6.14; cf. 1.21.19.

The comment concludes Orosius' explicit reflection on the parallelism between Babylon and Rome, and confirms the implicit reminders of Rome's fall woven into the narrative of the foundation of Rome in chapters 4–6. Orosius describes the anxiety of his contemporaries as *incircumspecta*: without due prudence, consideration, and care. The *nostri* are consequently not all of Orosius' contemporaries, but those who fail to see the suspension of Rome's demise because of Christianity.[50] They may be pagans who see Rome decline, but also Christians who fail to appreciate that God rewards true piety and can halt the seemingly inexorable course of history. Orosius is possibly alluding to a widespread uncertainty about the future of Rome. Indeed, the poet Claudian depicts many usurpers as threatening the very existence of Rome.[51] This is obviously a rhetorical ploy to enhance the saving of Rome by the virtuous Stilicho, but it does confirm Orosius' suggestion that the possibility of Rome's fall was at least entertained. The historian admits that it may have been a logical worry, given the previous course of history. But having this worry now, when God rewards Christian piety and morality by extending the lifespan of their earthly home, signals a lack of insight into what truly drives events.

Orosius thus challenges his contemporaries on two counts. He questions the authoritative Vergilian narrative of a glorious past and, especially, future for Rome through a set of allusions, quotations, parallelisms, and synchronisms. The constant references, covert and open, to the fall of Rome remind the reader that Rome was and is fragile, and block any attempt to hark back to an idealized past. At the same time, Orosius rejects the resigned attitude that would see Rome fall right now, as such a view underestimates the way in which God has trumped the ordained course of history in favour of Christianity. Together they form a strong repudiation of Vergil's *imperium sine fine*: had Rome stayed pagan, Orosius suggests, it would have gone down already. Not only does he question the pagan master narrative, he also provides a Christian alternative: only Christian faith and morality can lead God to postpone the inevitable. This twin argument underpins the narrative of the *Historiae*.

[50] Orosius 7.26.10, where he picks up the 'four empire theory' again, also emphasizes the importance of correctly understanding the past.

[51] Claudian, *De consulatu Stilichonis* 1.374–85, *In Rufinum* 1.273–4, 2.50–4, *De bello gildonico* 17.

The strong emphasis on the fall of Rome at the beginning of book 2 is balanced by the conclusion of the book (2.19), where Orosius picks up the theme again. The intervening chapters (7–18) chart Persian, Greek, and Roman history until 387 BC, the sack of Rome by the Gauls. The parallel with the sack of 410 is obvious, and Orosius announces the return to the themes of 2.1–6 by recording in 2.18.4 lines from the *Aeneid* describing the sack of Troy (2.361–2), drawn from the same passage used in 2.5.10 to picture the state of the world. The parallelism with Troy is again highlighted in 2.19.11, the conclusion to the description of the sack of 387: the great silence that struck the Gauls when entering the deserted city of Rome is drawn from Vergil's description of the sack of Troy.[52] These references in themselves would be enough to recall the reflection on the fate of Rome that opened book 2. But Orosius is anxious to get his message across: he spells out the comparison between Gauls in 387 BC and Goths in 410 AD (2.19.12–15) and shows how much less disastrous the second event was.

It is possible to explain the repeated references to book 2 of the *Aeneid* by the wish to focus attention on the sack of Troy, and thus Rome. But another target can be imagined too. Augustine engages repeatedly in books 2 and 3 of the *City of God* with *Aeneid* 2.351: *excessere omnes adytis arisque relictis*, a verse apparently used by pagan apologists to vouchsafe the link between divine protection and the survival of Rome: Troy could be sacked by the Greeks because its gods had already abandoned the city.[53] Orosius will quote the verse later in 6.1.23, but it is possible to understand his emphasis on the demise of Troy as an implicit reminder of the Christian counter-argument that the gods were unable to save the city. Interestingly, the verses Orosius quotes are just a couple of lines removed from 2.351.

Just as the synchronisms with Babylon with which book 2 are embedded in common historiographical practice in Antiquity, the conclusion of the book is rooted in established habits. Indeed, Roman historians had used the ruin of Rome by the Gauls for contemporary

[52] Orosius 2.19.11: horror quatiebat animos, silentia ipsa terrebant; Vergil, *Aeneis* 2.755: horror ubique animo simul ipsa silentia terrere. There is also an allusion to *Georgica* 4.50 (vocisque offensa resultat imago) in Orosius 2.19.10 (offensae vocis imago respondens): see Courcelle 1984: 214 and Arnaud-Lindet 1990–1: i.273.

[53] Augustine, *De civitate Dei* 2.22, 2.24, 2.25, 3.3, 3.7, 3.14, 3.15: see MacCormack 1998: 164–6; Tornau 2006: 220, 232, 241. The verse is alluded to by Symmachus, *Epistula* 1.51.

purposes before. Livy's book 5, which concludes on that event, is built around the theme of the re-foundation of Rome. The book starts with an implicit parallelism between Veii and Rome: both are sacked in the same book and in the face of the Gallic threat a transfer of Rome to the site of Veii is contemplated (5.24). Camillus, who is suspiciously like Augustus, is depicted as the new founder of Rome. Indeed, Livy famously points out that the sack of Rome is chronologically exactly halfway between 753 BC and 27 BC (5.54). C. Kraus has argued that one of Livy's messages was that Rome was doing better than Troy in that it was being founded anew.[54] Orosius is thus part of a historiographical tradition of establishing mirror images of Rome and styling calamities of the past as meaningful events for the present. He may well have drawn inspiration from Livy's construction: in 7.2.2, Orosius notes that Livy situates the sack of 387 BC halfway through the early history of Rome.[55] His message, however, is different from Livy's: his emphasis on the sack of Rome has the aim of showing that it is only because of God's benevolence that Rome survives today, not that it will be founded once again. His description of the fall of 387 BC is purposely not balanced by the triumphant resurgence of the Romans under Camillus, as in all traditional accounts.[56] Once Orosius does depict Brutus, the first consul, as a new founder of Rome, but only in a negative sense: just as Romulus, he constructs his new Rome on parricide and his actions bring the city to the brink of destruction.[57]

The fall of Rome as a real possibility is thus the theme that shapes book 2. The book is therefore quintessentially about Roman history, even when discussing other events, as is brought out when Orosius defines an episode of Greek history as a digression.[58] The book is relatively short, compared with the following ones: Orosius clearly

[54] Luce 1971; Kraus 1994.

[55] Inspiration may have been drawn from Augustine: Conybeare 1999 argues that *De civitate Dei* 5 closely engages with Livy's book 5. The argument is made less persuasive by the fact that Augustine discusses the sack of Rome in 387 BC in *De civitate Dei* 3.29.

[56] See Livy 5.50–5; Florus 1.7; Eutropius 1.20; Claudian, *In Eutropium* 2.598.

[57] Orosius 2.5.5–6 uses three times the term *pernicies* (destruction) to designate the state of Rome under Brutus.

[58] Orosius 2.12.1: *unde digressum*. See also 1.21.21, where Orosius notes that book 2 has more of a unity than book 1: ut ab urbe condita sequens libellus incipiat, qui contextiora illorum temporum mala (. . .) continebit, and 5.4.15, noting that he foregoes the crimes of other people to mention only those of the Romans. For Rome as the subject of Orosius, see Fear 2010a: 17.

wishes to cover exactly the period from Rome's foundation to the sack of 387 BC.[59] Indeed, he can be interpreted as consciously postponing the exploration of the sack of 410 to book 2, when he starts discussing Roman history. Book 1 can then be read as a mixture of preparation for the theme and reticence about it. The avenging power of God is illustrated by the fall of Sodom, which announces the link between punishment and sinfulness.[60] Twice in book 1 Orosius compares events of the distant past to the sack of 410: the invasions of the Amazons and, more importantly, the sack of Troy.[61] But he is remarkably coy about Aeneas, who is dismissed in a *praeteritio*.[62] It seems as if the historian is saving his engagement with the story of the founding father of Rome for the next book. Orosius also does not discuss the 'theory of the four empires' when narrating the fall of Assyria, and he just notes that 'such empires have been changed',[63] clearly reserving its discussion for the beginnings of book 2. But once that book has aroused the spectre of the fall of Rome, it recurs again and again. Like a stone thrown in a pond, the fall of Rome reverberates through the entire surface of the *Historiae*: Orosius repeatedly suggests or states that Rome could have fallen in the past and dwells on the destruction of other cities, so as to remind his readers of the benevolence of the Christian God he had demonstrated in book 2.[64]

III. HISTORY AND THEORY

Intertextuality has recently been argued to be a key to the work of Ammianus Marcellinus.[65] It would be rash to allow Orosius to put his

[59] At least in this case, thus, the book divisions are not purely inspired by practical concerns, as is stated by Arnaud-Lindet 1990–1: i.128 note 7 and i.xxxv.

[60] Orosius 1.6.6.

[61] Orosius 1.16–17.

[62] Orosius 1.18.1: Paucis praeterea annis interuenientibus, Aeneae Troia profugi aduentus in Italiam quae arma commouerit, qualia per triennium bella exciuerit, quantos populos inplicuerit odio excidioque adflixerit, ludi litterarii disciplina nostrae quoque memoriae inustum est.

[63] Orosius 1.19.3: talia regna mutata sunt.

[64] Orosius 3.1.1, 3.1.24, 3.3.2, 3.6.1, 3.13.1, 3.14.7, 3.21.1, 3.20.12, 3.22.15, 3.23.67, 4.6.11, 4.17.2–6, 4.23, 5.3.1, 5.6.1, 5.7, 5.16.4, 5.17.1, 5.17.7–11, 5.19.3, 5.24.5, 6.2.11. One wonders if it is accidental that Vergil's account of the sack of Troy is also narrated in book 2 of the *Aeneid*.

[65] Kelly 2008.

foot next to Ammianus, but understanding the intertextual engagement with Vergil—of which there is much more than usually granted—is a precondition for grasping the message Orosius wishes to convey to his readers. The tools of allusion, parallelism, and synchronism constantly remind the reader of the fact that Rome had run its course, were it not for Christianity. In the game of parallels and contrasts, the explicit point of reference for Rome is Babylon but the implicit one Troy: if Rome is repeatedly paralleled with Babylon, allusions to Vergil's *Aeneid* construe Troy as a symbol of Rome's fall rather than its rebirth, as was the case in Livy and Vergil himself. Orosius shares these tools with classical historians, but his aim is not to glorify Rome but to question its very greatness. His aim may be apologetic, but in order to achieve it, he works with the instruments other historians used as well. Even the famous 'four empire theory' must primarily be seen as a narrative tool to generate meaning in history. Orosius is far from unique in using apparently theoretical statements to that end, and not with the intention of proposing a fully coherent theory. Ancient historians regularly indulge in theoretical statements, but one rarely succeeds in constructing a coherent theory out of it. This has been observed for Livy's apparent stoicism, but also for late antique historians.[66] Indeed, the primary function of such statements is to serve the narrative: historians are not philosophers. A good parallel for Orosius is Polybius' famous cycle of constitutions, which argues that all states have to go through a series of constitutional changes. As has been observed, Polybius' description of the cycle is far from coherent and limpid, but its primary aim is to demonstrate the success of Rome, which escapes from the cycle in virtue of its mixed constitution. His theory is less an attempt at coherent theory making than a support for an explanation for Rome's rise to Mediterranean hegemony.[67] As this chapter has shown, Orosius' 'four empire theory' is similarly part of an argument, also conducted with other tools, that Rome's fall, and especially the divine suspension of it, should occupy a prominent place in the minds of his contemporaries.

[66] Veyne 1990; Levene 1993: 31; Van Nuffelen 2004a: 307–9.
[67] Walbank 1943 and 2002b.

3

The Past as Literature: exempla and the Culture of Rhetoric

Comparisons between the pagan past and the Christian present are ubiquitous in Orosius: already in the preface he announces that he has converted to the view that things are now much better than they were previously.[1] In such comparisons Orosius' true apologetic intentions are sometimes thought to surface: his, some scholars argue, is less a history than a theology of history.[2] Yet there is more to it. Comparison was a standard rhetorical technique: the amplification (*auxesis*) expected of an encomium also included a comparison (*synkrisis*).[3] To make comparisons, one needed a point of reference, which was provided by the illustrious past, digested and rehashed in the form of exempla.[4] Indeed, an orator needed to have an excellent grasp of the past, for its authority was a key rhetorical asset. In the words of Quintilian:

> Above all, the orator should be supplied with plenty of examples, both ancient and modern; indeed, he ought not only to know things which are recorded in histories or handed down by word of mouth, or which happen every day; he should not neglect the fictions of great poets either. For while historical examples can take the place of evidence or even legal precedents, those from the poets also are either sanctioned by

[1] Orosius 1.pr.13–14.

[2] Fainck 1951: 112; Schöndorf 1952: 70–1; Lacroix 1965: 70; Marrou 1970: 76; Lippold 1976: i.xxix; Koch-Peters 1984: 38.

[3] Pernot 1993: 690–8; Heath 1997: 96; Lausberg 1998: 191; Felmy 2001: 283–5.

[4] *Rhetorica ad Herrenium* 4.62 states that a *comparatio* and an exemplum have the same aim. See Valerius Maximus 1.pr and Augustine, *De doctrina christiana* 2.28.44 on history as a source of exempla. For comparisons between past and present in fourth-century rhetoric, see, e.g. Libanius, *Oratio* 15.1–2, 16.8, 18.53; Claudian, *In Eutropium* 2.60.

the guarantee of antiquity or believed to have been invented by great men as moral lessons.[5]

Quintilian is here in the first place concerned with emphasizing the value of poetry in rhetoric, and wishes it to be put alongside history, but in the process he highlights history as the more common source of authority.[6] History was indeed incorporated in rhetorical education as a set of exempla, mediated through authoritative texts and practical summaries. The prestige of the past was based on a standardized view, organized around examples to follow or to avoid, and, as other sources of rhetorical authority, 'incorporated into an immutable patrimony of knowledge through reading and memorization'.[7]

Against this background, Orosius' frequent use of comparison cannot be discussed without studying the way he deals with the authoritative view of the past inculcated in rhetorical education. Indeed, as we shall see, his use of exempla is specifically targeted to undermine the attitude towards the past his contemporaries developed at school: Orosius wishes to open their eyes for the true shape of past events.

The present chapter first analyses Orosius' views on the distorting impact of rhetorical training, symbolized by their use of exempla, as expressed in the preface to book 4. The surface message of that passage seems clear: Orosius pretends to have identified the prime reason why his contemporaries think the present is worse than the past: the school of rhetoric has inculcated in them a mistaken, glorious view of the past. This surface message is in itself of great interest, as it is one of the few ancient accounts that offer an analysis, albeit polemical, of the impact of rhetorical training on people's perception of reality. To counter this view, Orosius develops a double strategy. On the one hand, as the second section shows, he capitalizes on his audience's expectance that an account of Roman history should be built around exempla by consciously omitting traditional good exempla and highlighting negative ones. A close analysis of book 4 shows how the *Historiae* destabilize the fixed expectations of his readership and provide, as it were, a negative of traditional

[5] Quintilian 12.4.1–2. Tr. D. Russell (LCL). See also Quintilian 2.4.18–21, 5.11.17, 10.1.34.

[6] Franchet d'Esperey 2010 emphasizes that, for Quintilian, the historical example is the exemplum par excellence.

[7] Cribiore 2001: 224–5.

accounts of the Roman past. On the other hand, Orosius rejects the view that his history would be a mere 'anti-history'. As the third section shows, he presents the *Historiae* as the factual and truthful account that pagan historians have failed to write precisely because of their rhetorical mindset. In doing so, however, he picks up a traditional trope of the polemic among historians, who would accuse each other of writing rhetorically and not truthfully. These three sections show how strongly the *Historiae* are indebted to the rhetorical culture of his time, whilst underlining that Orosius does not substitute a theology of history for pagan histories but a better history—one that truly lives up to the standards set by classical historians themselves. This double strategy shows that Orosius remains deeply indebted to classical rhetorical education and historiography, notwithstanding his loud criticism of both. This need not cause surprise: in a society where rhetoric determined all forms of literary expression, the use of rhetorical tropes to attack a rhetorical mindset is only superficially paradoxical.[8] Moreover, as the fourth section argues, historiography and the school of rhetoric were closely intertwined in the fourth and fifth centuries and it is thus understandable that Orosius framed his arguments in a rhetorical way. The last section provides another element of context. Classical exempla, as moral models drawn from an authoritative past, were obviously disputed at a time when Christianity challenged long-established ethical codes and perceptions of the pagan past. Whilst Orosius is part of a wider Christian debate on the acceptance of pagan exempla, he also occupies a very specific position in it. He shares the explicit assessment of the power of exempla with other authors, such as Augustine and Sulpicius Severus. In contrast to these, however, he does not systematically put forward Christian exempla as superior models, but rather draws his arguments from the classical tradition itself. His polemical intention is surely part of the explanation for this different focus, but also the desire to challenge pagan historiography on its own playing field by writing a history that is superior to what his pagan predecessors could achieve.

[8] Fox 2001 shows how ancient arguments about the relationship between rhetoric and history are determined by implicit views about the nature of rhetoric. See also Kempshall 2011: 5.

I. A RHETORICALLY OVER-DETERMINED CULTURE

As if obeying Quintilian's instructions on the exemplary value of poetry, Orosius opens the preface to his fourth book with a *sententia* from Vergil.[9] Aeneas famously consoles his fellow travellers after another bout of troubles: 'Perchance even this distress it will some day be a joy to recall.'[10] The sentiment is commonplace[11] and, Orosius explains, suits all possible timeframes. The past is held to be much more agreeable in words when it was in fact hard to bear in reality. The future is, in turn, thought to be better than the present by disgust of current circumstances. The present, finally, is impossible to compare correctly with either past or future, as only present events can cause real pain; past and future events are not yet or no longer present. Only the present, indeed, can hurt precisely because it is present—even if the pain is insignificant.[12] Orosius repeatedly bemoans our inability to properly judge the present,[13] but in this preface he addresses the issue head-on. Two hilarious examples make clear that we may misjudge present woes. Trying to sleep in a bed with fleas surely is annoying, and may seem at that very instant the greatest of evils, but is it really worse than insomnia because of a mortal fever? Someone getting up from a cosy bed and seeing that it has frozen at night, has the right to say 'it is cold today'. What is reprehensible, according to Orosius, is that such a man would hide under his sheets and exclaim that:

> It is truly so cold as it never ever was in the Apennines, when Hannibal, overcome and closed in by snow, lost his elephants, horses, and the greatest part of his army. Not only would I not be able to endure a man talking like that, vomiting forth in puerile outspokenness, but I would

[9] See also Quintilian 8.5; *Rhetorica ad Herrenium* 4.24–5.

[10] Vergil, *Aeneis* 1.203: forsan et haec olim meminisse iuvabit. Tr. Rushton Fairclough (LCL).

[11] Cicero, *Ad familiares* 5.12.4; Seneca, *Hercules furens* 656–7; Macrobius, *Saturnalia* 7.2.9; Claudian, *De bello Gothico* 207.

[12] Orosius 4.pr.2–3: haec sententia, semel apte ficta, semper uim sui triplicem diuersissimis effectibus refert, cum et praeterita tanto gratiora habentur in uerbis quanto grauiora referuntur in gestis et futura dum desiderabilia fastidio praesentium fiunt semper meliora creduntur, ipsis autem praesentibus ob hoc nulla in parte miseriarum iusta conparatio adhiberi potest, quia multo maiore molestia adficiunt quantulacumque sint ista quae sunt quam illa quae siue transacta siue uentura, etsi magna dicuntur, interim omnino tunc non sunt.

[13] Orosius 1.pr.9, 2.11.9, 3.2.12.

drag him from under his sheets, witnesses to his laziness, into the public and the people, and once outside, I would show him the children playing, enjoying themselves and sweating in the cold and because of the cold. Then his verbose nonsense, corrupted by his elegant upbringing, will be taught that there is no violence in the temperature but sluggishness in him, and it will be proven by a comparison based on facts that the people of old endured no minor things but that he cannot endure minor things.

tantum omnino frigus esse quantum nec in Appennino aliquando fuerit, cum Hannibal elephantos equos plurimamque exercitus sui partem niuibus clausus atque oppressus amisit: hunc ego puerilibus licentiis nausiantem non modo dicentem ista non ferrem, sed etiam ab ipsis stratis, otii sui testibus, in populum publicumque protraherem, eique foras producto infantes in eo atque ex eo gelu ludentes iucundantes sudantesque monstrarem, ut uerbosa nugacitas delicatis uitiata nutrimentis non in tempore uiolentiam sed in se esse segnitiam doceretur et in conparatione rerum diiudicanda non maiores parua tolerasse sed se nec parua tolerare sufficere probaretur.[14]

This is a dense passage that is more than a simple illustration of the superiority of the Christian present. Orosius attacks a cultural *habitus* determined by literary practice. The image of the man who gets out in the cold and compares himself to Hannibal crossing the Alps is funny, but also goes to the heart of the issue at stake: Hannibal's crossing over the Alps is obviously an exemplum,[15] a great event of the past against which the present is measured. The man thus rhetorically situates himself in a historical context. But the history he positions himself in is not a series of facts: it is a past shaped and transmitted by literature. Indeed, Orosius' caricature carefully collapses social class and education: the man has enjoyed a luxurious upbringing with all the obvious ensuing defects, contrasted with the children of the populace playing outside in winter.[16] Unable to translate his experience of cold into normal, common language and to say simply that it is rather cold today,[17] he has recourse to

[14] Orosius 4.pr.8–10. Cf. 5.14.8 for the description of Hannibal with similar vocabulary.

[15] Lippold 1976: i.430.

[16] Orosius 4.pr.6: delicatis istis et querulis nostris; 4.pr.7: e mollissimis stratis cubiciloque percommondo; 4.pr.9: otii sui testibus; 4.pr.10: delicitis vitiata nutrimentis (...) segnitia. Note 4.pr.9: in populum publicumque.

[17] Orosius 4.pr.7: hic mihi nequaquam reprehendendus uideretur, quia uel communi usu uel proprio sensu locutus esset.

verbosity; instead of taking normal experience as a point of comparison, he reaches for an exemplum of the past.[18] It is infantile thinking masked as outspokenness,[19] which detaches one from reality—a reality that is replaced by a heroic past.

Rhetorical education thus distorts one's perception of reality. At the end of his account of fifth-century Greek history, Orosius remarks: 'In truth, all these events, because they have faded through the long interval of time, have for us been turned into exercises for our mind and delightful stories' (2.18.5: uerumtamen haec ipsa, quia multo interiectu saeculorum exoleuerunt, facta sunt nobis exercitia ingeniorum et oblectamenta fabularum). The former (*exercitio ingeniorum*) refers to rhetorical exercises, the latter (*oblectamenta fabularum*) to harmless stories about the distant past.[20] The distance of time as well as the repeated encounter of old tales in education render the reader insensitive to what has really happened; he stops listening carefully.[21] The past has been turned into a realm of stories without real pain and suffering.

Not only does the rhetorical culture denude the past of its reality, it also makes one's moral compass spin. Developing a critique already voiced by Augustine,[22] Orosius accuses his pagan adversaries of putting glory above everything else. The number of dead does not count, as long as wars add to the glory of Rome (5.1.1–3). In such a skewed rhetorical universe, the *magnitudo laudis* is determined by the *magnitudo sceleris* (5.19.14–16). For polemical purposes, however, Orosius is ready to recognize a positive side to the desire of glory. He concludes his lachrymose account of the rise of Carthage (4.6) with a renewed polemic against contemporary pagans who think the present is much worse than that period: distorted by their hate of Christianity, they cannot perceive how small present sufferings

[18] Orosius 4.pr.10: maiores.

[19] Orosius 4.pr.9: puerilibus licentiis nausiantem. *Licentia* was, theoretically, a true virtue in speech: cf. *Rhetorica ad Herrenium* 4.48. Orosius' caricature draws on established traditions: one is struck, for example, by parallels with Plutarch's *De garrulitate*: see Van Hoof 2010a: 158–65.

[20] Orosius 3.14.8, where he criticizes those who take history for *dulces fabulas*. Cf. Orosius 2.19.4.

[21] Orosius 1.6.5, 1.12.6: quae quia in fabulis celebrari solita sunt, neglegentius audiuntur.

[22] Augustine, *De civitate Dei* 5.22: sed quia non diligebant gloriam propter iustitiam, sed iustitiam propter gloriam diligere videbantur, pacem factam foedusque ruperunt.

actually are. In a reversal of his normal depreciation for ancient exempla, Orosius chides: 'However, they can learn the disregard of suffering from their own, for whom the greatest trouble was the greatest good, as long as it resulted in the celebrated and illustrious glory of fame.'[23] Orosius does not go as far as Augustine, who had set Roman exempla as examples for Christians,[24] but he does recognize, like his dedicatee, the positive effect on one's endurance that the desire for glory and fame had. This is easily contrasted with the contemporary pagans, weak and soft, who hide under their sheets at the first bout of frost and blame Christianity for it.

The rhetorical culture thus has a double distorting effect, for it disfigures the perception of both past and present: the former is deemed uniformly glorious, the latter infamous and dire. Such an attitude comes at the price of sanitizing the past: as Orosius remarks, ancient (given his apologetic slant, that label equals pagan) historians systematically leave out the number of dead on the Roman side so as to enhance the glory of the victory—except when remarkably few actually fell in battle.[25] Over-determined by their education, contemporary pagans have no idea what real suffering is and how much blood the rise of Rome has cost.[26] They are weaklings, who, because they create a rhetorical past, cannot live up to that past. It is hardly surprising, therefore, that they blame Christianity for the dire situation of the present, when the opposite is true.

II. THE WHETTING-STONE AND THE RUST: BOOK 4

This insight in to Orosius' basic criticism of the rhetorical culture of his age helps us to understand the most striking feature of the *Historiae*, namely that it is a story of calamities (*misteriae*: e.g. 1. pr.9; 3.15.1). He does not narrate an alternative and unknown history to his pagan audience: just as most of his sources, he basically retells a

[23] Orosius 6.4.41: quamquam contemptus miseriarum possunt etiam a suis discere, apud quos summa mala pro summis bonis aestimata sunt, tantum ut gloriam famae celebrem atque inlustrem consequerentur.

[24] Augustine, *De civitate Dei* 5.16–8.

[25] Orosius 4.1.12. He picks up a critique already found in Livy: Pelikan-Pittinger 2008: 105–14. See Valerius Maximus 2.8.1, showing that battle reports by generals often fiddled the numbers.

[26] The theme of the preface to book 5.

past already familiar from the basic works of history one read as part of the rhetorical curriculum. The aim of this redefinition of the past as a series of *miseriae* is to make his adversaries realize their misapprehension of the past and, hence, also of the present: the world they are living in is actually much better off than that of their supposedly glorious fathers. This is combined with a constant indictment of earlier, pagan historians for not narrating the past in its true, gruesome, colours. This general attitude, combined with the explicit attacks on the rhetorical culture of his age, may give the impression that Orosius wishes to do away with the exemplum. In fact, his attitude is more complex than that. Orosius pursues a double strategy in his narrative when dealing with exemplary acts of the past: he either suppresses them to make the past look undesirable, or he highlights them. The latter option can take, again, two forms: either he emphasizes that events do not deserve the status of exemplum, or he points to good actions of the past that were not sufficiently imitated. In this view he undermines the pagan view from within. This section takes a closer look at book 4, which starts with the long prefatory reflection on the distorting effect of the rhetorical culture that we have just discussed, in order to see how Orosius challenges the exemplary status of the past. My suggestion is that this book can be read as articulated around the issues raised in its preface. It questions the creation of an exemplary past in all three aspects, that is, its actual reality, its creation by ancient historians, and its impact on contemporary perception.

Book 4 is largely dedicated to the three wars with Carthage, and Orosius concludes the book with a reflection on the well-known theme of the *metus punicus*.[27] Carthage was, in Orosius' imagery, the whetting-stone that kept the rust off Roman *virtus*. Having decided to destroy Carthage, the Romans themselves are to blame for their current weaknesses, their moral bluntness and rust, their exterior obesity and spiritual anorexia. Christianity bears no guilt for that situation.[28] The wars against Carthage had traditionally been

[27] Sallust, *Historiae* 1.11 = Augustine, *De civitate Dei* 2.18; Diodorus Siculus 36.33; Plutarch, *Cato* 27; Augustine, *De civitate Dei* 1.31–3. On the theme in Orosius and Augustine, see Bonamente 1975.

[28] Orosius 4.23.10: quod cum ita sit, cur Christianis temporibus imputant hebetationem ac robiginem suam, qua foris crassi, intus exesi sunt? qui porro ante sescentos fere annos, sicut sui prudentes timentesque praedixerant, cotem illam magnam splendoris et acuminis sui Carthaginem perdiderunt.

seen as a fertile humus for *virtus* and exemplum—an image that Orosius consciously seeks to overturn. To that end he questions the exemplary nature of the Carthaginian wars, whilst hoping that this work of criticism can function as a new whetting-stone that will remove the rust of, and restore the edge to, contemporary Roman moral consciousness.[29]

The book opens with an account of the war against Pyrrhus, which immediately draws attention to the high numbers of casualties.[30] Orosius notices that he can give the right number of fallen for the Romans, but not for Pyrrhus. This is due to the fact, he asserts, that older historians deliberately obscured these, so that the price of the victory did not blemish its glory—unless, that is, when just a few died: small numbers of dead on one's own side were mentioned so that they would enhance the admiration of, and fear for, the greatness of the victor (admirationem terroremque virtutis augeat paucitas perditorum).[31] This is elaborated a few chapters later, where Orosius notes that, in the few years he has surveyed so far, he always had to report lamentable facts. But the other historians who have treated this period have left most of them out, 'having rather set themselves the task of praising' (proposito sibi magis laudandi negotio). They did this so as 'not to offend the people for whom and about whom they wrote and not to seem to frighten their readers with examples of the past rather than educate them'.[32] Apart from impugning the objectivity of classical historians, Orosius here also identifies their task as educating for glorious action, instead of saying the truth and thus sowing fear for the reality of warfare.

With their combined stress on the drama of the events and its negation in classical literature, the preliminary five chapters set the tone for the rest of the book which deals with the wars against Carthage. Both characteristics recur throughout the book. Orosius offers his readers a brief introduction to the history of Carthage,

[29] Orosius 4.23.10: Itaque finem uolumini faciam, ne forsitan conlidendo uehementius discussa ad tempus robigine ubi necessarium acumen elicere non possum, superuacuam asperitatem inueniam. quamquam obuiantem asperitatem nequaquam expauescerem, si interioris spem acuminis inuenirem.

[30] Orosius 4.1.11, 13, 18, 22.

[31] Orosius 4.1.12–13.

[32] Orosius 4.5.11: ne eosdem quibus haec et de quibus scribebantur offenderent auditoresque suos exemplis praeteritorum terrere potius quam instituere uiderentur. See also Orosius 4.20.7.

designed to make tears well up in their eyes.[33] It is, obviously, only the corrupted eye (*vitioso oculo*, 4.6.38) of the pagans that stays dry. Allusions to the dramatic nature of the wars abound,[34] and one brief example can suffice. After having described the start of the first Punic war, Orosius exclaims:

> Who, I ask, will be able to unfold in speech one war waged for twenty-three years between two cities, how many kings of Carthage, how many Roman consuls, how many army columns, what number of war ships were assembled, crushed, and destroyed?
>
> Quis, rogo, duarum ciuitatum unum bellum per annos tres et uiginti gestum fando explicet, quot reges Carthaginiensium, quot consules Romanorum, quot agmina exercituum, quantum numerum nauium contraxerit profligarit oppresserit? (4.11.4).

Fando explicet is, in fact, drawn from Vergil's description of the destruction of Troy.[35] It is unlikely that this is a stray recollection: not only has Orosius already quoted the same verse in 2.18.4, but it conjures up precisely the tearfulness that the entire book tries to convey. The rhetorical question and the anaphora evoke the greatness of the suffering during the war, and suggest that nothing of today can match it. Classical historians consciously negate this fact, and Orosius twice attacks them explicitly for this. In 4.12.11–3 he notes the misplaced joy found in his sources (and shared by their contemporary readers) about the year of peace in 235 BC when the gates of the Janus temple were closed. But, as Orosius remarks, such a joy about peace in a single year only shows how bad the situation was. In 4.20.6–10 the disagreement between Polybius, Valerius Antias, and Claudius Quadrigarius on the number of fallen leads Orosius to a severe

[33] Note the vocabulary in 4.6.12–15: omnia ululatibus personabant, clausae ubique ianuae, cuncta publica priuataque officia damnata, uniuersi ad portum decurrunt egredientesque de nauibus paucos, qui cladi superfuerant, de suis percontantur. postquam de clade suorum, tacentibus illis uel gementibus, miseri intellegunt, tunc toto litore plangentium voces, tunc infelicium matrum ululatus et flebiles querellae audiebantur. inter haec procedit et ipse de naui sua imperator sordida seruilique tunica discinctus; ad cuius conspectum plangentia iunguntur agmina; ipse quoque manus ad caelum tendens nunc suam nunc publicam infelicitatem accusat et deflet; ad postremum uociferans per urbem, tandem ingressus domum, cunctos, qui lacrimantes prosequebantur, ultimo dimisit adloquio ac deinde obseratis ianuis exclusisque etiam filiis gladio dolorem uitamque finiuit.

[34] e.g. Orosius 4.12.9, 4.13.6–8, 4.19.1, 4.22.9, 4.23.4.

[35] Vergil, *Aeneis* 2.361–2: quis cladem illius noctis, quis funera fando/explicet aut posit lacrimis aequare labores.

condemnation of the lies of ancient historians: 'the cause of these lies surely is adulation, as they wished to increase the praises for the victory and to extol the virtue of the fatherland either in the eyes of their contemporaries or in those of posterity.'[36] Again, Orosius' criticism on his predecessors as historians targets two interrelated aspects: their partisanship and their desire to reshape the past as glorious and exemplary.

Whilst these reflections question the way the past has come to be seen as exemplary, Orosius also sheds doubts on the standard view of the past as transmitted in rhetorical education. To that end, he employs the twin technique of omission and highlighting. Just as he had omitted any reference to the heroic actions of Camillus during the sack of Rome by the Gauls (387 BC), he deliberately suppresses key exempla related to the Carthaginian wars: there is nothing, for example, on Appius Claudius and Cineas in the context of Pyrrhus' invasion of Italy. Others, such as Regulus' conscientiousness of returning to Carthaginian captivity and torture after an embassy to Rome, are just briefly mentioned, without any elaboration.[37] Cannae and Lake Trasimene, sources of endless exempla in Valerius Maximus, are reduced to two, not even convoluted, sentences.[38] Fabius Maximus 'Cuncator' is barely mentioned.[39] The exemplary nature of events is not only questioned by methodical silence. Orosius several times stigmatizes Roman behaviour as dishonourable and ignominious: fleeing in battle,[40] parricide,[41] and fighting to the last man,[42] it is all condemned. Rome may have won, but it was rather out of desperation: the past was not a pleasant *otium* similar to that of Orosius' contemporaries.[43] Whilst many traditional exempla are silenced, others that illustrate the disjunction between morality and the glorifying view of the past are highlighted. The *licentia* of the

[36] Orosius 4.20.9: Sed haec uarietas scriptorum utique fallacia est; fallaciae autem causa profecto adulatio est, dum uictoris laudes accumulare uirtutemque patriae extollere uel praesentibus uel posteris student.

[37] Orosius 4.10.1.

[38] Orosius 4.15.6–7. For similar procedures in other books, see, e.g. 3.16–20. For Camillus, see Felmy 2001: 125–59.

[39] Orosius 4.15.7, 4.16.12.

[40] Orosius 4.13.9, 5.1.11.

[41] Orosius 4.13.17. See also Orosius 4.8.1–3, 4.12.7.

[42] Orosius 4.16.18. For similar procedures in other books, see Orosius 2.16.15, 3.1.2–3, 5.4.7, 5.15.21–2, 6.19.1.

[43] Orosius 4.16.21. See also Orosius 3.1.2–3, 3.2.1.

Volsians, which led to them being exiled from their own city by their slaves, was a stock element of the rhetorical historiography, but is spread out by Orosius at greater length than any previous author.[44] Scipio Nasica's injunction not to construct a theatre is discussed extensively—drawing inspiration from Augustine—as an exemplum which was not followed: had the Romans displayed more virtue of Scipio's kind, Orosius suggests, they would have suffered less.[45]

Exempla thus profoundly shape the narrative of the *Historiae*, through either their studied absence or the emphatic presence of negative precedent. Orosius hence writes a negative history not only in the sense that he lists the miseries of the past, but also as a conscious counterpoint to the traditional, glorious account with which his audience has grown up. If his own use of exempla shows that the exemplum itself, as a rhetorical tool, is not rejected, his critique implies that it has become part of a mindset that creates blindness for the true nature of the past.

III. FACT AND FICTION

The preface of book 4 not only diagnoses the disease, it also proposes a remedy: a comparison of facts (*in conparatione rerum*).[46] Pretending to narrate the facts and accusing other historians of bias and rhetorical inclinations is a standard part of the polemic among historians: discrediting the status of the others means raising one's own.[47] We have already noticed some of the techniques used by Orosius to that effect. He accuses rhetoric exercises of reducing the past to a *fabula*,[48] a fiction that is pleasant to listen to but bears no relation to reality.[49] The opposition between verbose and rhetorical

[44] Valerius Maximus 9.1.ext.2; Florus 1.16; *De viris illustribus* 36; Orosius 4.5.3–5.

[45] Orosius 4.21.5–9; *Periochae* 48; Valerius Maximus 2.4.2; Augustine, *De civitate Dei* 1.33. For similar procedures in other books, see 1.15–16, 2.17.17, 2.19.6, 3.10, 3.17.7, 3.22.8, 4.21, 5.5, 5.7, 5.16.13, 5.17.12–13, 5.21.7, 6.2.30, 6.15.17, 6.17.1, 7.

[46] See also Orosius 7.3.3.

[47] Marincola 1997: 218–36. A further indication (if need be) that Orosius sees himself as a true historian is the use of digressions: Orosius 4.8.10–15, 6.7.13–14.

[48] Orosius 1.6.5, 1.12.6, 2.18.4, 3.14.8.

[49] *Rhetorica ad Herrenium* 1.12; Cicero, *De inventione* 1.27; Sextus Empiricus, *Mathesis* 1.263–4; Plutarchus, *Artaxerxes* 6.9; Augustine, *Confessiones* 3.(6)11, *De civitate Dei* 4.1; Prudentius, *Peristephanon* 9.17–20.

historians and truthful depictions of reality was also used by the *Historia augusta*:[50] Orosius is thus drawing on a standard item of late antique historiographical polemic. We have seen how book 4 contains several attacks on pagan historians for distorting the facts and omitting casualty reports. Such accusations occur in unusual density in the first part of book 1, where Orosius notes several times that pagan authors such as Tacitus and Pompeius Trogus hide the facts,[51] and that he and his source Moses narrate the events 'more fully and in the order in which they happened'.[52] It looks as if Orosius wishes to establish the superiority of the Bible as a historical narrative and of the Christian as historian. Yet, the argument is not that the Bible has a higher authority, but that it gives the facts more fully and better. Indeed, in 1.1.8, Orosius expressly refuses to appeal to the authority of the Bible.[53] In that same sentence, an allusion to the first words of the preface of Livy (*operae pretium*) aligns Orosius with the classical historiographical tradition.[54] Therefore, apart from setting out the earliest history of mankind, the first chapters of book 1 assert the ultimate superiority of Christian historiography, not because it is inspired but because it gets the facts right. Repeated polemic with his sources, as we noticed in book 4, keeps that message alive in the mind of the reader.[55]

Orosius goes even one step further. Comparing facts also means doing away with the literary mediation between the fact and the reader. As we have seen in the discussion of the preface to book 4, Orosius sees contemporary rhetorical culture as a screen obfuscating the sight of those trained in it. Ancient historians cannot be trusted for the same reason: they are equally over-determined by the rhetorical mindset to see the facts the way they are—or they are simply biased. In order to see the facts for what they are, one therefore has to do away with the mediation of literature. This expresses itself in

[50] Scriptores Historiae Augustae, *Probus* 2.7, *Tyranni triginta* 33.8.

[51] Orosius 1.5.10, 1.6.2, 1.10.10.

[52] Orosius 1.3.6: plenius, ipso a quo incurrerit ordo. Cf. 1.5.5, 1.8.6.

[53] Augustine's reply against pagan criticism after the sack of 410 also refers the pagans back to their own writings: *Sermo Dolbeau* 5.13. Orosius 3.23.67 suggests that the Bible has a higher moral authority.

[54] Orosius 1.1.8: non quo auctoritatem eorum cuiquam uideamur ingerere, sed quo operae pretium sit de opinione uulgata quae nobis cum omnibus communis est commonere.

[55] In addition to the passages already discussed, see Orosius 5.3.3–4, 5.19.2, 6.1.30, 7.9.7, 7.10.4, 7.11.1, 7.19.4.

Orosius in a tendency to identify text and author, fact and diction. The writings of Moses are much more trustworthy than those of pagan historians, as he narrates 'more fully and truthfully the events as they are done by himself and his followers'.[56] Moses is at once actor and author. Orosius curiously interprets the Athenian amnesty after the rule of the thirty tyrants as an *abolitio malorum* and not, as all others do, as an injunction to forget.[57] He can then rail the pagans who think they can erase facts from history. Both passages imply the idea that text and reality are virtually identical: erasing from the record is seen as erasing from the past; the best historians are those who narrate reality as they have experienced it.[58] Orosius obviously relies on the assumption, common in ancient historiography, that eyewitness accounts are most trustworthy.[59] Yet there is more to his tendency to obscure literary mediation: as we shall see in chapter 5, Orosius often writes in the rhetorical mode of *enargeia*, vivid descriptions that set the events as they are before the reader's eyes. According to one ancient theoretical account, *enargeia* transforms the reader into an eyewitness.[60] Orosius' narrative thus achieves what pagan historians, too versed in their exemplary culture, cannot: he presents the facts as they are, to a reader who is virtually present himself.

IV. HISTORIOGRAPHY AND RHETORIC IN THE FOURTH CENTURY

Both Orosius' critique of contemporary rhetorical culture and his own rhetorical reply to it demonstrate the close intertwining of rhetoric and historiography in late Antiquity. Whilst he challenges his contemporaries for casting a rhetorically distorted regard on the past, he does not really step outside that rhetorical culture. Orosius thus provides excellent testimony of the close interaction of what we may think of as two separate realms.

56 Orosius 1.8.6: plenius veriusque per se suosque gesta conscripsit.

57 Orosius 2.17.5. See, e.g. Valerius Maximus 4.1.ext.4.

58 Orosius 1.1.1, 1.1.6 (where *actores scriptoresque* of the past are identified), 2.2.4, 3.pr.1, 2, 3.2.9, 3.2.13, 4.pr.2, 4.11.4.

59 Cf. Marincola 1997.

60 Dionysius of Halicarnassus, *Lysias* 7.

Whilst we have been taught to be sensitive to the impact of rhetoric on the writing of history,[61] the degree of symbiosis between the writing of history and rhetorical education has yet not been fully appreciated, especially for later Antiquity. That history was a source of exempla and the subject of declamations at school, needs little elaboration.[62] It is possible, however, to go a step further. It has been argued that many works of history, written under the Empire, were aimed at those studying history for rhetorical purposes and hence written by orators. The new comprehensive accounts of Roman history in the second century AD, such as those of Cassius Dio and Florus, are then interpreted as counteracting the focus on classical Greek history in most books of history, caused by the dominance of Greek rhetorical education.[63] This suggestion finds support in a linguistic study of Justin's summary of Pompeius Trogus (dated to the second to fourth century AD),[64] which has shown up the close connection in vocabulary with Cicero and the declamations ascribed to Quintilian. The work probably was 'some sort of aid for the prospective orator'.[65]

In the fourth century, the relationship between rhetoric as a taught discipline and historiography was, if anything, as close as in previous centuries. Obviously history remained part of the rhetorical exercises, but engagement with it went beyond what was needed for composing a proper speech. Teachers of lower rank would sometimes master an impressive array of knowledge about the past, reading even by this time obscure chronicles likes those of Castor.[66] In his *Teachers of Bordeaux* Ausonius praises Staphylius for not just being a grammarian and a rhetorician, but also knowing the entire Livy and Herodotus—undoubtedly metonymical for an excellent knowledge of the

[61] Peter 1911; Rosen 1970; Wiseman 1979 and 1994; Woodman 1988; Moles 1993; Fox 1996 and 2001; Kelly 2008; Laird 2009; Kempshall 2011. The issue of the relationship between rhetoric and history is further discussed in chapter 5.

[62] Russell 1983: 106–28; Kaster 1988: 12–18; Ax 1990; Nicolai 1992; Rebenich 1997: 288; Hose 1994: 5–18, 481–6; Cribiore 2001: 231–8; Wittchow 2001: 34–44; Sehlmeyer 2009.

[63] Hose 1994: 481–6.

[64] If he is not to be dated to the fourth century, at least Justin surfaces for the first time in the early fifth century as a source for Orosius and Augustine (*De civitate Dei* 4.5). For the fourth-century date, see Syme 1988. Yardley 1994: 4 prefers an earlier date.

[65] Yardley 2003: 214.

[66] Ausonius XI (Prof.).22

past—as well as Varro.[67] For Ausonius, history was one of the main occupations of orators, besides poetry, forensic rhetoric, medicine, and philosophy: they not only read such works but also practised these genres. Ausonius himself published the *Caesares*, a verse summary and continuation of Suetonius, and a *Consularis liber*,[68] besides the lost *Chronicle*, *Tyrants from Decius to Diocletian*, and a work on pre-Roman kings.[69] As these titles indicate, involvement with history often entailed a return to glorious periods of the rather distant Roman past, when the great examples for the present were set.[70] But contemporary history was not spurned either, although it is much more visible in Greek than it is in Latin. A list would include such names as Praxagoras and Bemarchius[71] and a number of individuals in contact with the sophist of Antioch, Libanius.[72] Eunapius is another obvious example of a sophist doubling as a historian of his times. The emperor Julian could, satirically but not implausibly, suggest to the Christian sophist Prohaeresius to write a history of his accession to power.[73] But the same happened in Latin: Symmachus praises an anonymous senator for his orations and the work of history he is now composing.[74]

Active interest in history, including the writing of it, was thus intense and widespread among the orators of the late fourth century. Depictions of the inexorable decline of historiography in that century, with Ammianus as the last Roman historian, are thus profoundly misleading.[75] The works that for us define ancient historiography, full-scale contemporary histories, never were as popular as the flowering of 'lesser' works that revisited well-known territories and exalted the greatness of what was known to be grand. The writing of

[67] Ausonius XI (Prof.). 20.8.

[68] Ausonius XI (Prof.).26.1–6 (For the title *Consularis liber*, see Coskun 2002). See also Ausonius XI (Prof.).2.21, XXVII(Epistulae).10.21; Symmachus, *Epistula* 1.3.2.

[69] Green 1991: 160–8, 720.

[70] Symmachus, *Epistula* 1.4, with Bruggisser 1993: 124–7; Nicomachus Flavianus, *CIL* 6.1783, with Hedrick 2000: 145–7.

[71] Praxagoras: *FGrHist* 219; Bemarchius: *FGrHist* 220. One can also think of Paeanius, the translator of Eutropius.

[72] Libanius, *Epistula* 1434, 1508, and Uranius *FGrHist* 675. For this tradition, see Janiszewski 2006.

[73] Julian, *Epistula* 31.

[74] Symmachus, *Epistula* 9.110. Callu 2002: 125 proposes to identify the anonymous with Nicomachus Flavianus senior. See also Symmachus, *Epistulae* 3.11.3 and 4.18.5.

[75] It is an impression still maintained by Marincola 2007.

breviaria was in the fourth century an occupation for the top brass of Roman society (Eutropius, Aurelius Victor, Festus). These works were not written for the common: the extraordinary success of Eutropius can only be explained by his rapid spread in rhetorical schools and stands in marked contrast with the limited traces we have of Ammianus actually being read. As is shown by the group of works attached to the *De caesaribus* of Aurelius Victor, the writing of history often entailed a return to the more distant past, using classical, canonical texts: the *Origo gentis romanae* possibly summarizes Verrius Flaccus,[76] whereas the *De viris illustribus* reviews figures of Roman history from Procas to Cleopatra. The exemplum collection of Valerius Maximus, neatly dividing up the glorious past, was epitomized twice, probably in the fourth century, by Julius Paris and Nepotianus for educational purposes. History was, then, a key element in the rhetorical education and practice, even when not practised with the critical regard at one's own past we expect today of historians: fourth-century culture was one of conscious knowledge of, and engagement with, the great exempla of the past.[77]

Orosius partakes in that culture. Most of the works he used in composing his *Historiae* precisely wish to draw attention again to the great and glorious past: Livy's history sets the past as exemplary for a renewal of the present;[78] for Florus, the history of Rome up to Octavian is not just an example of greatness, but also sums up what is to be known about mankind (see his preface); in the preface to his summary of Pompeius Trogus' history, Justin states to have left out the events 'which were neither pleasant for the desire to know nor necessary by their exemplary nature';[79] Eutropius' *breviarium* has the aim of setting out the *inlustrium virorum facta* (pr.); for the poet Claudian, the past is basically a series of exempla.[80] As set out in chapter 4, Orosius also knew Valerius Maximus and Pseudo-Aurelius Victor's *Epitome de caesaribus*, works that were obviously aimed at the orator. This dependence on the works of history that circulated in

[76] Sehlmeyer 2004: 119–26.

[77] Eigler 2003: 192–204; Sehlmeyer 2009: 115–39.

[78] Livy pr. 9. For the argument, see Chaplin 2000.

[79] Justin pr.4: omissis his, quae nec cognoscendi voluptate iucunda nec exemplo erant necessaria.

[80] Cameron 1970: 350; Eigler 2003: 12–17. See, e.g. Claudian, *In Eutropium* 1.435–65, *Panegyricus de quarto consulatu Honorii* 398–418.

rhetorical schools lends credence to the suggestion that Orosius' criticism of the rhetorical culture of his age is based on a close and intimate knowledge of that culture. In other words, even when criticizing the impact of rhetoric on history, Orosius is another example of the rhetorical nature of historiography in late Antiquity and an illustration of how it is rooted in the school of rhetoric.

Whilst he is thus dependent on works that project a glorious image of the Roman past, Orosius refuses to subscribe to that image. On the contrary, the *Historiae* are a conscious attack on the rhetorical culture of glorifying the past and consistently suggest that his opponents overestimate and idealize the past at the expense of the present. Orosius wishes to demonstrate the superiority of the *tempora christiana*, but also the distortive effect contemporary rhetorical culture has on the perception of reality and the past in particular. His reasons for doing so are obvious. The *Histories* can rightly be described as apologetic, in the sense that they aim at convincing an adversary. To gain cause, however, one needs 'to confirm one's own points and refute those advanced on the other side'—as the majority of rhetoricians held according to Quintilian.[81] To sway one's adversary, it is not enough to demonstrate the truth of one's own views; one also needs to convince him that his perspective is wrong. Orosius can very well assert that the present is superior to the past, but he also needs to show why his opponents think the opposite is true and why their opinion is mistaken. His *Historiae* are therefore also an attack on the rhetorical culture of the past that imbued Orosius' pagan contemporaries: he questions the basic coordinates of the pagan understanding of the past. His enterprise is for that reason similar to that of Augustine in the *City of God*, who also questions some long-held assumptions about, and perceptions of, the Roman past.[82]

Orosius' polemic invites us to see a wide chasm between his *Historiae* and pagan works of history. Indeed, it is his express aim of presenting the only true narrative of the past, which does not suffer from the blindness and bias of earlier histories. As this book suggests, we should not buy into that self-presentation: as much as his pagan contemporaries, Orosius illustrates the rhetorical nature of fourth-

[81] Quintilian 5.pr.2: plures (. . .) hoc tamen proprium atque praecipuum crederent opus, sua confirmare et quae ex adverso proponerentur refutare.

[82] Tornau 2006: 119: 'den Angriff auf verfestigte Denk- und Wahrnehmungsstrukturen.'

and fifth-century historiography. He remains largely indebted to the culture he attacks. The parallels and differences can be best grasped by briefly comparing Orosius' opinions on the exemplum to a famous passage in Ammianus (31.5.10–17). After his account of the battle of Adrianopolis (378 AD), Ammianus apologizes for not being able to offer an absolutely precise account of the battle: in history it suffices to tell the 'main points of events' with 'faithful honesty'.[83] He then criticizes his contemporaries, ignorant of ancient history and morally depraved, for thinking that nothing like the battle of Adrianopolis happened before: he singles out the invasion of Cimbri and Teutons (113–101 BC), the Marcomannic wars (166–180 AD), and the Gothic invasions of the third century to show that the defeat of 378 was not a totally new catastrophe. In fact, the virtue of past ages has always assured the subsequent recovery of the empire. Ammianus' criticism of the dissolute morals of his own day is thus an exhortation to his contemporaries to mend their ways so as to restore the Roman Empire once again.[84] There are striking parallels with Orosius. Both he and Ammianus argue that present catastrophes are not on the same level as the past, and hence that the past is not always better. Both chide contemporary immorality for misinterpreting the present[85] and combine this critique of the misperceptions of their contemporaries with a claim to the factuality of their narrative. Yet Orosius' critique mutates into an attack on the rhetorically transmitted authoritative view of the past, whereas Ammianus continues to use and defend the normative status of the past. The three exempla convey an important message for the present: if we Romans get our act together, we will be able to restore the empire to its time-honoured power. Even though he argues, just like Orosius, that the present is not worse than the past, Ammianus' exempla still betray a belief in the authority of the past: looking at the past, one knows how to judge the present and how to act today.[86]

In his recent study of Ammianus, Gavin Kelly summarizes the role of exempla in Ammianus as follows:

[83] Ammianus 31.5.10: sufficiet enim, veritate nullo velata mendacio, ipsas rerum digere summitates: cum explicandae rerum memoriae ubique debeatur integritas fida.

[84] Barnes 1998: 175–7 (partially followed by Kelly 2008: 282–3) thinks this passage criticizes Christians, but the parallel with the Rome-digressions (14.6 and 28.4) shows that Ammianus' critique is meant generally.

[85] See Orosius 1.6.1, 1.8.14, 1.12.1, 1.16.4, 1.21.17, 3.2.12, 3.3.3, 6.17.9, 7.10.2, 7.35.22.

[86] See Cicero, *De oratore* 169.

> Ammianus' history constantly proclaims the value of historical learning. It also proclaims the continuity and unity of its subject, the Roman Empire, across time and space. In the remarkable timelessness of the digressions, and the geographical sweep of the narrative, the idealized combination of Roman virtue and Hellenic civilisation is constantly reaffirmed. In the main the engine that drives these two ideals forward is the historical example. Ammianus' characters are constantly compared to those of previous history, and their quality is constantly judged by their own ability to recognize their historical context. Knowledge of history consists of knowledge of *exempla*, and successful characters imitate the good and avoid the bad.[87]

In Orosius, on the other hand, the authority of the past is under attack, because it is part of a rhetorical culture that creates an ideal past and distorts the facts. Significantly, whereas Ammianus chides his readers for having too little knowledge of the past and hence misjudging the present, Orosius presumes his readers to know all the events he describes. What they prefer to ignore, however, is their bloody and horrifying nature: they cannot judge the present well, because their heads are stuffed with glorious actions of the past. For Ammianus, his characters have to situate themselves in the past so as to act correctly in the present. Orosius thinks this is a rhetorical attitude which stands in the way of a true judgment of the present.

The striking closeness of Ammianus and Orosius better highlights the fundamental issue on which they part ways, namely that of the authority of the past as perpetuated in rhetorical training. A further comparison, with Christian discussions of pagan exempla, will provide additional insight into how Orosius' views fit into the Christian discourse of his own time. That is the subject of the last section of this chapter.

V. DEBATING EXEMPLA AMONG CHRISTIANS

Ancient discussions of exempla are largely technical, assigning them to a specific place in the catalogue of rhetorical figures.[88] But Roman

[87] Kelly 2008: 294. See already Rosen 1970: 230 for Ammianus and Chaplin 2000: 82 for Livy.

[88] For an overview, see Demoen 1997; Loutsch 1998.

authors also regularly emphasize the educational value of examples,[89] obviously praising how the exempla *maiorum* shape the as yet unformed view of the student on the world. Quintilian, as usual, spells this out most clearly: the pupil should copy lines that convey a moral message and in that way 'he will remember such aphorisms even when he is an old man, and the impression made upon his unformed mind will contribute to the formation of his character'.[90] Just knowing the past is not enough, it must be translated into action:

> But the man who does not believe that it is enough to fix his eyes merely on his own ages and his own transitory life, but regards the space allotted for an honourable life and the course in which glory's race is run as conditioned solely by the memory of posterity, will not rest content with a mere knowledge of the events of history.[91]

Exempla thus establish a link between past, present, and future: the past inspires one in the present to become, in the future, part of a glorious past. The past can only be normative if it has become part of one's own history: parallel to the anchoring of Roman history to Greek history through temporal synchronism, as noticed in chapter 2, Romans start to make famous Greeks part of their moral universe by comparing them to Romans. Nepos wrote about lives of famous Greek generals, and Valerius Maximus included 'foreign' examples after the Roman ones.[92] Just as the temporal synchronism, this moral synchronism ultimately aimed at showing the superiority of Roman virtue. Even so, both synchronisms created a more or less unified temporal and moral past, which, ultimately, was a glorious one, although not necessarily in every particular instance a successful one. Livy's history, for example, sees a contemplation of the distant past as key to the regeneration of the present (pr.9–11). Although he, in line with most contemporary historians, constructed history as a story of decline, the existence of at least an original, glorious past was never questioned.

A lot therefore comes together in a mere story about, say, Camillus or Torquatus: it conjures up a perception of the past and a

[89] Cicero, *Pro Archia* 14, *De legibus* 2.62, *Ad familiares* 6.6, *De oratore* 2.335; Vergil, *Aeneis* 12.438–40; Horace, *Satyra* 1.4; Seneca, *Epistula* 24.11, *De tranquillitate animi* 1.12. Cf. Skidmore 1996: 22–7; Walter 2002.

[90] Quintilian 1.1.35–6. See also Plutarch, *Praecepta gerendae reipublicae* 814A–C.

[91] Quintilian 12.2.31. Tr. D. Russell (LCL). See also Quintilian 12.2.29–30.

[92] Cornelius Nepos pr.; Valerius Maximus 1.6.pr.

prescription of action.[93] In a period when the rise of Christianity challenged both, the exemplum became a vicarious battleground for wider issues of Christian identity in relation to the classical past. Just as that relationship was negotiated in various ways, Christian responses to the classical exemplum varied from acceptance, incorporation into a Christian moral framework, to attempts at substitution.[94] It will be useful to briefly review some of these debates to understand where Orosius is to be situated.

Jerome's attitude towards classical learning has often been seen as 'oscillating between aversion and adhesion',[95] with the troubled dream of *Letter* 22, accusing him of being a Ciceronian,[96] and the defence of classical exempla in *Letter* 70 as the two poles of his attitude. Jerome is one of the Church fathers who, in certain contexts, could incorporate pagan learning without much ado.[97] As has recently been shown by Ann Mohr, these apparent vacillations obscure a more moderate and traditional attitude: classical learning can be accommodated in Christian teaching as long as it serves Christian ends.[98] This basic attitude also underpins *Letter* 70, with its defence of classical exempla.[99] In 397 Jerome received the following demand from the clearly Christian orator of the city of Rome, Magnus: 'why do we include, from time to time, examples from secular literature in our works, and why do we pollute the purity of the Church with dirt of the gentiles?'[100] Jerome's answer is curt: Christian literature, starting with Moses, over Paul, to the apologists of the early Church all used pagan learning, not just in controversy with pagans, but also

[93] Chaplin 2000: 197 notes that the exemplum involves two timeframes: the past is recollected and applied to the present, and the present is envisioned as a source of models for the future. The moral nature of history connects both.

[94] For the history of the exemplum in later Antiquity, see Vitale-Brovarone 1980; Inglebert 1994; Jaffelin 2000; Fournet 2003; Fratantuono 2006; Felmy 2001: 42 states, mistakenly in my view, that the exemplum was never a battleground. For a recent synthesis on Christianity and pagan *Bildung*, see Gemeinhardt 2007. Rather unsatisfactory is Sehlmeyer 2009: 203–11, who ignores all this literature.

[95] Hagendahl 1958: 22. See also Kelly 1975: 335.

[96] Jerome, *Epistula* 22.30.

[97] Tornau 2006: 73–105. This point was already made, with specific reference to exempla, in Schneiderhan 1921.

[98] Mohr 2007. The following is indebted to her reading of the letter.

[99] On exempla in Jerome, see Rebenich 1992; Clausi 1995; Hamblenne 1996.

[100] Jerome, *Epistula* 70.2: quod autem quaeris in calce epistulae cur in opusculis nostris saecularium litterarum interdum ponamus exempla, et candorem ecclesiae ethnicorum sordibus polluamus, breviter responsum habeto.

in exegesis and doctrinal works. There is more going on in this exchange than literary conventions. Jerome's rather blunt reply can be explained by his conviction that his archenemy, Rufinus of Aquileia, is behind this attack (70.6). Both had fallen out over the orthodoxy of Origen, and the argument of authority serves to make the point that his own attitude to pagan exempla is fully in line with tradition. The long list of respectable predecessors Jerome is capable of citing suggests that his own, accommodating, attitude is the rule, and that Rufinus deviates from established practice. In turn, Magnus' question illustrates that the use of classical exempla could mutate into a litmus test of orthodoxy.

Rhetorically trained, Ambrose knew the value of the exemplum and he consciously tried to put forward new, Christian models to take the place of classical ones[101]—even in imperial contexts where classical examples of warfare and virtue would seem, at first sight, better suited. In *De fide*, addressed to the emperor Gratian, Ambrose strongly banks on the traditional virtue of the emperor as an 'imitator of ancient history' (1.1: veteris imitator historiae): he opens by depicting Gratian as imitating the Queen of Sheba and King Hiram who came to consult Solomon's wisdom. He immediately deflates the implicit pretension of personal superiority over the emperor by stating that he is not Solomon and Gratian not a barbarian king.[102] Two other examples, that of Abraham leading 318 men to numerous victories (*Genesis* 14.14), and that of Joshua bringing down the walls of Jericho (*Joshua* 5.14), demonstrate to Gratian the value of piety in warfare. Ambrose concludes with the point that the participants of the council of Nicaea, which provides the foundation of the faith set out in the work, were equal in number to the pious of Abraham. The last words of the preface explicitly designate Abraham as 'an example of piety from history' (in historia pietatis exemplum). The emphatic position of this expression lays out the meaning of the preface: Ambrose suggests that Gratian sets as exempla to himself not the heroes of the pagan Roman past, who overcame their enemies through military prowess, but the patriarchs of the Old Testament

[101] Lanéry 2007; Sehlmeyer 2009: 199.

[102] Ambrose, *De fide* 1.1: Regina Austri venit audire sapientiam Solomonis, ut in libro regnorum legimus. Hiram quoque rex ad Solomonem misit, ut cognoscet eum. Tu quoque, sancte imperator Gratiane, veteris imitator historiae, fidem meam audire voluisti. Sed non ego Solomon, cuius mirere sapientiam; neque tu unius gentis, sed totius orbis Augustus fidem libello exprimi censuisti, non ut disceres, sed ut probares.

who did so through piety. Whilst this is an obvious point to make in a work on the Christian faith, so as to remind Gratian again of the value of the (Catholic) faith, it is also a reflection on the use of exempla: Ambrose does not reject their utility, but he wishes to substitute biblical figures for the heroes of the Roman past.

The query put to Jerome by Magnus and Ambrose's conscious attempt at substitution show that the use of pagan exempla in a Christian context was far from uncontroversial. It is not just in Christian literature that this battle was fought. Only one poem of Claudian is explicitly anti-Christian in tone: *Against Jacob the master of the horse* (poem L).[103] It deserves to be quoted in full:

> (1) By the ashes of Paul, by the shrine of old Peter,/do not pull my verses to pieces, general Jacob./So may Thomas defend your breast in stead of a shield/and Bartholomew go as a companion into war./(5) So may the barbarian not invade the Alps because of the throng of saints/So may saint Susanna give you her strength./So, should any savage swing across the icy Danube,/may he be drowned like the swift chariots of Pharaoh./So may the avenging sword strike the Gothic hordes/(10) and the favour of Thecla guide the Roman troops./So may the dying guest give you a great triumph/and the broken casks overcome your thirst./So may your hand never be stained by enemy blood;/do not pull my verses to pieces, general Jacob.
>
> (1) Per cineres Pauli, per cani limina Petri,/ne laceres versus, dux Iacobe, meos./sic tua pro clipeo defendat pectora Thomas/et comes ad bellum Bartholomaeus eat/(5) sic ope sanctorum non barbarus inruat Alpes,/sic tibi det vires sancta Susanna suas/sic quicumque ferox gelidum transnaverit Histrum,/mergatur volucres ceu Pharaonis equi/sic Geticas ultrix feriat romphaea catervas/(10) Romanasque regat prospera Thecla manus/si tibi det magnum moriens conviva triumphum/atque tuam vincant dolia fusa sitim/sic numquam hostile maculetur sanguine dextra./ne laceres versus, dux Iacobe, meos.[104]

Jacob, *magister equitum* during Alaric's invasion of Italy (401/2), obviously had criticized Claudian's poetry, although it is impossible to know precisely what for. If Claudian's satirical riposte is anything to go by, it must have been on his use of pagan imagery and exempla.

[103] Dated to 402/3 by Cameron 1970: 218. On Claudian's position as a pagan at a Christian court, see Cameron 1970: 189–227; Doepp 1980; Sebesta 1980; Vanderspoel 1986; Moreschini 2004.

[104] Tr. M. Platnauer (LCL), modified.

Indeed, the bulk of the poem sets Jacob in the company of a series of saints and biblical figures, a list which transforms into an assault on his military stamina. The poem can be read as if Claudian complies with Jacob's desire to use more Christian exempla: it ironically begs the *magister equitum* to show mercy on his verses and wishes him well in his future exploits with the support of Christian examples. Claudian's wishes, however, carry a sharp sting. The apostle Thomas is an unlikely defender of one's breast: not only did he waver in his support for Christ, but he also needed to put his fingers into the wound of Christ in his side (*Gospel of John* 20.24–9).[105] Bartholomew remains an obscure figure. According to Eusebius, he spread the Gospel in India, and later became the apostle of Armenia, where late legends have him martyred.[106] This particular lack of success, which Bartholomew shared with most Apostles, probably made him suited as an unwarlike companion for Jacob. Susanna is a Christian exemplum of chastity: in *Daniel* 13, she is falsely accused by two lecherous old men after she refuses to satisfy them. This is a better identification than with the martyr Susanna,[107] as it allows us to detect a pun on *viros* in Claudian's *tibi det vires*: will Susanna give strength (*vires*) to Jacob or old, feeble men (*viros*)? The identification of barbarian invaders with Pharaoh's chariots needs little explanation. The use of the Greek *romphaea* for the 'avenging sword' might be an allusion to *Genesis* 3.24, where God posits an angel with a fiery sword to keep Adam and Eve out of paradise. The references to God's avenging sword and the exodus conjure up an image of Rome as the Promised Land, its enemies held at bay by God. The sting probably lies in the ineffectiveness of this divine help: Goths had crossed the Danube and the Alps, and Roman armies were fighting to control them. Thecla was another famous virgin who battled hard to keep her virginity and whose cult took a high flight in the fourth and fifth

[105] I see this as a better interpretation than the one proposed by Vanderspoel 1986: 249, who refers to the apocryphal acts of Thomas. It is far from clear if these circulated in the West at this time (see Myers 2006 for issues of dating and composition). He seems to underestimate the Bible as point of reference for the poem.

[106] Eusebius, *Historia ecclesiastica* 5.10.3. For the development of the legend, see Leloir 1992: 479–83.

[107] Suggested by Platnauer 1956: 278; Vanderspoel 1986: 250. The martyr Susanna is, after all, rather obscure. Vanderspoel's argument that the adjective *sancta* cannot refer to a figure of the Old Testament is mistaken: see Augustine, *In psalmos enarratio* 52.

centuries.[108] She closes off the list of exempla: being the companion of Paul who is the first Christian figure mentioned in Claudian's poem, she occupies a suitable position. She seems here to become the substitute of the personified Roma, who plays a large role in several of Claudian's poems,[109] just as Peter and Paul can be seen as stand-ins for Romulus and Remus. Lines 10 and 11 remain hard to interpret. In the translation of Platnauer in the Loeb Classical Library, they are taken as references to banquets. On that reading, Claudian, after having put Jacob in the company of unwarlike and ineffective helpers, shows where the general can achieve victory, namely in feasting and drinking. Alternatively, as the stimulating suggestion of J. Vanderspoel goes, *moriens conviva* refers to Christ during the Last Supper and *dolia fusa* to the Eucharist: Claudian thus challenges the Christian propaganda that attributes military victory to Christ.[110] At any rate, the ironic wish in the penultimate line, that Jacob's hands may stay clean of enemy's blood, captures the message of the poem well: it is an allusion to the Christian ideal that one should not shed blood[111] and to the misplaced trust put by Jacob in his saints and biblical exempla, as well as a plea not to commit metaphorical violence on Claudian's poems by thrashing them. The poem is remarkable for its depth of engagement with Christian themes and literature: this is a learned poet showing off that he could write poems with a Christian content as well—if he wished to. Whilst Claudian is attacking Jacob's misplaced piety and excessive trust in the power of the saints,[112] he also challenges a way of writing poetry, which seeks to substitute a Christian glorified past and moral framework for the classical one to which he is attached, and thus ironically surrounds Jacob with Christian anti-exempla. Jacob probably wished that Claudian was more of a Prudentius, who precisely substituted

[108] Gregory of Nazianzus, *Oratio* 24.10 mentions Susanna and Thecla together. For the cult, see Dagron 1978.

[109] See Claudian, *Panegyricus dictus Probino et Olybrio consulibus* 75–173, *De bello gildonico* 28–127, *In Eutropium* 1.371–513, *De consulatu Stilichonis* 2.223–407, *De sexto consulatu Honorii* 356–493 with Gärtner 1996–7; Roberts 2001.

[110] Vanderspoel 1986: 246–7.

[111] Van Nuffelen 2004b.

[112] Cameron 1970: 225; Vanderspoel 1986; Consolino 2004. I am not convinced that the poem is ultimately about the battle of Pollentia (402), as suggested by Vanderspoel. At any rate, the poem should also be read as part of a literary debate, and not just a political one.

Christian for pagan exempla,[113] but, although Claudian knew Prudentius' work, he was having none of it.

In Jerome, Ambrose, and Claudian, the intellectual battle being fought about exempla seems to focus on the content of the exempla, namely whether it is acceptable for Christians to use pagan exempla and whether they should be replaced with Christian ones. Orosius' criticism has a wider aim: he challenges, as we have seen, the rhetorical culture of which the exemplum is an expression. His attack is less a matter of purifying Christian literature than questioning the view of the past and the morality that too much reliance on traditional exempla generates. These are matters that can be seen as underpinning the debates that surface in Jerome, Ambrose, and Claudian, although they are not explicitly articulated there.

The wider perspective of Orosius can be explained by two factors: Augustine and apologetic. In his *Confessions*, Augustine pondered on the disjunction between morality and education: in school, good acts that were badly discussed were deemed reprehensible, whereas evil actions described in beautiful periods were praised.[114] As shown by C. Tornau, this exemplifies Augustine's attitude towards rhetorical education: his critique did not aim primarily at the content of education, but at the attitude it generated.[115] As a consequence, the *City of God* questions the perception of past and present, fixed by rhetorical education[116]—an enterprise very similar to what we have detected in Orosius and which may very well have influenced the *Historiae*. In that work this does not lead to a wholesale condemnation of the Roman past. Whilst Augustine questions the desire for *gloria* that drives the Romans,[117] he does admit that some good may come out of it: even when aimed at a wrong or imperfect goal, deeds performed out of a desire for glory may set some example, even to Christians—be it just for the latter to realize that they are doing much better.[118]

[113] See, e.g. Prudentius, *Peristephanon* 2.14, 2.413–84. See also Paulinus of Nola, *Carmina* 25.9–10.

[114] Augustine, *Confessiones* 1.(18)28, cf. 1(13)22, 1.(17)27.

[115] Tornau 2006: 32–3.

[116] Tornau 2006: 119.

[117] Augustine, *Confessiones* 6.(4)6, *De civitate Dei* 2.29, 5.12, 5.17.

[118] Augustine, *De civitate Dei* 5.16–8, with Swift 1986 and 1987, and in particular Tornau 2006: 320. See also Augustine, *De civitate Dei* 1.15, 1.24 and Lactantius, *Institutiones* 5.13.13.

Augustine, in a sense, saves Roman virtues by devaluating them and giving them such a place in his Christian world view.

Because of his strident polemic, Orosius has a less positive appreciation of ancient Roman virtue than Augustine[119] and his argument focuses strongly on the distorting *habitus* created by rhetorical training among his contemporaries. The negative thrust of Orosius' apologetic can be better sensed when comparing him with his contemporary Sulpicius Severus. The preface to the *Life of Saint Martin* develops a contrast between pagan and thus vain exempla for temporal life and Christian exempla for the life to come. Sulpicius starts out by recognizing the imitational value of exempla: many a secular (i.e. pagan) author hoped to gain eternal glory by writing down the lives of great men. He dismisses this as vain, but admits that they had some success: 'Having set down the examples of great men, not a little emulation was incited among the readers.' He does not attack the mechanism, but rather the choice of exempla by pagan authors: 'What profit did posterity draw from reading how Hector fought and Socrates philosophized?'[120] People have put their faith in fables and thus confided their souls to tombs. Indeed, literature is powerful: 'And this human error, transmitted in literature, has become so strong, that one finds very many imitators of inane philosophy or this vain virtue.'[121] Sulpicius proposes a double change of perspective: he will set the readers a proper, Christian exemplum with Martin, and he, as an author, will derive true, divine profit from it (1.6). Similarly to Orosius, Sulpicius Severus here recognizes that it is literature that shapes the exemplary past. The desire for glory is everywhere: not just in the heads of the great men, but also in the heads of the authors of their lives and those of the audiences reading them. Literature is the place where glory is eternalized and displayed to be imitated. What pagan exempla lack, according to Sulpicius, is the right moral aim: inspired by the wrong moral code, they lead the reader to eternal damnation rather than to everlasting glory. But the mechanism of

[119] See Inglebert 1996: 536–9 for an inventory of the kind of virtues that he detects among the Romans.

[120] Sulpicius Severus, *Vita Martini* 1.2–3: propositis magnorum virorum exemplis non parvua aemulatio legentibus excitabatur. (. . .) at quid posteritas emolumenti tulit legend Hectorem aut Socrates philosophantem?

[121] Sulpicius Severus, *Vita Martini* 1.5: qui quidem error humanus litteris traditus in tantum valuit, ut multos plane aemulos vel inanis philosophiae vel stultae illius virtutis invenerit.

exempla is basically sound: the preface ends with Sulpicius consciously (but humbly) assuming the position of the author who will receive true glory for having shown a true exemplum to mankind.[122] In a work with a different aim, Orosius might have subscribed to Sulpicius' combination of analysis and substitution: indeed, the rare instances that he does use a positive exemplum show that he is capable of proposing alternative models of conduct.[123] But he writes *Historiae adversus paganos* and he thus banks by and large on criticism. Because his polemic is directed in the first place against his contemporaries, his criticism targets mainly their distorted perception. This entails also a criticism of those responsible for that misleading perception: ancient authors, who systematically downplay the gruesome nature of supposedly glorious events. There is, however, no suggestion that Christian exempla, i.e. a Christian history and morality, need to be substituted for its pagan counterpart. Indeed, Orosius is writing a secular history aimed at subverting pagan categories of thought from within: the traditional glorious view of the past, inculcated by rhetorical education, needs to be challenged by focusing on its most explicit expression, the exemplum. Orosius wishes to open the eyes of his adversaries for the true nature of their past and he does so by shaping his history as the explicit mirror image of the sanitized exemplary one he is questioning.[124]

Paradoxically, thus, Orosius' attack on the contemporary rhetorical culture is at once wide ranging and rather narrow. It draws attention to the mindset, conditioned by rhetorical training, which underpins the high value attributed to a specific reading of the past. In that way he reveals aspects of rhetorical education that ancient theoreticians of rhetoric often fail to spell out but are emphasized in modern analyses, such as its importance in forming the pupil's view of the past and their authority in guiding conduct.[125] Even in Christian debates about the role of the exemplum, Orosius occupies a peculiar position: whilst

[122] Tanner 1989: 110 argues that Sulpicius is writing for Christian orators. This would explain his desire to keep the mechanism but change the content.

[123] Orosius 7.4.12, 7.34.2–3, 5, 7.42.13. I fail to see why Sehlmeyer 2009: 203 writes 'Orosius ist eher exempla-Quelle denn exempla-Nutzer'.

[124] The fact that Orosius is capable of using Vergil in the *Commonitorium* (see chapter 1), shows that he is not simply conforming to the idea that the use of classical culture is justified in an apologetic context but not in properly Christian works (cf. Jerome, *Epistula* 70.6).

[125] Skidmore 1994: 22–7; David 1998; Cribiore 2001: 238–42; Walter 2002.

he shares with Augustine and Sulpicius Severus an explicit awareness of how the exemplary culture functions, he does not propose to substitute pagan exempla with Christian ones, as does Severus, or to insert pagan virtues into a re-jigged moral hierarchy, as one finds in the *City of God*. Here one senses well that Orosius does not write a theological treatise, where more attention would go to the Christian alternative, but a history which aims at substituting a true view of the past for the distorted one his contemporaries usually read. In this way, Orosius' criticism has a rather narrow focus, in that it remains one-sided. By and large, he is content with questioning the mindset of his contemporaries, whilst even suggesting their general moral weakness and inability to live up to their own exempla.

To what extent Orosius' critique of his contemporaries is justified is a largely irrelevant question, although it has been noted by astute observers that Claudian and Ammianus, two of the foremost pagan authors of the fourth century, admire the Rome of literature, not of reality,[126] and that the degree to which both rely on exempla is higher than ever before.[127] Even if an increased late antique awareness of, and fascination for, the classical past is thus a possible background, Orosius' argument against exempla is primarily triggered by the anti-Christian arguments after the sack of Rome, suggesting that the pagan past was superior to the Christian present. From his own rhetorical training, Orosius sensed that this was based on a culturally and educationally determined esteem for an idealized past. His polemic allowed him to depict pagan culture, including pagan historians, as rhetorically over-determined and unable to state the facts as they are. Embracing the self-definition of the classical historian as unbiased, factual, and prosaic, Orosius succeeds in proposing Christian historians, and himself in particular, as the only true historians who can live up to what is expected of a historian. Rather than abandoning classical history for Christian apologetic, as is often asserted, Orosius turns elements of the classical tradition against itself, in order to claim pride of place in that tradition for himself. It is a strategy that was well suited for the target audience of elite sympathisers of Christians, troubled by recent events: they are invited to adjust their perception of reality and to notice the distorting mirrors of the past that pagan histories actually are.

[126] Cameron 1970: 360–1.
[127] Demandt 1965: 112.

4

(Re)sources of Narrative

The preceding chapters have suggested that we should understand Orosius in the context of late antique rhetorical practice. He draws on, and engages with, the techniques and mindset that were inculcated in the school of rhetoric: literary allusions and the conscious manipulation of traditional exempla lend his message strength and depth. Rather than merely blurting out apologetic, Orosius consciously situates himself in the historiographical tradition, itself strongly marked by rhetoric. The image of a much more sophisticated historian than usually sketched is emerging. The present chapter wishes to take that revision one step further and argues that Orosius' attitude towards his sources has been judged much more passive than it actually is. The view of Orosius as the prototype of the late ancient historian, who supposedly merely copies his sources, needs to be abandoned.

Research on the sources of Orosius has been extensive,[1] although it often served ulterior ends. O. Seel, for example, was mainly interested in the information the *Historiae* could provide for establishing the text of Justin's epitome of Pompeius Trogus. Other scholars have tried to reconstruct the Livian epitome, supposedly produced in the early empire,[2] and a hypothetical pagan history[3] from the *Historiae*. Many of these studies share the basic assumption that Orosius is a copyist, that is, someone who faithfully transcribes a single source.[4] On such a view, one can relatively easily ascribe entire passages to

[1] A start was made by Beck 1834: 1–9. For overviews, see Lippold 1976: i.xxiv–vi; Goetz 1980a: 25–8; Arnaud-Lindet 1990–1: i.xxv–ix. Detailed investigations are Hingst 1973; Polichetti 2000.

[2] Bessone 1982 is a useful guide to the extensive bibliography on the subject. For Orosius, see Lippold 1976: i.xxv.

[3] Paschoud 1975: 164 and 1980: 132–3; Nelson 1977; Escribaño Paño 2007: 709.

[4] Mörner 1844: 51; Lippold 1976: i.xxxv–ix; Arnaud-Lindet 1990–1: i.xxv.

now lost sources. Such a 'mechanical' method has been attributed to late antique historians in general by L. Bessone, with the aim of justifying the use of Orosius as a reliable source for the epitome of Livy.[5] To a certain extent, it is indeed true that Orosius sometimes includes entire sentences, for example drawn from Justin and Suetonius.[6] Nevertheless, this chapter argues that as a general characterization of Orosius' practice it is demonstrably wrong. The point has, in fact, been made before, but bears restating and expanding.[7] Orosius normally rephrased his sources,[8] and, whilst he indeed tended to use a single source as the backbone of blocks of narrative, this does not imply an exclusive reliance on that source in every detail of the section, as the fleeting use of Lactantius in 7.22.4 demonstrates.[9] In line with the general argument of this book about the importance of rhetoric, this chapter wishes to add to this scholarship in two specific ways. First, I shall show that Orosius used the exempla collection of Valerius Maximus and contaminated it with various other sources in order to create his own version. Such a dependency shows again that we must understand Orosius against the background of contemporary rhetorical education and practice, for which such exempla collections were designed. Moreover, the use of multiple sources at the same time cautions against the idea that we can reconstruct lost sources out of Orosius with any degree of confidence. The second point this chapter wishes to make is that, especially in the last book, Orosius had recourse to the technique of amplification in order to construct a narrative out of brief indications in *breviaria* and chronicles. This shows again not only the use of rhetorical techniques, but also that there did not seem to exist a continuous historical narrative on which Orosius could draw for the last decades of the *Historiae* (or if it existed, he was unable to access it). The chapter thus shows that the idea of a 'mechanical' use of sources seriously underestimates the priority that Orosius (as most historians) accorded to his narrative, over and against strict fidelity to his sources.

[5] Bessone 1982: 1241. For a similar view, see Vittinghoff 1964: 560. Kelly 2008: 222–55 and Cameron 2011: 686 discuss similar assumptions that underpin late antique *Quellenforschung*.

[6] e.g. Orosius 2.17.14, 7.7.1.

[7] Hingst 1973: 44, 96; Fear 2010a: 15.

[8] A point made by Hagendhal 1941 in relation to Justin.

[9] Orosius 7.22.4 and Lactantius, *De mortibus persecutorum* 5.2–3: cf. Polichetti 2000: 154. See Salzman 2010: 212 on Orosius 7.20 and 7.35.

I. CONSTRUCTING EXEMPLA: VALERIUS MAXIMUS

The obvious interest Orosius has in exempla raises the question whether Orosius used one of the typical rhetorical tools, namely exempla collections, in particular that of Valerius Maximus. Valerius Maximus dedicated his collection of memorable deeds and sayings to the emperor Tiberius (14–37 AD). It enjoyed quite some popularity in later Antiquity, in particular in schools of rhetoric: two fourth-century *epitomai*, by Julius Paris and Nepotianus, still exist. That Orosius used Valerius is a priori likely given his rhetorical training and the fact that other late antique historians, such as Ammianus Marcellinus, did so as well.[10] It can, in fact, be demonstrated in a number of precise instances,[11] whilst I could not detect a link with the *epitomai*. Yet, as the following examples make clear, the picture is complicated by two factors. First, Orosius used several sources at the same time to construct his own narrative, thus making it sometimes hard to disentangle what derives from a particular source. Second, Valerius Maximus relied on Livy—although not exclusively—for many of his anecdotes.[12] Because Orosius used several other sources from the Livian tradition, in particular Florus and the *Periochae*, it can be hard to determine with certainty which sources were drawn on in a given passage. The following three examples will set out the methodological problems involved.

In the middle of book 5, Orosius narrates the well-known exemplum of the 'soldier of Pompey',[13] who the day after a battle in the civil war stumbles upon the corpse of his brother. He realizes that he himself has killed him and commits suicide. As the following table makes clear, Orosius drew on (at least) two different sources:

[10] Finke 1904; Kelly 2008: 249.

[11] Hingst 1972: 98–102 provides in-depth analyses of some passages with conclusions that run parallel to mine: Orosius 5.19.7 may have used *De viris illustribus* 67.4, Symmachus, *Oratio* 1.5, Valerius Maximus 2.10.6, and *Periochae* 77.6, whilst Orosius 4.16.5 draws on Eutropius 3.11, Valerius Maximus 7.2.ext.16, *Periochae* 23, and Augustine, *De civitate Dei* 18. Fear 2010a: 176 on 4.10.1 suggests a common source with Valerius Maximus 9.2.ext.1, but direct use is more plausible. I shall not discuss these passages.

[12] Maslakov 1984.

[13] See Tacitus, *Historiae* 3.51.

Orosius 5.19.12–3	Valerius Maximus 5.5.4	Augustine, *De civitate Dei* 2.25	*Periochae* 79
postera die cum permixtim corpora ad sepulturam discernerentur, miles Pompeianus fratris sui, quem ipse interfecerat, corpus agnouit: in concursu enim utrique cognitionem uultus galea, considerationem furor ademerat; quamuis parum sit culpae circa *ignorantiam*, ut uideatur nescisse de fratre quem non ambigitur scisse de ciue. itaque uictor uicto infelicior, ubi et *fratris corpus* agnouit et parricidium suum, exsecratus bella ciuilia ilico *pectus suum gladio transuerberans* simulque lacrimas et sanguinem fundens super *fraternum* sese cadauer abiecit.	Sed omnis memoriae clarissimis imperatoribus profecto non erit ingratum, si militis summa erga fratrem suum pietas huic parti uoluminis adhaeserit: is namque in castris Cn. Pompei stipendia peragens, cum Sertorianum militem acrius sibi in acie instantem comminus interemisset iacentemque spoliaret, ut fratrem germanum esse cognouit, multum ac diu conuicio deos ob donum impiae uictoriae insecutus, prope castra transtulit et pretiosa ueste opertum rogo inposuit. ac deinde subiecta face protinus eodem *gladio*, quo illum interemerat, *pectus suum transuerberauit* seque super *corpus fratris* prostratum communibus flammis cremandum tradidit. licebat *ignorantiae* beneficio innocenti uiuere, sed ut sua potius pietate quam aliena uenia uteretur, comes *fraternae* neci non defuit.	Iam multos moverat, quod miles quidam, dum occiso spolia detraheret, fratrem nudato cadaver agnovit ac detestatus bella civilia se ipsum ibi perimens fraterno corpora adiunxit.	In quo bello duo fratres, alter ex Pompei exercitu, alter ex Cinnae, ignorantes concurrerunt, et cum uictor spoliaret occisum, agnito fratre ingenti lamentatione edita, rogo ei extructo, ipse se supra rogum transfodit et eodem igne consumptus est.

The obvious borrowings demonstrate that Orosius constructed his version from Augustine and Valerius Maximus. There is no link with the *Periochae* in terms of vocabulary, which suggests that Orosius' version does not derive from Livy, the common source of the *Periochae* and Valerius Maximus, but directly from the latter. At the same time, Orosius does not slavishly follow his sources, but in this case strikes a balance between the extreme brevity of Augustine and the, in his eyes, misguided prolixity of Maximus. Orosius focuses the episode on its key moment and heightens the drama by postponing the recognition scene to the day after the battle. The recognition takes place in isolation, thus increasing its intensity. The funeral pyre plays a key role in Valerius but seems to have been judged a distracting detail by Orosius and is left out, probably in imitation of Augustine. Even more importantly, Orosius also changes the meaning of the exemplum. For Valerius, it is an example of brotherly piety: the civil war is the tragic context for an act of brotherly love and dedication. Indeed, Valerius concludes the story by commenting that the soldier's ignorance might have excused his crime. This triggers Orosius' criticism, first expressed in 5.19.12 and immediately repeated at greater length in 5.19.14–16, that if the soldier did not know he was fighting his brother, he surely did not ignore that he was fighting a fellow citizen. The civil war is thus not a tragedy but a moral depravity; committing suicide after the murder of one's own brother is not an example of piety in dire circumstances, but impiety heaped on impiety. The subversion of this classic exemplum thus starts with a refocusing of the anecdote, which then allows a different moral framework to be applied to it, different from the one in which Valerius wished it to be understood.

It should cause no surprise that most connections with Valerius can be established in the context of negative exempla or, at least, exempla that are negatively interpreted. Another illustration is the gruesome death of M. Marius Gratidianus, a well-known event from 82 BC,[14] for which possible links with four sources can be established.

[14] Sallust, *Historiae* 1.44; Quintus Cicero, *Commentariolum petitionis* 10; Lucan, *De bello civile* 2.173–93; Cassius Dio 48.14.2.

Orosius 5.21.7	Augustine, *De civitate Dei* 3.28	Valerius Maximus 9.2.1	Florus 2.9.26[15]	*Periochae* 88
M. Marium siquidem de caprili casa extractum uinciri Sylla iussit DUCTUMQUE trans Tiberim AD LUTATIORUM SEPULCHRUM effossis oculis *membrisque minutatim desectis* uel etiam fractis trucidari.	alius *oculis effosis* et *particulatim membris amputates* in tantis cruciatibus diu vivere vel potius die mori coactus est.	quam porro crudeliter se in M. Mario praetore gessit! quem per ora uulgi ad SEPULCRUM LUTATIAE GENTIS *PERTRACTUM* non prius uita priuauit quam oculos infelices erueret et singulas corporis partes confringeret.	apud Catuli sepulchrum oculis effosis, minibus cruribusque effractis servatum aliquamdiu, ut per singula membra moreretur	VIII milia dediticiorum in uilla publica trucidauit, tabulam proscriptionis posuit, urbem ac totam Italiam caedibus repleuit inter quas omnes Praenestinos inermes concidi iussit, Marium, senatorii ordinis uirum, cruribus bracchiisque fractis, auribus praesectis et oculis effossis necauit

[15] Florus is here (indirectly?) dependent on Sallust, *Historiae* 1.44: ut in M. Mario, cui fracta prius crura brachiaque et oculu effossi, scilicet ut per singulos artus expiraret.

Orosius implicitly acknowledges the use of at least two different sources, as he indicates that Marius' body was either dismembered or broken. Dismemberment is the version chosen by Augustine, on whose description of Marius' execution Orosius clearly depends. The Livian tradition, represented by the three other sources, only records breaking. Orosius thus was also aware of that version. Whilst there are some slight parallels with Florus and the *Periochae* (although nothing that necessitates direct use), Orosius must have used Valerius Maximus for the indication that Marius was brought to the grave of the Lutatii, a detail in which the latter differs from the rest of the Livian tradition. There is little amplification in this passage, unless one counts the inclusion of amputation as such, nor was it necessary to change the message of the exemplum: it was already the illustration of cruelty in the preceding tradition.

There are other passages where a use of Valerius Maximus is likely,[16] but rather than reviewing them all in detail, I wish to discuss one final example that illustrates the difficulties involved in source hunting in Orosius. The famous *devotio* of M. Curtius is, possibly, composed out of four sources.

Valerius Maximus, the *Periochae*, and Livy belong to the same tradition, the latter being the ultimate source of the other two. There is no direct proof that Orosius used Valerius in this case, but he shares more vocabulary with him than with any of the other two, even Livy himself. Some words Orosius only shares with Valerius and the *Periochae*, and not with Livy, suggesting that both Livy and the other two were used. The references to Vergil are not certain, but the discovery of the cave of Cacus and its dramatic account of the opening up of the earth would be a fitting passage to allude to in the context of the story of Curtius, as Cacus had supposedly lived on the site of Rome.[17] Indeed, the parallel with Vergil deepens the negative tone of Orosius' version. In the traditional account, Curtius' *devotio* has a positive result, restoring peace with the gods. In Livy's version, it guarantees the eternity of Rome, whereas for Valerius, Curtius symbolizes the unique Roman

[16] Orosius 1.20.3–4: Valerius Maximus 9.2.ext.9; Orosius 2.11.9: Valerius Maximus 3.2.ext.3; Orosius 2.17.15: Valerius Maximus 4.1.4; Orosius 3.2.8: Justin 6.8.2 and Valerius Maximus 3.2.ext.5; Orosius 3.9.2: Valerius Maximus 2.7.6 (note in particular the use of the verb *occurrere* and the use of *victoria/victor*, absent in Livy 8.12.1 and *Periochae* 8); Orosius 4.21.5: Valerius Maximus 2.4.2 (see also Augustine, *De civitate Dei* 1.33). See also the parallels noted in note 11 above.

[17] See Augustine, *De civitate Dei* 19.12 on the same story, with MacCormack 1998: 214–16.

Orosius 3.5	Valerius Maximus 5.6.2	*Periochae* 7	Livy 7.6.1–5	Vergil, *Aeneis* 8.238–50
Sequitur hanc	Cum autem in	Tunc omnia	Eodem anno, seu	inde
miseram luem	*media* parte fori	pretiosa	motu *terrae* seu qua	REPENTE/impulit;
miserioremque	*uasto* ac *repentino*	missa sunt in	ui alia, forum	impulsu quo
eius	*hiatu terra*	praealtam	*medium* ferme	maximus intonat
expiationem	subsideret	uoraginem	specu *uasto*	aether,/dissultant
proximo anno	responsumque	urbis	conlapsum in	ripae refluitque
satis triste	esset ea re illum	Romanae. In	immensam	exterritus amnis/at
prodigium.	tantum modo	eam Curtius	altitudinem dicitur;	specus et Caci
REPENTE	conpleri posse,	armatus	neque eam	detecta apparuit
siquidem	qua populus	sedens equo	*uoraginem* coniectu	ingens/regia, et
medio *urbis*	Romanus	praecipitauit	*terrae*, cum pro se	umbrosae penitus
terra dissiluit,	plurimum ualeret,		quisque gereret,	PATUERE
uastoque	Curtius et animi et		expleri potuisse,	cauernae,/non
praeruptu	generis nobilissimi		priusquam deum	secus ac si qua
hiantia subito	adulescens		monitu quaeri	penitus ui terra
INFERNA	interpretatus		coeptum quo	dehiscens/INFERNAS
PATUERUNT.	*urbem* nostram		plurimum populus	reseret sedes et
manebat diu ad	uirtute armisque		Romanus posset; id	regna
spectaculum	praecipue		enim illi loco	recludat/pallida,
terroremque	excellere,		dicandum uates	dis inuisa,
cunctorum	militaribus		canebant, si rem	superque immane
patenti	insignibus ornatus		publicam Romanam	barathrum/cernatur,
uoragine	*equum* conscendit		perpetuam esse	trepident immisso
inpudens	eumque		uellent. Tum M.	lumine
specus	uehementer		Curtium, iuuenem	Manes./ergo
nefariamque	admotis calcaribus		bello egregium,	insperata

uiui hominis sepulturam diis interpretibus expetebat. satisfecit inprobis FAUCIBUS praecipitio sui M. Curtius, uir ***eques armatus***, *iniecitque* crudeli terrae inopimam satietatem, cui parum esset, quod ex tanta pestilentia mortuos per sepulchra susciperet, nisi etiam uiuos scissa sorberet.	*praecipitem* in illud profundum egit, super quem uniuersi ciues honoris gratia certatim fruges *iniecerunt*, continuoque terra pristinum habitum recuperauit. magna postea decora in foro Romano fulserunt, nullum tamen hodieque pietate Curtii erga patriam clarius obuersatur exemplum. cui principatum gloriae obtinenti consimile factum subnectam.		castigasse ferunt dubitantes an ullum magis Romanum bonum quam arma uirtusque esset, et silentio facto templa deorum immortalium, quae foro imminent, Capitoliumque intuentem et manus nunc in caelum, nunc in **patentes** terrae **hiatus** ad deos manes porrigentem, se deuouisse; **equo** deinde quam poterat maxime exornato insidentem, **armatum** se in specum immisisse.	deprensum luce repente/inclusumque cauo saxo atque insueta rudentem/desuper Alcides telis premit, omniaque arma/aduocat et ramis uastisque molaribus instat, cf. 267 FAUCIBUS ignis

combination of virtue and martiality prowess. Such admiration for Curtius' act is obviously removed by Orosius, who sees the story as an illustration of the debasement of pagan religion, which asks for human sacrifices. Thus, in Orosius it is a story of unjust death, for a useless cause, an interpretation to which the allusion to Vergil adds hellish undertones.[18] The reference to the Cacus scene turns, in fact, the Livian welcoming earth into a monstrous one. On a maximalist interpretation, then, Orosius may have looked at all four possible sources in order to construct his own version.

From the preceding case studies, one can conclude that Orosius' use of Valerius is firmly established. The reliance on such a rhetorical tool-book fits well with the argument formulated earlier about Orosius' rhetorical background. If many of the sources he used were classics, such as Sallust, he also relied on works tailored for the school of rhetoric. The *Histories* of Florus and Justin are examples of this, but even very specific tools such as collections of exempla should be added to that list. The use of other types of tools is likely. The quotation from Ennius in 1.12.10 probably comes from a rhetorical handbook too: Ennius was hardly read in late Antiquity,[19] and the very same verse was quoted by the *Rhetorica ad Herrenium* (2.34). Orosius may even have found it in that particular work.[20] A comparison in book 6 between the civil wars that sprung up after Caesar's death and the dragon's teeth sown by Medea which generated soldiers, is obviously rhetorical in its inspiration: Medea was a traditional topic of declamations.[21]

Orosius' use of multiple sources has an important consequence for his relationship with the Livian tradition.[22] In 1882 the editor of the *Historiae*, Zangemeister, argued that Orosius had used a now lost epitome of Livy, produced in the early empire, an idea that has been accepted by subsequent editors.[23] Parallels with the different

[18] The expression *uastoque praeruptu hiantia subito* in Orosius also recalls Vergil's description of the underworld: *Aeneis* 6.237: vastoque immanis hiatu.

[19] Suerbaum 1997; Cameron 2011: 406–10.

[20] For parallels with the *Rhetorica ad Herrenium*, see pp. 32 and 118–32.

[21] Orosius 6.17.7; see Augustine, *Confessiones* 3.(6)11.

[22] On Livy in the fourth and fifth centuries, see Cameron 2011: 498–526, noting (513) his popularity among Christians.

[23] Zangemeister 1882: xxv. He is followed by Lippold 1976: i.xxxviii. Arnaud-Lindet 1990–1: i.xxv rejects the idea that Orosius used a pre-existing epitome of Livy, but supposes one was made by Orosius himself as a preliminary work. This is not very convincing.

representatives of the Livian tradition, such as the *Periochae* or Valerius Maximus, should then be understood as reflecting that epitome, rather than direct use of these sources. Such a view accords well with the classic one-source theory and Orosius' supposedly mechanical way of proceeding. Yet, as I have argued, Orosius combined several sources, selected elements from them, and amplified them. In fact, rather than copying a single source, he contaminates the different traditions deriving from Livy, drawing on Valerius Maximus, the *Periochae*, Florus, and Livy—sometimes all at the same time. This conclusion obviously does not disprove the existence of a Livian epitome, nor is it my intention to argue against it. Rather, it reinforces the conclusion that P. L. Schmidt drew several decades ago: as ancient historians engaged much more dynamically with their sources than often thought, it is impossible to reconstruct the epitome in any coherent fashion, if it ever existed.[24] Although scholars have continued to deduce specific features of the Livian epitome from later sources, including Orosius,[25] the preceding discussion strongly endorses Schmidt's position.

II. FROM CHRONICLE TO HISTORY

Towards the end of his history, Orosius was faced with a specific problem. Whereas for the earlier parts he could draw on a wide range of mainly historiographical sources, that source of information petered out when he started writing about his own times. If in earlier sections he could use a single source as the backbone for his narrative, that was now impossible. His main sources for the Roman Empire were Florus[26] and Eutropius, but the latter concluded his *breviarium* in 364. Many of the sources used by Orosius thereafter remain unclear: one suspects that rhetorical pieces formed the basis of some of the later elaborated sections, such as the sack of Rome in 410 (7.39), or the invasion of Radagaisus in 405/6 (7.34.4–7), for which an unknown source is combined with Augustine, *De civitate Dei* 5.23.[27] Other Christian authors are used too, such as Jerome's

24 Schmidt 1968 and 1989: 191. See also Beschorner 1999; Cameron 2011: 513–14.

25 Bessone 1982: 1262, 1984, and 2002–3; Bird 1995; Zecchini 2003: 321.

26 See Fear 2010a: 219 n. 65 and 222 n. 78.

27 Mörner 1844: 55 noticed the parallel, but scholars seem to have failed to pick it up since.

chronicle,[28] the Church history of Rufinus,[29] and Paulinus' *Life of Ambrose.*[30] A reference to anonymous 'historians' might indicate the use of a further unknown chronicle or history,[31] and on one occasion Orosius states to have used oral sources.[32] Some of his information may indeed have been based on reports and rumours that reached Africa, but most of it can still be plausibly traced to written sources.[33]

[28] See Orosius 7.33.1–4 and 7, which rely on Jerome, *Chronicon* a. 377.

[29] See, e.g. Orosius 7.33.13–5, which combines Jerome, *Chronicon* a. 378 and Rufinus, *Historia ecclesiastica* 11.13.

[30] Paulinus, *Vita Ambrosii* 51: Mascezeli etiam *desperanti* de salute sua vel exercitus quem ductubat contra Gildonem, baculum tenens *manu in visu noctis adparuit,* atque cum provolveretur ad pedes sancti viri Mascezel, *percutiens* in *terram* senex *baculo* quo regebatur *tertio*—hac enim illi specie adparuerat -, *ait*: *'hic, hic, hic'*, *signans locum*; deditque *intellectum* viro, quem visitatione dignum fuerat arbitratus, ut agnosceret se in ipso loco in qui sanctum domini viderat *sacerdotem*, *die tertia victoriam* adepturum; atque ita securus bellum inchoavit et consummavit.

Orosius 7.36.5–8: igitur Mascezel, iam inde a Theodosio sciens, quantum in rebus *desperatissimis* oratio hominis per fidem Christi a clementia Dei impetraret, Caprariam insulam adiit, unde secum sanctos seruos Dei aliquot permotos precibus suis sumpsit: (. . .) ubi cum parua manu, hoc est cum quinque milibus (ut aiunt) militum, contra septuaginta milia hostium castra metatus, cum interiecta mora excedere loco oppositasque praeiacentis uallis angustias transgredi uellet, *incurrente nocte beatum Ambrosium episcopum Mediolani paulo ante defunctum per somnium sibi uidere uisus est* significantem *manu* et *inpacto* ad *humum ter baculo dicentem*: *hic, hic, hic.* quod ille prudenti coniectura *intellexit* merito adnuntiantis fidem *uictoriae*, uerbo *locum*, numero *diem significare.* substitit ac *tertio* demum *die* post noctem orationibus hymnisque peruigilem ab ipsis caelestium sacramentorum mysteriis in hostem circumfusum processit.

Orosius' dependence on Paulinus is obvious from the vocabulary; the fact that he shortens the latter's version makes it unlikely that Paulinus derives from Orosius. Orosius has streamlined the apparition in a slightly shorter but surely more elegant Latin: he has removed some of Paulinus' cumbersome subclauses and details, and has constructed an elegant parallelism *verbo/numero*. At the same time, he decreases the importance of the apparition of Ambrose. Orosius clearly knew more about Mascezel than Paulinus, and has him imitate Theodosius' prayers to the Egyptian monk John. In Orosius, the apparition of Ambrose is just part of a larger story, whereas in Paulinus it is a proof of Ambrose's powers beyond the grave. In line with Orosius' general argument, his Mascezel is much more confident than Paulinus'. The latter wishes to enhance the importance of Ambrose's intervention by having him save a desperate Mascezel. In Orosius, Mascezel is on the contrary already strengthened by the support of the monks of Capraria.

Orosius' use of Paulinus provides additional support for an early date of the *Life of Ambrose*, around 412–13: the other proposed date, 422, would be after the publication of Orosius' history and is therefore excluded: Duval 1964: 178–9; Lamirande 1981 and 1983: 21–4 for 413, followed by McLynn 1994: 370 n. 40.

[31] Orosius 7.38.1.

[32] Orosius 7.43.4.

[33] Van Nuffelen 2004a: 262–3 argues that fifth-century church historians also relied more on written sources than is usually accepted.

The absence of a single narrative source has important implications for Orosius' way of proceeding. Rather than combining different sources and adapting their perspective, he now had to expand often dire notices from chronicles into a narrative. As we shall see in chapter 6, the last pages of the *Historiae* are highly rhetorical and panegyrical. Whilst this is to be explained by the fact that they represent the climax of the history, it was also due to the necessity of amplifying brief snippets of information into a fully developed view of the period.

In this section I wish to show how Orosius went about doing so by focusing on two sources which have not yet received the attention they deserve. First, the *Epitome de Caesaribus*, dated between 395 and 408.[34] It is part of a group of works on Roman history wrongly ascribed to Aurelius Victor and covers imperial history up to Theodosius I. The latest editor of the *epitome* noted that Orosius knew this work, but only spotted some minor contacts.[35] In fact, Orosius heavily relied on the work, as the list below shows, in particular for the reigns of Gratian and Theodosius. It is likely that Orosius also knew the *Liber de viris illustribus*,[36] suggesting that he may have known the Pseudo-Aurelian corpus as a whole.

These parallels leave little doubt about Orosius' dependency on the *Epitome*. Especially 7.33.8 is amplified: out of a brief notice about Gratian's victory over the Alamanni, a grand demonstration of the need to confide in Christ's power is constructed. The other passages are less elaborated and could even be termed faithful reworkings, except for the fact that Orosius has a rather positive view of the usurper Maximus (7.34.9)—which could be explained by the latter's orthodoxy or by the use of another, unknown source. The use of the *Epitome* is uncertain for the battle of Adrianopolis. Orosius' primary source is Jerome, but Orosius also seems to have used the *Epitome* (suggested by the addition of *cum Gothis*). The picture is complicated by the fact that Jerome and Pseudo-Aurelius Victor obviously share much vocabulary, possibly because of a shared dependence on the so-called *Kaisergeschichte*. It is indeed impossible to discuss the *Epitome* without raising the spectre of the *Enmannsche Kaisergeschichte* (EKG), a hypothetical breviarium that underpins the Latin historical

[34] Festy 1999: liii.
[35] Festy 1999: lxi. Schlumberger 1974 does not spot any contacts.
[36] Lippold 1976: i.395; Fugmann 1990–2003: 317–21.

Orosius	*Epitome de Caesaribus*	
7.33.8: Gratianus interea imperator admodum iuuenis cum inaestimabilem multitudinem hostium Romanis infusam finibus cerneret, fretus Christi potentia, longe inpari militum numero sese in hostem dedit et continuo *apud Argentariam, oppidum Galliarum*, formidulosissimum *bellum* incredibili felicitate confecit. nam plus quam *triginta milia Alamannorum* minimo Romanorum detrimento in eo proelio interfecta narrantur	47.2: Hic apud *Argentariam oppidam Galliae triginta Alamannorum milia* in *bello* exstinxit	
7.33.13–15: Itaque quinto decimo imperii sui anno ***lacrimabile*** illud ***bellum*** **in Thracia** *cum Gothis* iam tunc exercitatione uirium rerumque abundantia instructissimis gessit. (. . .) **ipse imperator** cum ***sagitta saucius*** uersusque in **fugam** aegre in cuiusdam **uillulae** ***casam deportatus*** lateret, ab ***insequentibus hostibus*** deprehensus, subiecto *igne* consumptus est et, quo magis testimonium punitionis	46.2: Hic Valens *cum Gothis lacrimabili bello* commisso *sagittis saucius* in *casa deportatur* vilissima; ubi *supervenientibus Gothis ignique* supposito incendio concrematus est.	Jerome, *Chronicle* a. 378: **Lacrimabile bellum in Thracia.** In quo deserente equitum praesidio Romanae legiones a Gothis cinctae usque ad internecionem caesae sunt. **Ipse imperator** Valens, cum **sagitta saucius fugeret** et ob dolorem nimium saepe eque laberetur, **ad cuiusdam villulae casam deportatus** est. Quo

eius et diuinae indignationis terribili posteris esset exemplo, etiam communi **caruit sepultura**		**persquentibus barbaris** et incense domo **sepultura** quoque **caruit**.
7.34.1–2: Anno ab urbe condita MCXXXII Gratianus quadragesimus ab Augusto post mortem Valentis sex annis imperium tenuit, quamuis iamdudum antea cum *patruo* Valente et cum Valentiniano *fratre* regnaret. qui cum adflictum ac paene conlapsum reipublicae statum uideret, eadem prouisione, qua quondam legerat Nerua Hispanum uirum *Traianum*, per quem respublica reparata est, legit et ipse Theodosium aeque *Hispanum* uirum et restituendae reipublicae necessitate *apud Sirmium purpura induit* orientisque et Thraciae simul praefecit imperio. See also 7.34.3: *propagator* ecclesiae	48.1: Theodosius, genitus patre Honorio, matre Thermantia, genere *Hispanus*, originem a *Traiano* principe trahens, a Gratiano Augusto *apud Sirmium imperator effectus* regnavit annos decem et septem. The comparison with Trajan is made more explicit in 48.8. See also 48.5: *propagator* rei publicae; 47.1: Gratianus, genitus Sirmii, imperavit cum patre Valentiniano annos octo, dies octoginta quinque; cum *patruo et fratre* tres; cum eodem fratre ac Theodosio quattuor, et his omnibus accedente Arcadio menses sex.	
7.34.9: Maximus, uir quidem strenuus et probus atque Augusto dignus nisi contra sacramenti fidem per	47.7: Hoc tempore cum Maximus apud *Britanniam tyrannidem* arripuisset et *in Galliam transmisisset*, ab	

Continued

Continued

Orosius	*Epitome de Caesaribus*
tyrannidem emersisset, in *Britannia* inuitus propemodum ab exercitu imperator creatus *in Galliam transiit*	infensis Gratiano legionibus exceptus Gratianum fugavit nec mora exstinxit
7.35.10: Igitur Valentinianus iunior regno restitutus *extincto* Maximo *eiusque filio Victore, quem imperatorem Gallis Maximus* reliquerat, ipse in Galliam transiit: ubi cum tranquilla republica in pace ageret, apud Viennam dolo Arbogastis comitis sui, ut ferunt, strangulatus atque, ut uoluntariam sibi consciuisse mortem putaretur, laqueo suspensus est	48.7: *Maximum* autem tyrannum, qui Gratianum interfecerat et *sibi Gallias vindicabat*, apud Aquileiam *exstinxit Victoremque eius filium*, intra infantiae annos a Maximo patre Augustum factum, necavit[37]

[37] The *Consularia Constantinpolitana* a. 388, 392 are also used here: a. 388: sed et *filius eius Victor occiditur* post paucos dies in *Gallis* a com. Theudosii Aug.; a. 392: *Valentinianus iunior apud Viennam* est interfectus et levavit se Eugenius Tyrannum.

tradition of the fourth century.[38] It is usually supposed to have covered the history until 337, but later dates have been advocated, in particular 357 and, most recently, 378.[39] It is this later date that might suggest a dependency of Orosius on the EKG.[40] Indeed, Orosius' description of the battle of Adrianopolis seems to be dependent on both the *epitome* and the chronicle of Jerome, two works that presumably used the EKG. Nevertheless, Orosius certainly used both works elsewhere, and it is hence much more likely that he combined them independently for his version of the battle of Adrianopolis, rather than having recourse to the EKG.

It has been argued that the *Epitome de Caesaribus* was a pagan *Tendenzschrift* aimed at the uncultivated.[41] Orosius' dependency on it rather supports the idea of P.L. Schmidt that the work was written for an audience of rhetors, independently of specific aims of religious propaganda.[42] Indeed, this would fit well with the context that the previous chapters have sketched for the *Historiae*: a work profoundly influenced by the culture of rhetoric of his age.

A second brief historiographical work that helped Orosius to fill in the canvas for the last decades of the *Historiae* are the *Consularia Constantinopolitana*. Following Burgess' reconstruction of the genesis of the text, Orosius probably used a version composed in 405 and destined for Africa.[43] The main, but not only, use of it by Orosius is 7.34.[44]

Building on the brief notices from the *consularia*, Orosius succeeds in creating a brilliant narrative of triumph for Theodosius I. He starts out by amplifying the victories over the barbarians, in particular the Goths, by comparing Theodosius positively to Alexander the Great, who had avoided battling with the Scythians, the supposed forebears

[38] Enmann 1884 and most recently Burgess 1993b and 1995, and Bleckmann 1997, all with further references.

[39] Burgess 2005.

[40] Sehlmeyer 2009: 203.

[41] Festy 1999: liii.

[42] Schmidt 1988.

[43] Lippold 1952: 74 and 1976: ii.511; Burgess 1993a: 197–8, 203–4.

[44] See also Orosius 7.35.10: Igitur *Valentinianus iunior* regno restitutus *extincto* Maximo eiusque *filio Victore*, quem imperatorem *Gallis* Maximus reliquerat, ipse in Galliam transiit: ubi cum tranquilla republica in pace ageret, *apud Viennam* dolo Arbogastis comitis sui, ut ferunt, strangulatus atque, ut uoluntariam sibi consciuisse mortem putaretur, laqueo suspensus est; Orosius 7.35.23: *Theodosius* autem conposita tranquillataque republica *apud Mediolanium* constitutus *diem obit; Consularia Constantinopolitana* a. 395: *recessit apud Mediolanum* Theudosius Aug.

Orosius 7.34.5–10	*Consularia Constantinopolitana*
itaque Theodosius adflictam rempublicam ira Dei reparandam credidit misericordia Dei; omnem fiduciam sui ad opem Christi conferens maximas illas *Scythicas* gentes formidatasque cunctis maioribus, Alexandro quoque illi Magno, sicut Pompeius Corneliusque testati sunt, euitatas, nunc autem extincto Romano exercitu Romanis equis armisque instructissimas, hoc est *Alanos Hunos et Gothos*, incunctanter adgressus magnis *multisque proeliis uicit.*	a. 379: Ipso anno *multa bella* Romani cum *Gothis* commiserunt. Deinde *victoriae* nuntiatae sunt adversus *Gothos, Alanos, atque Hunos* die XV k. Dec.
urbem *Constantinopolim* uictor *intrauit* et ne paruam ipsam Romani exercitus manum adsidue bellando detereret, foedus cum Athanarico *Gothorum rege* percussit. *Athanaricus* autem continuo ut *Constantinopolim* uenit, *diem obiit. uniuersae Gothorum gentes* rege defuncto aspicientes uirtutem benignitatemque Theodosii Romano sese *imperio dediderunt.*[45] in isdem etiam diebus *Persae*, qui Iuliano interfecto aliisque imperatoribus saepe uictis, nunc etiam Valente in fugam acto recentissimae uictoriae satietatem cruda insultatione ructabant, ultro *Constantinopolim* ad Theodosium misere *legatos* pacemque supplices poposcerunt; ictumque tunc foedus est, quo uniuersus oriens usque ad nunc tranquillissime fruitur.	a. 380: . . . et ipso anno *ingressus* est Theodosius Aug. *Costantinopolim* die XVIII kl. Dec. a. 381: ingressus est *Aithanaricus rex Gothorum Constantinopolim* die II id. Ian. Eodem mense *diem functus* idem Aithanaricus VIII kl. Feb. a. 382: ipso anno *universa gens Gothorum* cum rege suo in *Romaniam* se *tradiderunt* die V non. Oct. a. 384: introierunt *Constantinopolim legati Persarum*
interea cum Theodosius in oriente subactis barbarorum gentibus Thracias tandem ab hoste liberas reddidisset et *Arcadium* filium suum *consortem fecisset imperii*,[46] Maximus, uir quidem strenuus et probus atque Augusto dignus nisi contra sacramenti fidem per tyrannidem emersisset, in Britannia inuitus propemodum ab exercitu imperator creatus in Galliam transiit: ubi Gratianum Augustum subita incursione perterritum atque in Italiam transire meditantem dolis circumuentum interfecit fratremque eius Valentinianum Augustum Italia expulit. Valentinianus in orientem refugiens a Theodosio paterna pietate susceptus, mox etiam imperio restitutus est.	a. 383: *levatus* est *Arcadius* Aug. Constantinopolim in miliario VII in tribunali a Theodosio Aug. Patre suo die XVII kl. Feb.[47]

[45] Orosius' account of the submission of Athanaric has been judged 'confused' by scholars who wish to determine the exact nature of the *foedus* with the Romans (Wirth 1997: 52 n. 172). In fact, Orosius' testimony is worthless as a legal source because he rhetorically elaborates what is said or implied in the *Consularia*. Moreover, he attributes the submission to the empire to Athanaric, who, according to the *Consularia*, had died the year before.

[46] The end of fifth-century chronicler Hydatius has for a. 383: Theodosius filium suum Augustum appellans regni facit sibi esse consortem. Unless one wishes to suppose that Orosius used the source of Hydatius, it is likely that the latter used the former as a source.

[47] From here onwards, the *Epitome de Caesaribus* is used, see above.

of the Goths. To prove this, Orosius refers to Pompeius Trogus (via Justin) and Tacitus.[48] Similarly, the negotiations with the Persians are contrasted with Julian's defeat at their hands and with Valens' troubles—the latter assertion being rather misleading, because the truce of 371, which resulted from Roman successes, is omitted. But the chance to contrast Theodosius with a pagan and a heretic could not be missed in the crucial final pages of the *Historiae*. For that same reason, the negotiations with the Persians as mentioned in the *Consularia* are assimilated to those taking place with the Goths: whilst the Goths surrender to the Romans, the Persians conclude a universal peace. The success of Theodosius is thus complete. Taking into account the panegyrical contractions and amplifications, the basic information given by Orosius is not very far removed from what he found in the *Consularia*. Yet it needs no further elaboration that he offers an interpretation of the entries of the chronicle, and one that aims at demonstrating the unique successes achieved by the emperor.

If the ideological and panegyrical use of amplification is thus well illustrated by this passage, it also informs us of its stylistic side. Amplification implies a raising of the style: Orosius uses the more classicizing 'Scythians' (7.35.5) to designate the Goths, although he uses 'Goths' as well. His desire to compare Theodosius' victory over the Goths to Alexander's fear of the Scythians obviously plays a role, but stylistic considerations were of importance too. Indeed, Orosius shows elsewhere that he is aware of the low Latin used by the *Consularia*. In 7.43.5, he notes that the term *Romania*, to indicate Roman territory, is 'vulgar'.[49] Precisely that term was used by the *Consularia* a. 382 (and later in a. 386), but replaced with *imperium* by Orosius.

III. BEYOND THE SCHOOL AUTHOR

The preceding series of brief investigations into Orosius' sources has provided additional evidence for Orosius' use of works that were

[48] Cf. Justin 12.2.16–17. On Alexander and the Scythians, see Orosius 1.16.2.

[49] Orosius 7.43.5: *ut vulgariter loquar, Gothia quod Romania fuisset*. This is clearly a linguistic comment and not an ideological one as Marchetta 1987: 53 thinks. The traditional opinion, that *ut vulgariter loquar* refers to *Romania* rather than *Gothia*, is hence likely: against Corsini 1968: 187; Martínez Cavero 2002: 261.

either manufactured for the rhetorical schools or intensively consulted there: this is evident for Valerius Maximus, and the preceding chapter has suggested that late antique *breviaria* also served to inform and support aspiring and practicing orators. Such a *Sitz im Leben* would indeed help to explain why Orosius shares some of these sources with, for example, the fifth-century Church historian Socrates, who, writing in Constantinople, also used Eutropius and the *Consularia constantinopolitana*,[50] and why the *Epitome de Caesaribus*, suggested to have been produced in Constantinople,[51] ended up fairly soon after its publication (after 395) in Hippo to be consulted by Orosius. The rhetorical culture seems to have guaranteed the rapid and wide circulation of practical and useful works.

The culture of rhetoric not only determines Orosius' access to his sources, but also his use of them. I have provided additional arguments against the old but still current theory that Orosius normally used a single source. That theory has led to a complicated search for intermediary sources when Orosius' practice did not comply with that theory. Such an approach has been taken to extremes in Lippold's 1976 commentary.[52] But it is easy to show that the hypothesis of an intermediary source is often superfluous. Besides the detailed discussions above, one final example can suffice. A. Lippold argued for the use of an unknown source for 7.24.4, since contrary to the known sources Jerome (*Chronicon* a. 285) and Eutropius (9.18), Orosius seems to know that Numerian was killed when he returned from Persia. Yet, just a few lines further, Eutropius 9.19.2 clearly refers to that emperor being killed whilst on his way back.[53] Orosius' more dynamic attitude also cautions against attempts to reconstruct lost sources out of the *Historiae*. In particular his habit of contaminating different strands of the Livian tradition makes it impossible to reconstruct the hypothetical Livian epitome on the basis of the *Historiae*. Rather, Orosius' now well-established habit of combining and amplifying multiple sources strongly argues against the idea that he actually used that work.

[50] Van Nuffelen 2004a: App. IV.

[51] Cameron 2011: 670.

[52] At one point he suggests an intermediate source combining Tacitus, Suetonius, Josephus, Jerome, and Eutropius: Lippold 1976: ii.481. Orosius most likely used all of these directly. See Kelly 2008: 273 for similar 'paroxysms of guesswork' relating to Ammianus.

[53] Lippold 1976: ii.494. The error goes back to Zangemeister 1882: 487.

Amplification is the other key characteristic of Orosius' use of his sources. Although he repeatedly merely copies his sources, he regularly intervenes in them to shape the narrative according to his wishes. As we have seen, this implies interventions regarding style and content. Harsh criticism has been directed to Orosius for not always faithfully copying his sources: 'falsification' and lack of objectivity are regular charges.[54] Such judgments correctly underscore that in some instances Orosius desires to transmit a certain message different from that of his source, but they presuppose that a good historian faithfully copies his sources. Few historians of Antiquity actually felt bound by their sources and considerable freedom was exercised to create the correct narrative with the right message.[55] Rhetorical elaboration is, in fact, part of the process of turning a series of sources into a coherent story and not necessarily an attempt to 'falsify' history. As must be clear by now, I do not wish to deny Orosius' ideological intentions, but before we judge them incompatible with the writing of history, we must understand Orosius in the context of ancient historiography.

To conclude this chapter, I wish to emphasize that, if the culture of rhetoric provides the context for the *Historiae*, they cannot be reduced to it. The preceding pages may have generated the impression that Orosius may have dealt independently with the texts he had read, but that the selection of what he read was made for him, in the school of rhetoric. To a certain extent that is true: in every culture there is a shared basis of knowledge, which is mediated through education. The reading list of Orosius, albeit more limited, is not fundamentally different from that of Ammianus.[56] Just as Ammianus drew on many contemporary sources to write his history, Orosius did not restrict his reading to the classics of the school. As was argued by G. Hingst, it is likely that he had actually read Claudian and Symmachus,[57] and we have suggested above that contemporary panegyrics provided some of the information for the last chapters. Obviously, Orosius also, and strongly, depended on Christian texts, of which Augustine's *City of God* is the most obvious example: much of the

[54] Corbellini 1984; Pardini 1988; Bessone 2000; Escribaño Paño 2007.

[55] To cite but two examples: Tacitus with Griffin 1982, Eck 2000, Polleichtner 2003, Riess 2003, and Talbert 1999; Ammianus with Rosen 1970 and 1982, Barnes 1998, and Kelly 2008.

[56] Cf. Sabbah 1978 and Kelly 2008.

[57] See note 11, p. 95.

panegyric of book 7 is, in fact, inspired by book 5 of Augustine's monument of learned apologetic. Augustine probably was an important mediator for Orosius. It can, for example, hardly be accidental that he also used Paulinus' *Life of Ambrose* in *Civitas Dei* 5.26:[58] Orosius may well have acquired access to the text via Augustine's library. Jerome and Rufinus were probably consulted there too. Such wider reading, however acquired, suggests that, if the *Historiae* are the outcome of the rhetorical culture of the fourth and fifth centuries, they remain an autonomous and original product, which should be approached with an eye for the creative skill of its author.

[58] Duval 1964: 165–6.

5

A Sense of the Past: The Truth of Rhetoric

The preceding pages have analysed the building blocks out of which Orosius constructed his *Historiae*: Vergilian allusions, the inversion of traditional exempla, and the contamination and amplification of his sources all lend depth to a narrative that may seem simple at first sight. The study of these literary tools has not only added to our insight into Orosius' working methods, but has also helped us to better understand his message. Writing from within a rich and esteemed rhetorical culture, he argues that his pagan opponents are blind-eyed: the glorious view of the past, mediated through education, renders it virtually impossible for them to apprehend both past and present as they really are. We have identified already one way in which Orosius sought to pierce the defence-wall thrown up by rhetorical education, namely his suggestion that he is the only true historian who presents the facts as they are.

This chapter explores another key technique: in order to make his audience see the suffering the supposedly glorious past was made up of, Orosius had to make them feel it.[1] As we have seen when discussing exempla in the *Historiae*, Orosius criticizes the habits and views created by education, but he does not reject the use of rhetoric. It should thus not cause surprise that he turns to a highly rhetorical mode of writing in order to show the reality of the past and challenge the rhetorical mindset of his opponents: his history is rich in appeals to emotions,[2] and to arouse these, Orosius uses *enargeia*, *oratio*

[1] Augustine may have been a source of inspiration for Orosius: he repeatedly resorts to *pathos* in the first five books of the *City of God*, which discuss the Roman past (Tornau 2006: 229).

[2] See the brief remarks by Svennung 1922: 174; Bartalucci 1976: 251. For *enargeia* in Orosius, see Mueller 2005.

gravis, and *pathos*. After an introduction to the rhetoric of pathos in Quintilian and the *Rhetorica ad Herrenium*, two possible sources of Orosius' rhetorical training, an analysis of book 5 shows how the *Historiae* are built on a staccato of emotions: several paragraphs of rather factual description are followed by highly rhetorical and emotional sections that draw on all the resources recommended by rhetorical handbooks. Although for us rhetoric and historical truth may seem opposites, Orosius does not conceptualize his rhetoric as an abandonment of the writing of history: again in line with the advice of Quintilian, pathetic descriptions are proposed as producing the most truthful version of the facts, one that makes the reader truly feel the horror of the events. The third section shows that Orosius is conscious of the fact that full verisimilitude is impossible: he cannot narrate all events of the past as they truly happened. He thus presents the *Historiae* as a synecdoche of the past: certain sections are fully elaborated, whereas in others the reader is invited to imagine what the events could have been like. The final section draws out some of the consequences of this argument for ancient historiography in general. It argues that Orosius' rhetorical historiography is not a new or alien element in ancient historiography: rather, his apparent idiosyncrasies can be more fruitfully understood as general tendencies intensified by his polemical intentions. In fact, Orosius' development of Quintilian's suggestion that rhetoric helps the reader to see the painful truths of the past can be understood as one of the ways in which the relationship between historiography and rhetoric and between truth and language was conceptualized in Antiquity.

I. SEEING AND FEELING: A RHETORIC OF PATHOS

'The life and soul of oratory, we may say, is in the emotions.'[3] The arousal of emotions in the audience and the judge was, for Quintilian, the hallmark of the real orator. It is worth perusing his reflection on *pathos*, as the trajectory it traces from the aim of convincing through the arousal of emotions to the use of vividness and a grand style is

[3] Quintilian 6.2.7: adeo velut spiritus operis huius atque animus est in adfectibus. Tr. D. Russell (LCL). The emphasis on emotions goes back at least to Aristotle (*Rhetorica* 2.1–11).

precisely what, as we shall see, undergirds Orosius' rhetoric in the *Historiae*. Quintilian distinguishes between *ethos*, more moderate and dignified emotions, and *pathos*, concerned with violent sentiments: anger, hatred, fear, envy, and pity (6.2.20: iram odium metum invidiam miserationem). The former is more associated with comedy, the latter with tragedy.[4] One way of arousing these is through comparison and amplification. Events that might seem tolerable have to be shown to be grievous through the use of *deinosis*: 'language that adds force to facts which are disgraceful, cruel, or odious.'[5] The heart of the matter, however, is that the orator needs to be moved himself: verisimilitude is only achieved when the orator becomes true to the 'emotions of those who really suffer'.[6] The orator thus has to conjure up in the minds of his audience the truthful image of what has happened. 'The result will be *enargeia*, what Cicero calls *inlustratio* and *evidentia*, a quality which makes us seem not so much to be talking about something as exhibiting it.'[7] This is, Quintilian confides to the reader, the secret of his own success: being moved, to the point of being overtaken by tears, pallor, and 'a grief which is very like the real thing'.[8] For Quintilian, emotions lie at the heart of oratory and link together several key stylistic choices such as *deinosis*, amplification, and verisimilitude. Most prominently, however, emotions are said to be aroused by *enargeia*: it is not only the strongest mean, but it also ties together the orator and the audience. True vividness can only be sustained if the author gets involved himself.[9] Implicitly in this passage, and explicitly elsewhere, the arousal of emotions is also linked to the use of the high style (*oratio gravis*).[10] The most dramatic occasions demanded the highest emotions. The sack of a city and (civil) warfare were among the gravest events Roman orators could imagine, and, as a consequence, figure prominently among the

[4] Quintilian 6.2.20. See also Aristotle, *Rhetorica* 3.19; Ps.-Longinus, *Peri hypsous* 9.15; Cicero, *Ad familiares* 5.12.5.

[5] Quintilian 6.2.24: haec est illa quae dinosis vocatur, rebus indignis asperis invidiosis addens vim oratio.

[6] Quintilian 6.2.27: Quare, in iis quae esse veri similia volemus, simus ipsi similes eorum qui vere patiuntur adfectibus. On this aspect, see Schrijvers 1982.

[7] Quintilian 6.2.32: insequetur ἐναργεῖα, quae a Cicerone inlustratio et evidentia nominatur, quae tam non dicere videtur quam ostendere.

[8] Quintilian 6.2.36: *et veri similis dolor.*

[9] Cf. Cicero, *De oratore* 2.188, 2.194.

[10] Quintilian 6.2.19, 12.10.59, 60–2. For the link between *pathos* and *enargeia*, see Plutarch, *De gloria Atheniensium* 3.347A.

illustrations in rhetorical handbooks. Quintilian refers to a sack as an example in a discussion of *enargeia* (vividness), whereas the *Rhetorica ad Herrenium* illustrates *oratio gravis* (grand style) with a speech denouncing a traitor in times of war and *oratio mediocris* (middle style) with a war waged by allies on Rome.[11]

Even a superficial perusal of Orosius already indicates his closeness to Quintilian's discussion. As argued in chapter 2, the sack of Rome is a prominent theme in the *Historiae*; that warfare is ubiquitous is stating the obvious. Of Quintilian's list of things that are grave in themselves and thus arouse emotions anyway, namely parricide, murder, and poisoning (6.2.22, *parricidia, caedes, veneficium*), Orosius' interest in the second needs no illustration,[12] whereas parricide, branded as the Roman disease since Romulus murdered Remus, is a recurring theme in the *Historiae.*[13] Poisoning is repeatedly highlighted as well.[14] Just as Quintilian asserts that oratory can add force to the facts by highlighting their cruel nature (6.2.24, addens vim), Orosius emphasizes, significantly, that he wishes to show the 'force of the facts' (3.pr.3, vim rerum). Of the range of emotions that Quintilian ranks under *pathos* (anger, hatred, fear, envy, and pity),[15] Orosius strongly banks on pity and fear, making the reader feel pain, shudder, and weep at the horror of the past.[16] *Deinosis* is ubiquitous. As we have noticed in the first chapter, already in his preface Orosius involved himself in his narrative, expressing his own doubts and feelings about the troubles of his own age.[17]

The match between the rhetoric of the *Historiae* and Quintilian's advice remains as yet superficial, but is a first stepping-stone in the

[11] Quintilian 8.3.67–9; *Rhetorica ad Herrenium* 4.11–3, 4.51 (a sack). These were popular topics for rhetorical display: see, e.g. Cicero, *In Catilinam* 4.11; Augustine, *De civitate Dei* 3.7–8, 3.20, and also in historiography: Polybius 2.56.7–12; Sallust, *De coniuratione Catilinae* 3; Diodorus Siculus 17.13, 17.35, 17.70, 19.6–8, 20.71.

[12] See the index of Zangemeister 1882: 783.

[13] Orosius 1.11, 3.9, 3.12.19, 4.13.17, 5.10.7, 5.16.23, 5.19.13, 6.5.3, 6.21.17, 7.7.9. Orosius may also have been inspired by the equally pathetic account of Augustine in *De civitate Dei* and its emphasis on parricide (2.14, 3.6, 3.12, 3.14, 15.5).

[14] Orosius 6.5.5, 7.5.10, 7.6.18.

[15] Cf. Cicero, *De oratore* 2.189: ut doleat, ut oderit, ut invideat, ut pertimescat aliquid, ut ad fletum misericordiamque deducatur.

[16] An indication of this is the following list of occurrences of a selection of emotional terms and their cognates, based on Brepols' *Library of Latin Texts*: *miseria* (147), *crudelitas* (83), *sanguis* (55), *atrocitas* (30), *metus* (28), *dolor* (25), *horror* (15), *terror* (15), *tristis* (13), *lacrimae* (12), *furor* (7), *luctus* (4), *pavor* (3), *fremens* (3).

[17] See also Orosius 3.20.

argument of this chapter, namely that the desire to arouse *pathos* in his audience is what drives the rhetoric of the *Historiae*. This is not an accidental choice on Orosius' part, for three reasons. First, *pathos* targets the hearts of the audience. As the preface of book 3 shows, Orosius wished to show to his obtuse contemporaries the reality of the past and all its suffering, something the rhetorically overdetermined culture of his age prevented them from doing. The definition of the past as a series of *miseriae* obviously betrays an apologetic intention, but it is also, fundamentally, a challenge to a tradition of looking at the past in terms of glory and success, and one that closely ties in with rhetorical prescriptions. Indeed, the *Rhetorica ad Herrenium* advises, as one way of inciting pity, the use of a comparison between the good old days and present misery.[18] This is possibly the most ubiquitous tool in the *Historiae*, yet in a reverse direction: the past was miserable and the present is much better. The choice for *pathos* is thus the cure for the disease we diagnosed in chapter 3. Second, as we have also seen in that chapter, Orosius wishes to cure his audience with the truth. In Quintilian's discussion *pathos* and the related style of *enargeia* aim at verisimilitude. This allows Orosius to present his *Historiae* as more truthful than those of his pagan predecessors. Third, Orosius is likely to have been directly inspired by rhetorical handbooks. The next section argues that the rhetoric of the *Historiae* adheres closely to the rules set out in Quintilian and the *Rhetorica ad Herrenium*. This may not be just because these two rhetorical handbooks are the most explicit expositions in extant Latin rhetorical writing. Quintilian and the *Rhetorica* also share the fact that the first signs of their reception and use in rhetorical schools are dated to the fourth and early fifth centuries.[19] Orosius may therefore have known them or works based on their teachings. Indeed, at times one gets the impression that he is writing by the book. I do not wish to argue for a direct use of either handbook, which would be very hard to prove, but at least an indirect awareness of the rules set out there is highly plausible.

[18] *Rhetorica ad Herrenium* 2.50. The exemplum is for this author a form of *enargeia* (4.62).

[19] Quintilian: Jerome, *Epistula* 107; Julius Victor, *Ars rhetorica* 371–448. *Rhetorica ad Herrenium*: Jerome, *Apologia adversus libros Rufini* PL 23.409, *Commentarii in Abdiam* PL 25.1098; Rufinus, *Versus* 577, 584.

Before we take a closer look at Orosius, we must first get a better insight into the techniques he uses to excite the passions of his audience. As Quintilian's discussion indicates, *pathos* is closely related to *oratio gravis* and *enargeia*. Although the didactic spirit of rhetorical handbooks aims at neatly categorizing and distinguishing these stylistic tools, it is maybe best to consider them as overlapping and interrelated rhetorical concepts, which in turn conjure up other figures. The *Rhetorica ad Herrenium* notes, for example, that the figure of description (*demonstratio*) is well suited for amplification and *pathos*. *Demonstratio* is, obviously, what other theorists called *enargeia*: it 'is expressing a fact with words in such a way that the action seems to happen and the fact to be before one's eyes'.[20] The example given by the author is the murder of Tiberius Gracchus—narrated by Orosius as well.[21] Nevertheless, it may be useful to take a brief look at how *enargeia* and *oratio gravis* were conceptualized, and which figures of style were linked to it, so as to set the scene for the closer analysis of book 5 of the *Historiae*.

Enargeia aims at representing events in such a way that the listener feels he is present himself and is therefore emotionally touched by the events.[22] For its most explicit theorist, Quintilian, *enargeia* is an enhancement of an essential feature of narrative, perspicuity (*perspicuitas*): 'instead of being merely transparent [as the latter], [the former] somehow shows itself off.'[23] Indeed, 'it is a great virtue to express our subject clearly and in such a way that it seems to be actually seen.'[24] In his usual systematic frame of mind, Quintilian subdivides *enargeia* into three categories, one that paints the whole scene, one that focuses on all the different details that make up the

[20] *Rhetorica ad Herrenium* 4.68: demonstratio est cum ita verbis res exprimitur ut geri negotium et res ante oculos esse videatur. It is close to, but more dramatic than, *descriptio*, also suitable for arousing pity (4.51).

[21] Orosius 5.9.1–3.

[22] Quintilian 6.2.32: adfectus non aliter quam si rebus ipsis intersimus sequentur. *Enargeia* was also known as *repaesentatio, sub oculos subiectio, evidentia, hypotyposis* (Quintilian 8.3.61, 9.2.40). See Cicero, *De oratore* 2.59, 2.56; Dionysius of Halicarnassus, *Lysias* 7. See Zanker 1981; Innocenti 1994. *Enargeia* is linked to *ekphrasis*: see Fowler 1991; Webb 2009. The term goes back to Stoic philosophical theory (see Plutarch, *De Stoicorum repugnantiis* 1051EF), where it designates a self-evident apprehension.

[23] Quintilian 8.3.61: illud patet, hoc se quodam modo ostendit.

[24] Quintilian 8.3.62: magna virtus res de quibus loquimur clare atque ut cerni videantur enuntiare. Tr. D. Russell (LCL).

scene, and one that focuses on specific details.[25] As we have seen, *enargeia* is particularly useful in conjuring up emotions to sway the judge: in order to be successful, the scene should not just reach his ears but also touch his heart.[26] Quintilian admits that it might be good to use rhetorical *inventio* and add something false to 'what would have happened'. But that is only a tool to help show the truth: *enargeia* aims at revealing the truth of the events, or rather at allowing the truth of the events to shine more forcefully,[27] by giving clear, almost picture-like[28] descriptions of events in all their details.[29] Indeed, the basic rule remains that one has to follow nature.[30] *Enargeia* was a prominent stylistic feature in late Antiquity: it has been argued by M. Roberts that it was a constitutive part of the late antique literary esthetic[31] and it surely figures prominently in late antique rhetorical handbooks.[32]

Pathetic emotions demand a high style, Quintilian notes,[33] although he immediately adds that the division into three styles is quite arbitrary. The earlier *Rhetorica ad Herrenium* makes a lot of these three styles, giving short sample speeches of each of them.[34] *Oratio gravis* demands the best vocabulary (*ornatissima verba*), the most noble thoughts suitable for amplification and appeal to pity (*amplificatione et conmiseratione*), and figures of thought and diction which have grandeur (*quae gravitatem habebunt*).[35] These figures include: *repetitio* (epanaphora) and *conversio* (antistrophe, 4.19),

[25] Quintilian 8.3.62–72.

[26] Quintilian 6.2.34, 8.3.62.

[27] Ps-Longinus, *Peri hypsous* 15.8.

[28] Quintilian 6.2.30. Orosius sometimes has explicit recourse to visual imagery and wishes to 'put things before the eyes' of the reader (3.23.2; 6.12.2: *constitui ante oculos*). In 2.17.12, the speech of Thrasybulus sets 'before the eyes' of the Athenians from whom they are fleeing. Orosius 5.15.11 is a brief *ekphrasis*.

[29] Demetrius, *On style* 209: *enargeia* implies leaving nothing out and cutting nothing short.

[30] Quintilian 8.3.61–71, 71: *naturam intueamur, hanc sequamur*. See also Quintilian 9.2.40–4.

[31] Roberts 1989: 39–40; Webb 2009: 87–106. See Kelly 2008: 161–221 for doubts about the idea of a 'late antique esthetic'.

[32] *Schemata dianoes quae ad rhetores pertinent* 71: enargeia est imaginatio, quae actum incorporeis oculis subicit; Isidorus, *Libellus de arte rhetorica* 517.10.

[33] Quintilian 12.10.59.

[34] The example of *oratio gravis* (4.12) reminds one immediately of Orosius' style, with its exclamations, use of questions, ornate but also repetitive vocabulary, and the claim of the impossibility of language to express the facts.

[35] *Rhetorica ad Herrenium* 4.11.

contentio (antithesis, 4.21), *exclamatio* (apostrophe), which in particular conjures up pain and indignation (*quae conficit significationem doloris aut indignationis*), and *interrogatio* (interrogation, 4.22), *subiectio* (hypophora—the use of questions, 4.33–4), *conduplicatio* (reduplication), particularly useful in amplification and commiseration, and *interpretatio* (synonym, 4.38), *expeditio* (elimination of various counterarguments, 4.40–1), *superlatio* (hyperbole, 4.44), and *similitudo* (simile, 4.59). According to the *Rhetorica*, amplification can be divided into two categories: exhortation (*cohortatio*), leading to anger in the audience, and bathos (*conquestio*), which arouses pity (3.24). In terms of speaking style, *pathos* demands frequent interruptions and long pauses; for corporal behaviour, dramatic gestures such as hitting one's head interrupted by calm gestures are recommended (3.26–7). By its very nature, the pathetic mode of amplification is closely linked to *conmiseratio*, as both aim at arousing pity (*misericordia*).[36] It has to be relatively brief, for, as the *Rhetorica* tersely notes, 'nothing dries as quickly as a tear'.[37] With this brief perusal of rhetorical theory in the back of our mind, we can now turn to a closer study of book 5 of the *Historiae*.

II. WAR INTO CIVIL WAR: TEARFUL SPECTACLES IN BOOK 5

Emotions often run high in the *Historiae*. But their expression is not random, nor ubiquitous. It is therefore important not to restrict one's analysis to a number of passages, but to take a look at an entire book. Book 5 presents itself as a suitable case-study. It covers Roman history from the sack of Corinth to the rebellion of Spartacus, one of the most troubled periods of Roman history, with, in particular, the first civil wars. Emotional involvement of the reader is immediately solicited in the very first sentence of book 5: 'I know that quite a number of people can now, after all this, be moved by the fact that Roman victories grew greater by the massacre of many peoples and cities.'[38]

[36] See, e.g. *Rhetorica ad Herrenium* 4.38.

[37] *Rhetorica ad Herrenium* 2.50: nihil enim lacrima citius arescit.

[38] Orosius 5.1.1: Scio aliquantos post haec deinceps permoueri posse, quod uictoriae Romanae multarum gentium et ciuitatum strage crebrescunt.

Yet, not all are and, Orosius notes, some stress the glory of all Roman victories. This counterargument, which is indebted to the distorted view of the past that was strongly attacked in book 4, is eliminated in a lengthy rebuke (5.1–2): Orosius first argues that this unduly privileges the glory of Roman triumph at the expense of the suffering of what were about to become provinces of the empire, and that the world offers now many more safe havens if one would have to flee today for an invasion.[39] The final sentence explicitly compares the good things of the present to the suffering of the *maiores*.

Proof is found in history. The first subject of Orosius is the destruction of Corinth, depicted as the sequel to that of Carthage: 'in a short period and at the same time the pitiful burning of two of the greatest cities shone through the various parts of the world.'[40] The hyperbole and the qualification of the fire as *miserabile* announce the dramatic nature of the description that follows. Whereas the military movements leading to the sack of Corinth are set out in a rather factual manner and in a simple style, the actual sack itself is dramatically highlighted. Orosius first draws attention to the fact that Corinth was the richest city and the arts capital of the world. Then he describes the destruction of the city itself:

> Once the licence to plunder is cruelly given, even to captives, everything is so filled with murder and fire that the fire burns from the circuit of the walls as if from a furnace massed into one flame. In that way, the greater part of the population is consumed by sword and fire and the rest is sold as slaves. After the city has burnt down, the walls are destroyed from their foundations. The stone of the walls is reduced to dust and an enormous plunder is taken.
>
> permissa crudeliter etiam captiuis praedandi licentia sic omnia caedibus ignibusque conpleta sunt, ut de murorum ambitu quasi e camino in unum apicem coartatum exundaret incendium. itaque plurima parte populi ferro flammisque consumpta reliqua sub corona uendita est; urbe incensa muri funditus diruti sunt; muralis lapis in puluerem redactus, praeda ingens erepta est (5.3.6).

One notes the repetitive vocabulary, typical for Orosius' dramatic descriptions, which serves to render the description more piteous and

[39] The argument is already in Cicero, *De republica* 3.20. See also Prudentius, *Contra Symmachum* 2.488–591.

[40] Orosius 5.3.1: duarumque potentissimarum urbium paruo unius temporis interuallo per diuersas mundi partes miserabile conluxit incendium.

was noted by the *Rhetorica ad Herrenium* to be especially suited in amplification and to arouse pity,[41] the simile of the city becoming a single flame, and the emphasis on the cruelty of the act. The generally repetitive nature of the description—fewer words would have said the same—recalls Quintilian's amplification through accumulation of words and sentences that say the same thing.[42] In a final paragraph, Orosius draws attention at once to the force of the fire and to Corinth's artistic past by explaining how all the statues of the city melted into one big chunk of metal, called Corinthian vase.

The next chapter focuses on the war in Spain, and ends on the 'tearful spectacle' (*lacrimabile . . . spectaculum*) of Mancinus, his hands bound, alone at night in front of the gates of Numantia, rejected by both the Numantians and the Romans. At this point Orosius interrupts his narrative: 'the pain forces one to cry out at this point',[43] thus spelling out the emotions his pathetic depiction of Mancinus should raise in his reader. In a series of rhetorical questions, Orosius then forcefully attacks the pride Romans take in their treatment of Mancinus: justice, loyalty, strength, and pity are to be found among the Numantians, rather than among the Romans. Moreover, Orosius challenges the arbitrary nature of Roman judgments of the past, as they rejected Mancinus after a disaster but actually rewarded Varro who was responsible for the disaster at Cannae. The sentiment aroused by Mancinus' unjust and cruel fate is thus used to question again the traditional exemplary nature of the past.[44] This procedure of using rhetoric to question rhetoric is paradigmatic for the entire *Historiae*. The highly rhetorical nature of this chapter can be illustrated by a single paragraph, which questions the justice of the Roman attitude towards Mancinus:

> If the treaty he made displeased them, why were the troops redeemed on such conditions? When they returned, why were they received? And when they were demanded back, why were they not returned? On the other hand, if they thought it right to save their troops on whatever

[41] Praedande/praeda; ignibus/incendium/flammis/incensa; muri/muralis. See *Rhetorica ad Herrenium* 4.38.

[42] Quintilian 8.4.27.

[43] Orosius 5.5.1: exclamare hoc loco dolor exigit.

[44] The reference to Varro is an obvious exemplum: see Valerius Maximus 3.4.4. See also Orosius 5.5.15 for another poignant description of the weakness of the Roman soldiers.

terms possible, why was Mancinus, who made this treaty, the only one to be handed over?

aut, si displicuit foedus quod pactum est, cur miles hoc pignore redemptus aut, cum reuerteretur, receptus est aut, cum repeteretur, redditus non ęst? aut, si placuit seruati militis qualiscumque prouisio, cur Mancinus, qui hoc pepigit, solus deditus fuit?[45]

Part of a larger *expeditio*, a refutation of counterarguments, one notices the use of anaphora (*aut . . . aut . . . aut*), *subiectio* (the use of questions), and even a *contentio* with a variation of vocabulary (*receptus/redditus, reverteretur/repeteretur*), procedures that the *Rhetorica ad Herrenium* prescribed for *oratio gravis.*

The rhythm of the first chapters of book 5 is typical for the *Historiae.* Several paragraphs of factual description are spiced with some rhetorically enhanced passages and followed by an exclamation that draws explicit attention to the drama of what the reader has just read, and which develops into a rhetorical dispute with the imaginary pagan opponents. Emotions are thus not continuously aroused, but allowed to rest before they are appealed to again. This choice can be taken to reflect the advice of the *Rhetorica ad Herrenium*, that *conmiseratio* cannot be continuous or last too long, and that in an *oratio gravis* one should combine periods of calm with outbursts of emotions. Otherwise, the orator risks draining the feelings of the audience.

The pattern is continued in the following chapters. With its discussion of slave revolts in Sicily, chapter 6 effectively announces what will become the main theme of book 5: warfare, and, in particular, civil war. In a typical rhetorical amplification driven by comparison,[46] Orosius states: 'A slave revolt, for being much rarer than other insurrections, is much more savage, in that the free masses are driven by the intention to increase the fatherland and slaves to destroy it'.[47] Paragraph 7 recalls the sack of Corinth, but outbids it in cruelty: not only is Rome almost defeated, but the Numantians are even forced to commit mass suicide. With the sack of Numantia, Rome had effectively lost all significant external opposition: from now on civil discord

[45] Orosius 5.5.6. Tr. Fear 2010a: 216.

[46] Quintilian 8.4.10–12.

[47] Orosius 5.6.6: in hoc autem seruilis tumultus excitatio quanto rarior ceteris tanto truculentior est, quia intentione commouetur libera multitudo ut patriam augeat, seruilis ut perdat.

will be Rome's fate.[48] The staccato of emotions is continued. Orosius concludes, after his account of the suppression of a slave rebellion on Sicily:

> Truly a sad thing, such a war, and impossible to find an issue out of. Without any doubt, the masters had to perish, unless one went against the slaves that had become too overbearing. But even in the most infelicitous losses of the battle and in the even more infelicitous gains of the victory, the victors lost as much as the number of vanquished who died.
>
> Misera profecto talis belli et inextricabilis causa. pereundum utique dominis erat, nisi insolescentibus seruis ferro obuiam iretur. sed tamen in ipsis quoque infelicissimis damnis pugnae et infelicioribus lucris uictoriae quanti periere uicti tantum perdidere uictores (5.9.8)

Again we notice repetitive vocabulary,[49] the comparison between the luckless defeat and even more regrettable victory, and Orosius' habitual use of assonance.[50] These tools serve to underline the dramatic and painful nature (*misera profecto*) of the event.

A brief account of various wars in the East is followed by an extensive and dramatic depiction of a locust plague in Africa, followed by an epidemic disease (5.11). Orosius regularly inserts such references to natural disasters, with the obvious aim of showing that the disorder of the times was not limited to the realm of politics.[51] This sympathy between man and nature is in a later passage artfully underlined, when Orosius describes the numerous executions by Sulla with a sentence drawn from a description of a plague in Vergil's *Georgics*.[52] The description of the locust plague is an obvious example of *enargeia*, with Orosius taking care to point out all the different details of the picture—which is, as we have seen, one of three forms *enargeia* can take according to Quintilian. The insects not only destroyed the harvest, but also the herbs with the roots, the leaves of the trees and part of the branches, and even the cortex and dry wood. When the locusts were swept into the sea, they rotted and

[48] Orosius 5.8.2: Carthagine Numantiaque deleta moritur apud Romanos utilis de prouisione conlatio et oritur infamis de ambitione contentio.

[49] Infelicissimis/infelicioribus; pereundum/perire; uictoriae/victi/victores.

[50] Perire/perdidere.

[51] In book 5 it is particularly eruptions of Mount Etna that draw Orosius' attention: 5.6, 5.10.11, 5.13.3.

[52] Orosius 5.21.6: nec ipsius mortis erat uia simplex aut una condicio; Vergil, *Georgica* 3.482: nec via mortis erat simplex.

caused a plague, which touched the birds and domestic and wild animals.[53] The description is dutifully amplified.[54] Orosius again explicitly appeals to his audience by showing his own emotions: 'at how great the destruction of men was, I myself, when narrating it, shiver in my entire body.'[55] The emphasis is strongly on a transfer of emotions from the speaker to his audience: ego ipse, dum refero, toto corpore perhorresco (note the o-sound).

Chapter 16 narrates Marius' war against the Cimbri and Teutones. Orosius particularly highlights the behaviour of the Gallic women and their manly strength and female fury:[56] when they do not obtain the permission to serve as priestesses, they smash their children in the first stage of a collective suicide (13).[57] At another battle, they fight as men and even scalp their enemies, before turning on their own men and themselves (17). This last mass-suicide is depicted by Orosius in graphic detail:

> Indeed, some slit their throats with mutual help, some strangled themselves grasping each other's throats, some attached ropes to the legs of horses and then incited the horses, after having put their heads into the ropes which they had attached to the legs of the horses, and were dragged and killed, others hung themselves with a noose from raised yoke-beams of chariots. There was even found one who attached her two sons to her feet, having put nooses around their heads and, when she made herself die through hanging, she dragged them along killing them.

[53] Orosius 5.11.2–3: namque cum per totam Africam inmensae lucustarum multitudines coaluissent et non modo iam cunctam spem frugum abrasissent herbasque omnes cum parte radicum, folia arborum cum teneritudine ramorum consumpsissent, uerum etiam amaras cortices atque arida ligna praeroderent, repentino abreptae uento atque in globos coactae portataeque diu per aerem, Africano pelago inmersae sunt. harum cum inmensos aceruos longe undis urguentibus fluctus per extenta late litora propulissent, taetrum nimis atque ultra opinionem pestiferum odorem tabida et putrefacta congeries exhalauit, unde omnium pariter animantum tanta pestilentia consecuta est, ut auium pecudum ac bestiarum corruptione aeris dissolutarum putrefacta passim cadauera uitium corruptionis augerent.

[54] See, e.g. the first sentence with its emphasis on total destruction in the whole of Africa by a huge crowd of locusts, and the second which shows that the rotting locusts arrived everywhere; the fact that the plague is 'beyond imagination'; the duplication of vocabulary (corruptione/corruptionis, pestiferum/pestilentia).

[55] Orosius 5.11.4: At vero quanta fuerit hominum lues, ego ipse, dum refero, toto corpore perhorresco.

[56] Orosius 5.16.21: quae se suosque paruulos femineo furore, ui autem uirili necauerunt.

[57] A well-known exemplum: Valerius Maximus 6.1.ext.3; Jerome, *Epistula* 123.7.

namque aliae concursu mutuo iugulatae, aliae apprehensis inuicem faucibus strangulatae, aliae funibus per equorum crura consertis ipsisque continuo equis exstimulatis, postquam suas isdem funibus, quibus equorum crura nexuerant, indidere ceruices, protractae atque exanimatae sunt, aliae laqueo de subrectis plaustrorum temonibus pependerunt. inuenta est etiam quaedam, quae duos filios traiectis per colla eorum laqueis ad suos pedes uinxerit et, cum se ipsam suspendio morituram dimisisset, secum traxerit occidendos (5.16.18–19).

Women overstepping the limits of their sex often fascinated Orosius,[58] and the episode obviously serves well the purpose of showing the unusual quality of the events. He focuses on a series of modes of suicide, each described in detail. Added *enargeia* is created by almost over-describing the suicide with the horses, where the fact of attaching the rope to the horse is repeated in almost identical words. The narration consciously builds up to the last event, when a mother hangs herself and her two sons at the same time: the scenes get longer and the last scene is the only one that is not included in the anaphora (*aliae . . . aliae . . . aliae*).

The Social and Mithridatic Wars provide the material for chapters 18 and 19, and sufficient occasion for drama. Again the same rhythm is detectable: sections of factual narrative are interrupted by dramatic descriptions.[59] The most harrowing scene, probably of the entire *Historiae*, is the description of a group of Italians who during the Social War had retreated onto a mountain:

But four thousand Italian men who had fled this massacre had climbed by chance to the rim of a mountain, together as one battalion. There, pressed and suffocated by the snow, they froze into a terrible death. Indeed, they stood as if paralyzed by fear for the enemy, some leaning on roots or stones, some resting on their arms, and all appeared with their eyes wide open and their teeth shown in the manner of the living. There was no sign of death at all for those looking from afar except the

[58] See his description of Semiramis (1.4.4), the Amazons (1.15–16, 3.18.5), Thamyris (2.7.4), Artemidora (2.10.3), the matrons poisoning Rome (3.10), and the Gallic and Germanic women (5.16.17, 6.21.17). This is not uncommon: see, e.g. Claudian, *In Eutropium* 1.499.

[59] Another vivid scene is the well-known story of a soldier killing his brother in the civil war (5.19.12–13; see pp. 95–7), shortly afterwards followed by a new exclamation drawing attention to the unwelcome horror, even today, of the civil war (5.19.20–2).

long immobility, which in no way the normal energy of human life can sustain for long.

quattuor milia autem Italici uiri ex ea caede profugi iugum montis coacto in unum agmine forte conscenderant, ubi oppressi exanimatique niuibus miserabili morte riguerunt. namque ita, ut attoniti timore hostium steterant, alii stirpibus uel saxis reclines, alii armis suis innitentes, patentibus cuncti oculis dentibusque nudatis uiuentium in modum uisebantur; nec ullum erat procul intuentibus mortis indicium nisi diuturna immobilitas, quam nullo modo humanae uitae uegetatio diu perpeti potest (5.18.19–20)

The strength of this scene lies not just in its vivid description, detailing the various positions of the dead soldiers, but also in the paradoxical horror of being looked at by a dead person. The *enargeia* of the depiction is increased by a subversion of traditional *enargeia*. Normally, a scene is set before our eyes so as to make at once that scene vivid and full of life and ourselves present at the scene. Here, although the scene is vivid and full of appearance of life, it is actually a semblance of life that is depicted. Moreover, while we look at the dead soldiers, they stare back at us, returning our gaze of the living with the eyes of the dead. Whilst Orosius may have found this scene in his source,[60] it is obviously his choice to exploit the potential of this paradoxical *enargeia* for inspiring horror in his audience.[61]

The last chapters of the book develop into a lengthy peroration, which picks up the key elements ascribed to a conclusion by the *Rhetorica ad Herrenium*. According to the handbook, a conclusion consists of a summing-up, amplification, and an appeal to pity (*enumeratio, amplificatio, conmiseratio*, 2.47). Chapter 5.22 of the *Historiae* inventorizes the number of dead of the Social and Sullanic wars, asserting that it supersedes the number of Roman citizens of the fourth century BC (5.22.3)—an obvious amplification through comparison.[62] This develops, quite naturally for Orosius, into an argument for the superiority of the Christian present (5.22.5–15). The exclamation *pro pudor* opens the argument, followed by a series of questions (5.22.5)—a rhetorical tool used a few paragraphs further as

[60] The battle is mentioned in *Periochae* 76.

[61] See also Orosius 5.24.3: Spartacus has Romans fight as gladiators and his followers, former gladiators, watch the games. Orosius notes that he thus reverses the normal roles of spectator and participant. An interesting parallel can be found in *Chronicle of Zuqnin*, part III, 101, 108.

[62] *Rhetorica ad Herrenium* 2.49.

well (5.22.12–14). Orosius concludes the argument with a return to the figure with which he opened it: the number of ordinary soldiers who died in the present wars hardly equals the number of noblemen who lost their lives in the wars of the first century BC (5.22.15). The last chapter of the book (24) makes the same argument all over again. Having graphically recalled that the revolt of Spartacus inspired equal fear as did Hannibal,[63] Orosius again bursts out in questions to make his readers feel the horror of the facts usually disguised by rhetoric:

> Who, I ask, would not shudder when hearing about, I would not say such wars, but even just so many names of wars, foreign, slave, social, civil, against fugitives? They do not even follow one another as the waves of an agitated sea, huge though they are, but they come running from all sides, with various causes, appellations, forms, and evils, roused and massed.
>
> quis rogo audire non horreat non dicam bella talia, sed uel nomina tanta bellorum, externa, seruilia, socialia, ciuilia, fugitiuorum? quae ne sic saltem sese, ut commoti maris fluctus quamuis molibus magnis sequuntur, sed undique diuersis causis uocabulis formis malisque excitata coaceruataque concurrunt (5.24.9–10)

The already dramatic metaphor of huge waves crashing onto the ship of state is dismissed in favour of a fundamentally anarchic image: even the formidable but at least orderly menace of waves following one another is insufficient to describe the confused state of affairs in the first century BC: the wars are a chaotic mass of events, with an equally tumultuous amount of terms attached to them. As much as the reader gets lost in the words, he will get lost in the events. Orosius' true picture of the past is thus predicated on the fact that the past may be fundamentally muddled. It creates a loss of orientation among the readers, which helps to undermine the glorious and limpid narrative of Roman success that Orosius supposes to be rife among his audience.

Orosius then sums up the various wars that he has reviewed in the present book, from the Jugurthine war to that against Spartacus (5.24.11–19). It concludes with a strong appeal to self-pity in the mind of the Italians:

[63] Orosius 5.24.5: itaque exterrita ciuitate non minore propemodum metu, quam sub Hannibale circa portas fremente trepidauerat (. . .). One notes the repeated vocabulary referring to fear and trembling.

> On the basis of this, we exhort Italy to console herself for the troubles caused by current foreign enemies through the remembrance of those caused in the past by her, from herself and in herself, and which destroyed her in an incomparably more cruel way.
>
> ex quo admonemus ut ipsa se consoletur Italia de uexatione externorum praesentium per recordationem praeteritorum ex se atque in se et ipsam se inconparabiliter crudelius dilacerantum suorum (5.24.20)

The last chapters, construed as a *conclusio*, thus turn the entire book into a plea. Indeed, Orosius is not simply depicting the past: he is highlighting its terrible nature in order to persuade his audience that they have misinterpreted the past so far. Fittingly, the conclusion also puts an end to rhetoric: the past was more cruel 'beyond comparison'.

The *Historiae* are at once a narrative of the past and an argument on how to interpret that past. As the preceding pages have shown, neither can be separated. Orosius not only represents the past in a dramatic way, but he also intervenes to appeal to the audience and to direct its interpretation of the facts—just as a deliberative speech is never solely narrative.[64] More profoundly, the choice for *pathos* as the mode of narrative is part of the demonstration that pagan accounts are less truthful than the *Historiae*. The latter shows the true, sour flavour of the past, in conscious contrast with the sweet tones of the traditional accounts. Whilst the pathetic description of events is Orosius' main way of doing so, he also strongly banks on expression of his personal involvement, usually by suggesting that he experiences the horror, fear, or dread that they should feel too.[65] Already in the preface, Orosius had set himself as an example for his audience: first convinced that the past was better than the present, his research showed him otherwise. The repeated self-references are thus part of a conscious strategy of using himself as the explicit gateway for his audience to get a true sense of the past. Given the fact that the *Historiae* are aimed at an audience that is in doubt about Christianity's claims, this is an obvious strategy of persuasion. Here one may

[64] Arnaud-Lindet 1990–1: i.xxxviii has suggested that book 1 can be read as an oration too. One could argue that book 7 also builds up to a highly rhetorical climax: see the dramatic passages in 7.22.6, 7.35.14–19, 7.39.5–10, 7.40.

[65] The autobiographical passages referring to Orosius' flight from barbarians (3.20.6–7; 7.41.4–5) are also part of this rhetorical strategy of self-involvement. This does not preclude their historicity, but this cannot be accepted without due caution: cf. Fear 2010a: 2 n. 15.

detect the influence of Quintilian's advice, discussed at the start of this chapter, that the orator should feel the emotions himself in order to sway the judge. Yet personal involvement can also be a strategy for literary authority. As the author of the *Historiae*, Orosius is already *de facto* the access to the past that his readers have. By setting himself up as such in a more explicit way, he becomes also the paradigm of how one should react to the past. Orosius not only controls the narrative, but also hopes to steer the audience's response to it.

For Quintilian, and Orosius with him, *pathos* aims at a greater verisimilitude, at a true depiction of the events that, in *enargeia*, is put before the reader's eyes. This may suggest a strong belief in the power of rhetoric to depict reality. Nevertheless, Orosius has a clear awareness that even his own rhetoric may fall short of fully representing the chaos and drama of the past. In another twist of Orosius' engagement with rhetoric, he betrays a clear sense that verisimilitude can overstretch the demands of rhetoric.

III. EXPLORING THE LIMITS OF NARRATIVE

Theorists of rhetoric were conscious of the fact that they sometimes put contradictory demands on the orator. Quintilian comments in particular on the fact that the virtues of brevity and lucidity can clash: 'But we must be no less on our guard against the obscurity that comes from compressing everything too much: it is better for there to be too much in a narrative than too little.'[66] This is a concern echoed at length by Orosius in the preface to book 3. The preface opens with a sense of defeatism: It is impossible 'to set out everything and in every detail what happened and how they happened' (nec omnia nec per omnia posse quae gesta sunt et sicut gesta sunt explicari). There are simply too many facts described by too many authors. Moreover, Orosius is not interested in the facts themselves but in the misery of the facts. *Brevitas* is thus a necessary quality of his history. Yet it is a problematic one: too much brevity may earn him the accusation of

[66] Quintilian 4.2.44: non minus autem cavenda est, quae nimium corripientes omnia sequitur, obscuritas, satiusque aliquid narrationi superesse quam deesse. Tr. D. Russell (LCL). See also Quintilian 8.3.82; *Rhetorica ad Herrenium* 1.15, 4.69; Cicero, *De inventione* 1.29.

omitting key events for the sake of brevity, but if he includes all events he lapses into the vice of obscurity. Obscurity would greatly damage Orosius' ultimate aim of giving the audience a flavour of the true nature of the events: 'we, on the contrary, shall take care in particular to give a sense of the force of the events and not present an image' (3.pr.3: maxime cum e contrario nos vim rerum non imaginem commendare curemus). The danger of *brevitas*, in turn, is that the *intellegendi vigorem* is taken away,[67] that it chips away at the true understanding of the events, at its *enargeia*.[68] For Quintilian, a good orator could balance brevity and lucidity. Orosius, on the contrary, suggests that this is impossible:

> Brevity and obscurity, or rather brevity, as it is always obscure, takes away the rigour of understanding, even if it offers a semblance of knowledge. But I, as I know that either has to be avoided, will aim for both so that they balance each other out in some way, on condition that not a lot of events will seem to have been left out nor that they seem too restricted.
>
> breuitas autem atque obscuritas, immo ut est semper obscura breuitas, etsi cognoscendi imaginem praefert, aufert tamen intellegendi uigorem. sed ego cum utrumque uitandum sciam, utrumque faciam ut quocumque modo alterutra temperentur, si nec multa praetermissa nec multum constricta uideantur (3.pr.3)

This is a remarkable statement for an otherwise rhetorically astute author: Orosius proclaims here that two of the cardinal virtues of narrative, brevity and lucidity, can hardly be successfully reconciled: brevity always tends to be obscure (*obscura brevitas*).[69] He proposes a vague compromise: he will try to be as brief as possible, hoping not to reduce the understanding of the events. At one level, one can read this as an honest confession by Orosius who realizes the conflict that is developing in his narrative. Indeed, the general preface to the *Historiae* claims the cardinal rhetorical virtue of *brevitas* and seems to situate the work in the tradition of writing *breviaria* rather than that of full-scale historiography: Augustine's order was *ut (...) ordinato breviter voluminis textu explicarem* (1.pr.10). Yet the actual

[67] Note the parallel with Ammianus 15.1.1: tunc enim laudanda est brevitas cum moras rumpens intempestivas nihil subtrahit cognitioni gestorum, a passage discussed on p. 136.

[68] Cf. Orosius 2.18.5, 3.14.8, 3.20.5.

[69] See Augustine, *Retractationes* 1.5 and 2.13 for similar reflections.

result, seven books, is far from brief, and shares few characteristics with the extant *breviaria* of the fourth century—except that Orosius used them as sources. The preface to book 3 would then be an apology for the clash between *brevitas* and *enargeia*—a rhetorically informed admission of failure.[70] On this reading, Orosius' apologetic enthusiasm leads to him transcending the boundaries of the genre of the *breviarium* in which he started out.

Such an interpretation takes Orosius at face value. But admissions of failure by ancient authors are rarely straightforward and Orosius is actually up to much more. There is, first, an obvious element of modesty in the assertion of failing to fulfil the demands of rhetoric: just as Orosius could style himself a sinner in the *Commonitorium*, he presents himself here as an unaccomplished writer. At the same time, it raises Orosius' standing as an author, because it demonstrates the difficulty of the task. Second, the appeal to 'obscure brevity' draws attention to the double strategy of persuasion in the *Historiae*. We have seen that Orosius alternates more descriptive passages with emotional ones. Whereas the latter show the true, miserable, nature of the events, the former serve to indicate the extent of suffering of the past. The reference to 'obscure brevity' can be taken to hint at the absence of the vividness in these other passages and at the general incompleteness of Orosius' narrative. It invites the reader to extrapolate, from the few dramatic descriptions that are actually given, all that remains hidden behind the names and numbers in the other passages. In such a way, Orosius is not obliged to perform the impossible task of dramatizing the entire course of history, which would not only be impossible, but would also contravene the rhetorical precepts that *pathos* should be punctual and brief. The apparent modest admission to the presence of obscurity in his narrative thus serves to highlight the lucidity that shines elsewhere and to suggest to the reader what drama remains hidden in the other passages.

The admission of the failure to achieve full lucidity in the preface of book 3 is thus an invitation to the reader to fill in the skeleton offered in the *Historiae*. The drama punctually supplied by Orosius is to be extended imaginatively by the audience to the other events that

[70] This is most explicitly argued in De Coninck 1992. Orosius' *brevitas* is usually seen as problematic or feigned: Lacroix 1965: 75–7; Corbellini 1984; Escribaño Paño 1996; Cesa 2003: 28; Sehlmeyer 2009: 302. An interpretation going in the direction here suggested is put forward by Kempshall 2011: 74–6.

are merely summed up. Read in this light, the repeated references throughout the narrative to the necessity to abbreviate, and the omissions this implies, take on a different meaning.[71] As statements of imperfection, they are constant reminders of what is not in the work and how many more examples and details of suffering from the past could be given. Orosius therefore does not write a *breviarium*. Traditional *breviaria* pretend to be comprehensive: they do not contain all events, but give a complete picture in the sense that the reader will know all he needs to.[72] Indeed, in rhetorical theory brevity does not mean truncation: a brief account is still a full account, reduced to its essentials. Orosius, on the contrary, is at pains to emphasize his own incompleteness, as a rhetorical suggestion that he has even more proof of the misery of the past than he actually offers to the reader.

There is a further level on which to understand Orosius' qualms about brevity and lucidity, namely as a statement of the difficulty of translating the chaos of the past into a clear narrative. Indeed, in his desire to represent to the reader the true nature of events, Orosius confesses to abandoning the rules of a well-ordered narrative, and to prefer a chaotic narrative that truly reflects the disordered state of things. In book 3, he excuses himself for having produced a disordered narrative—because the facts themselves are completely topsy-turvy:

> I have woven an inextricable hurdle of confused history and entwined the uncertain courses of wars waged here and there with a mad fury, having followed them with words from their traces. And, as I see it, I have written about these in a so much more disordered way as I have tried to maintain their order.[73]

As we noted in chapter 3, Orosius sometimes elides fact and text and tries to describe the events in the way they present themselves. This generates disorder in his narrative—but this allows him to distance

[71] See, e.g. Orosius 1.6.1, 1.12.1, 1.12.7–10, 1.19.2–3, 4.5.6, 4.10.4, 4.20.40, 5.15.2, 5.17.2, 5.19.2, 5.23.3, 6.7.2, 6.18.2, 7.37.1. Orosius sometimes has recourse to the vocabulary of 'counting' (*numerare*) instead of telling the facts (1.12.2–3, 3.2.10–11, 3.7.1). He shares this with the *breviarium* of Festus (see the preface).

[72] Eutropius, pr.; Festus, pr.

[73] Orosius 3.2.9: Contexui indigestae historiae inextricabilem cratem atque incertos bellorum orbes huc et illuc lymphatico furore gestorum uerbis e uestigio secutus inplicui, quoniam tanto, ut uideo, inordinatius scripsi, quanto magis ordinem custodiui.

himself from more rhetorical ways of writing in which the nature of events is sacrificed to the virtues of narrative.

In aspiring to truth in disorder, Orosius consciously wrong-foots a traditional way of writing history, as exemplified in Ammianus. At the beginning of his fifteenth book, Ammianus notes:

> So far as I could investigate the truth, I have, after putting the various events in clear order, related what I myself was allowed to witness in the course of my life, or to learn by meticulous questioning of those directly concerned. The rest, which the text to follow will disclose, we shall set forth to the best of our ability with still greater accuracy, feeling no fear of critics of the prolixity of our work, as they consider it. For brevity is to be praised only when it breaks off ill-timed discursiveness, without detracting at all from an understanding of the course of events.[74]

The passage is often read as Ammianus' critique on the tradition of *breviaria* of the fourth century.[75] Yet a more rhetorical reading is also possible and, I would argue, to be preferred: in line with rhetorical theory, Ammianus links clarity and order,[76] and, just as Orosius, takes his distances from excessive brevity. In essence, Ammianus' argument is similar to that of Orosius: excessive brevity leads to obscurity and takes away the *cognitio gestorum*. But Ammianus solves the conflict in a traditional way, by consciously arguing that one should describe events at the length their importance demands. In doing so, he puts himself as the author at the centre of attention: he as authoritative author has researched the events and will set out what the reader needs to know in relation to the magnitude of the events. This makes Ammianus' work self-contained: contrary to Orosius, who constantly reminds his reader that there is much more than he can report in vivid detail and thus draws attention to what lies beyond the narrative, he presents his work as all one needs to know. Equally, in contrast with Orosius, who sacrifices narrative order to the reality and disorder of events, Ammianus sticks to a rhetorically constructed

[74] Ammianus 15.1.1: Vtcumque potuimus veritatem scrutari, ea quae videre licuit per aetatem, vel perplexe interrogando versatos in medio scire, narravimus ordine casuum exposito diversorum: residua quae secuturus aperiet textus, pro virium captu limatius absolvemus, nihil obtrectatores longi, ut putant, operis formidantes. tunc enim laudanda est brevitas cum moras rumpens intempestivas nihil subtrahit cognitioni gestorum. Tr. J. Rolfe (LCL).

[75] De Jonge 1948: 6; Rosen 1970: 5; Barnes 1998: 66; Kelly 2008: 240; Sehlmeyer 2009: 22–3.

[76] *Rhetorica ad Herrenium* 1.15.

structure that allows the events to stand out in all clarity without addressing the difficulty of making reality fit with the rhetorical demands of such an ordered narrative.[77] Although Orosius constructed his work as rhetorically as Ammianus did, he nevertheless betrays the awareness that the demands of narrative limit one's ability to represent reality in its true colours.

It is Orosius' overriding concern with giving the most truthful narrative that makes him explore the limits of rhetorical narrative. Yet exploration it is, not explosion. The impossibility to narrate everything in due lucidity is caused by the number of events, not by a fundamental impossibility to represent facts with words. The admission that the chaotic nature of the events forces him to abandon traditional criteria for an ordered narrative still maintains the belief that words can fully depict events, although it points to the inadequacy of a narrative that adheres to the demands of order and lucidity. As the comparison with Ammianus shows, this can be interpreted as a criticism of traditional historiography. Indeed, Orosius' attention to the limits of rhetoric is predicated on the polemical claim that his is the truest depiction of the past. Depicting the *Historiae* as only in part a full and truthful exposition of all the drama of history turns the rest of the work into an *aide-mémoire* that invites the reader to imagine the true nature of events. The *Historiae* are, hence, presented as a synecdoche of the full reality of the events. If the part is already so dramatic, how much more must the full story be. It is this kind of rhetorical outbidding that pushes Orosius to question the power of rhetoric.

IV. THE TRUTH OF VIVIDNESS

Drawing on Quintilian's understanding of *enargeia* as a way of displaying truth, I have argued that the highly rhetorical historiography of Orosius aims at almost literally showing the truth to his audience. Here we touch on a more general problem: to our modern understanding, rhetoric and truth are mutually exclusive.[78] Rhetoric is for us a synonym of fiction, to be avoided at all costs in history.

[77] On this issue, see Quintilian 4.2.55.
[78] Cf. Ginzburg 1999; Fox 2001.

In addition, the arousal of emotions, bathos, and drama are supposed to be alien to the writing of history and, indeed, Orosius' rhetorical outbursts have been used to disqualify him as a historian.[79] At best, he is a quasi-historian who talks the talk but lacks the substance. In this final section, I shall first argue that such a view of Orosius fails to situate him in the context of ancient historiography, to which such apparently outrageous rhetoric is less alien than some have thought. Then, I suggest that Orosius' use of *enargeia* and *pathos* as modes of displaying truth is one particular way in which the relationship between history and rhetoric could be conceptualized in Antiquity—one that may deserve more attention in current discussions of that relationship.

Although he strongly distances himself from classical historians, Orosius does not stand alone in the history of historiography in choosing highly rhetorical modes of expression. As we have seen, Quintilian assimilates the kind of emotions expressed in *pathos* with those depicted in tragedy. Orosius' emphasis on *pathos* thus puts him in the tradition of so-called 'tragic historiography'. The term goes back to the criticism by the Hellenistic historian Polybius on some of his predecessors, in particular Phylarchus, for trying to show the drama of the past and arousing the emotions of his readers. In his habitual way, Polybius draws a strong contrast between such historians and himself, and distinguishes firmly tragedy from history: the former has to charm and to please, and can thus tell lies, the latter has to tell the truth and thus be useful.[80] Scholarship is still in two minds about 'tragic historiography'. It was argued by E. Schwartz that Hellenistic tragic history was based on a peripatetic theory which reversed Aristotle's own separation of history and poetry.[81] Tragic history was thus a subgenre based on a theoretical choice. Schwartz's theory was challenged early on by F. Walbank, who argued that 'the link between tragedy and history (...) is in fact a fundamental affinity going back to the earliest days of both history and tragedy,

[79] Corbellini 1984; Pardini 1988; Bessone 2000.

[80] Polybius 2.56. See also 2.16.14, 3.48.8, 7.7.2, 15.34. See Plutarch, *Life of Themistocles* 32.4 and *Life of Alexander* 75. On Phylarchus, see Pédech 1989: 391–493. The other main proponent of 'tragic history' was Duris of Samos: see *FGrHist* 76 F1 with Pédech 1989: 368–72.

[81] Aristotle, *Poetica* 9.2–9, 1451b1–32. See Schwartz 1897: 560, 1900: 107, and 1909: 491; Scheller 1911; von Fritz 1958; Brink 1960; Landucci Gattinoni 1997; Foucher 2000a: 773–80 and 2000b; Candau Morón 2001; Cozzoli 2002.

and insisted upon throughout almost the whole of the classical and later periods down to the Byzantine scholiasts'.[82] That this is the more fruitful line of inquiry has become clear in the past decades. The accusations voiced by Polybius against Phylarchus have been turned against himself,[83] and his polemic unmasked as consciously misrepresenting his own practice and that of his predecessors.[84] Polybius' seemingly theoretical statements thus started off a wild goose chase for the 'genre' of tragic historiography, whereas in fact the use of dramatic elements was very widespread in all forms of historiography. Scholars have detected *enargeia*, appeal to emotions, dramatic language, theatricality, and imitation of tragic structures in almost all major historians, including those of the Latin tradition.[85] *Enargeia* was regularly praised as a quality in historiography,[86] but also debated.[87] Ammianus' reliance on *energeia* and *pathos* was noted a long time ago,[88] and, as we have seen above, his history explores some of the same rhetorical issues as the *Historiae*. How far an author verged towards dramatization depended on his motives and intentions. Entertainment has been alleged as the main motive for Phylarchus, but another aim may have been more important: one of the most dramatic passages in his history was the extreme punishment meted out by the Achaeans to the Mantinaeans in 223 BC. A strong anti-Achaean bias must have played a role in him embracing *pathos* in his narrative of these events:[89] strikingly displaying the immoral behaviour of the Achaeans may well have been a conscious attempt to coax people into sympathizing with their enemies. In the case of the

[82] Walbank 1960: 240. See also Meister 1975: 109–22; Pédech 1989: 371–2; Marincola 2003.

[83] Schepens 1975.

[84] Walbank 1962; Schepens 1980.

[85] Mellor 1993: 118–22; Walker 1993; Levene 1997; Feldherr 1998: 4–12, 165–211; Woodman 1998: 190–217; Shumate 1997; Dué 2000; Foucher 2000a and 2000b; Marincola 2003; MacMullen 2004: 15–72; Mahé-Simon 2006; Santoro L'Hoir 2006.

[86] e.g. Plutarch, *De gloria Atheniensium* 347AC on Thucydides; Lucian, *Quomodo historia conscribenda est* 51.

[87] Zangara 2004.

[88] Rosen 1970: 193–200, 1982: 149–63. Rosen's approach was controversial (see Austin 1973; Calboli 1974), as it questioned Ammianus' reliability, but has on the whole turned out to be very fruitful. The direction pointed by Rosen has been pursued by Kelly 2004 and 2008 and Mratschek 2007, but not always with the same attention for the rhetorical background.

[89] Phylarchus, *FGrHist* 81 F53–6. McCaslin 1985–1986 compares Polybius and Phylarchus.

Historiae, the accusation of immorality is extended to the whole of pre-Christian history: just as Phylarchus accuses the Achaeans, Orosius attacks the pagans for misrepresenting the horrors of the past. He can, thus, be fruitfully seen as belonging to the more 'tragic' or 'rhetorical' mode of historiography, as long as this is not understood as a claim for the continuity of a hypothetical genre. Rather, drama and high rhetoric were resources that each ancient historian could draw on, if his aims prompted him to do so. The difference between historians, then, lies in the degree to which this rhetoric was embraced, rather than whether rhetoric was used or not.

As the example of Polybius shows, it is part of the tropes of historiography to accuse other historians of writing in a rhetorical mode and not doing justice to reality. But that is in itself a rhetorical pose, which, moreover, usually only means that one rhetorical mode of writing is substituted for the other, or hides the fact that the historian is relying on the very procedures he accuses the others of. We moderns are easily seduced into sympathizing with the side that makes the accusations and asserts its own objectivity, but that temptation is to be resisted.[90] As Orosius shows, the claim to give a truthful account is itself rhetorical and the way he constructs such an account is quintessentially rhetorical.

The fact that historians, as all ancient authors, were rhetorically informed, to a greater or lesser degree, is a trivial fact. But too great an influence of rhetoric on historiography has been seen as imperilling the very nature of history. As rhetoric is seen as concerned with elaboration and amplification, and less with getting the facts right, its use in historiography impugns the hallmark of history, namely veracity. Scholarship has long been aware of this tension,[91] although it was often minimized by arguing that rhetoric was just a matter of style and not of substance. Ancient historians stick to the facts, so the suggestion went, but they obviously have to present their material in an attractive way.[92] In 1988 Tony Woodman challenged that view. He contended that earlier scholars had failed to take the rhetorical nature of ancient historiography seriously and detected among them a desire to see ancient and modern historiography as fundamentally identical undertakings that aim at establishing the facts. Against this he pleaded for the discontinuity of ancient and modern

[90] See, e.g. Schepens 1975 on Polybius and Phylarchus.
[91] See Peter 1911.
[92] For a polemical restatement of that view, see Lendon 2009.

historiography: for the ancients, historiography was literature, and they could freely draw on the rhetorical resource of *inventio* not only to embellish the narrative, but also to invent facts.[93]

Woodman's *Rhetoric in Classical Historiography* has had the great merit of trying to conceptualize a long neglected problem in the study of historiography, but it also had the effect of focusing discussions of the relationship between rhetoric and historiography on one particular element, namely the use of *inventio*, and hence the presence of fiction in historiography.[94] Indeed, his suggestion that ancient historians were free to make up facts shows that he interpreted the opposition between rhetoric and historiography as one between fact and fiction: since the former distinction did not exist in Antiquity, nor did the latter. Having established that fiction was admitted into the historical narrative in Antiquity, Woodman used this feature as the crucial distinction between ancient and modern historiography. Woodman's position has hence been interpreted as undermining the traditional idea that historiography is undergirded by a referential truth, namely that history represents true events.[95] Nevertheless, he explicitly concedes that a historian is usually limited by the facts: he compares ancient historiography to modern documentaries that add dramatic detail to enliven history.[96]

Woodman's contribution has been crucial in seeing rhetoric not as a problem, but as part of the very nature of ancient historiography.[97] Scholars have become more sensitive to how historians construct meaning instead of simply conveying facts, and it has been argued that what constitutes truth is relative to the specific historical position of author and audience.[98] This has implied a weakening of the very notion of truth, which as a relative category is supposed to be 'not subject to refutation'.[99] Implicitly, such views still presuppose the

[93] The use of *inventio* by early Roman historians had also been argued for by Wiseman 1979 and 1994.

[94] See Woodman 1988: ch. 2; Paschoud 1989, 1995, and 1997; Moles 1993; Wiseman 1993; Bosworth 2003; Zangara 2004; Bleckmann 2006 and 2010; Marincola 2009. For a good discussion of these issues for Medieval historiography, see Kempshall 2011: 4–9, 350–427.

[95] Blockley 2001; Bosworth 2003; Brodka 2007; Lendon 2009: 50.

[96] Woodman 1988: 92. For truth in history, see Avenarius 1956: 76–9.

[97] Cf. Laird 2009: 212.

[98] Fox 1996: 29–48; Laird 1999: 116–52.

[99] Laird 2009: 197. Fox 1996: 33 justifies his 'relativism' with reference to H.-G. Gadamer and P. Ricoeur—two philosophers who would, I suppose, not appreciate that label.

identification of the opposition between rhetoric and history with that between fiction and fact. The argument that truth is relative and irrefutable weakens the notion of 'fact' and hence opens up a much wider realm in which rhetoric, which we think of as creating fiction, can perform its part.

Such arguments correctly draw attention to one of the key issues in this debate, namely how we and the ancients understood historical truth. Yet the preceding discussion of Orosius suggests still another way of conceptualizing the relationship between rhetoric and history than the one just sketched. In ancient rhetorical theory the appeal to emotions was closely related to the third of the three traditional qualities of narrative, namely credibility (or verisimilitude), besides brevity and lucidity.[100] Quintilian notes that, even for some theorists, grandeur (*megaloprepeia*) was another virtue of narrative, and for still others *enargeia*.[101] For him, the latter is indeed an important quality of narrative, 'when a truth requires not only to be told but in a sense to be presented to the sight'.[102] All of these are important properties of narrative, depending on the occasion, but, for Quintilian, they can be classed under the traditional three headings: *enargeia*, for example, can go under lucidity.[103] Vividness and the display of emotions therefore do not distance the text from reality: on the contrary, they approach speech and reality by making the former conform to nature.[104] A vivid description 'sets out the whole event and as it were puts it before the eyes'.[105] When Orosius is thus writing in a rhetorical mode, this does not contradict his assertion, explored above in chapter 3, that he wishes to deconstruct the distorted rhetorical image of his contemporaries by having recourse to the true facts. Indeed, according to rhetorical theory, events vividly described help to show their real nature. Amplification and commiseration thus have their place in a work of history. Paradoxically, then, but only to the modern mind, rhetoric is a tool to represent reality

[100] *Rhetorica ad Herrenium* 1.14; Quintilian 4.2.31–2.

[101] See Cicero, *Topica* 97.

[102] Quintilian 4.2.64: cum quid veri non dicendum ses quodammodo etiam ostendum est.

[103] Quintilian 4.2.64.

[104] See Quintilian 6.2.27: in iis quae esse veri similia volemus, simis ipsi similes eorum qui vere patiuntur adfectibus. See also *Rhetorica ad Herrenium* 1.16.

[105] *Rhetorica ad Herrenium* 4.69: Statuit enim rem totam et prope ponit ante oculos.

better: Orosius would have felt unable to give a true sense of the facts had he not had the tool of *enargeia* at hand.

In the *Historiae*, and I would dare to suggest for many other ancient historians as well, 'reality' does not lie so much in describing the events exactly as they were, but rather in displaying them in such a way that the reader can feel present and experience them as if he were present. The measure of truth is not the simple correspondence of words to an external reality, but the correspondence of the recreated experience of the reader's perception with that of a real spectator. Referential truth is hence not absent in ancient historiography, but mediated through the reader's apperception of the events as presented in the narrative. Truth has to be created in the reader's mind, not in the text.[106] To phrase it differently: we tend to think of historical truth as the correspondence between the events as they happened in reality and their description by the historian. Orosius (or, not to give too much credit to him, Quintilian) suggests another correspondence. The text is only a mediator between the reader and the event, which aims at creating a contact as direct as possible between the reconstituted event and the reader. Helped by the text, the reader becomes, as it were, an eyewitness. This is more than a semantic (and pedantic) distinction, as shown by Orosius. His entire *Historiae* aim at challenging the mindset of his audience and opening its eyes through *pathos*. In this framework, one understands that the role of fiction in historiography is of limited importance. Quintilian does mention making details up as a possibility when aiming at a truthful, vivid narrative, but it remains subordinated to general truthfulness.[107] As such, rhetoric is a matter not of fiction, but of truth: it is a way of displaying reality, rather than distorting it. The relationship between rhetoric and history was conceptualized in various ways in Antiquity,[108] and Orosius' understanding of it can thus not be a priori extended to all ancient historians. Yet, I would like to suggest, it deserves attention in current discussions about this relationship among classicists.

[106] Cf. Morgan 1993: 184, commenting on Duris of Samos, one of the so-called tragic historians. This view is not entirely different from the one espoused by Pomian 1999: 59–78 regarding the role of fiction in contemporary historiography. Pomian's view is implicitly dependent on Collingwood 1946.

[107] Quintilian 8.3.62.

[108] Fox 2001.

Contrary to the tendency to separate Orosius off from ancient historiography, he can fruitfully be seen as exemplifying tendencies that are fundamental to ancient historiography in general. His apologetic tendency does not catapult the *Historiae* outside the realm of historiography; rather, it exacerbates and highlights general characteristics of the writing of history in Antiquity. Admittedly, Orosius is obviously a historian with an axe to grind and his agenda unsurprisingly affects the way he presents events.[109] But that is true for all ancient historians,[110] and it remains to be demonstrated that writing with a Christian bias is substantially different from writing with an Athenian, senatorial, Alexandrian, or Achaean bias, to the degree that it relegates one from the realm of ancient historiography. On the contrary, there is great profit in locating Orosius in the context of ancient historiography. His apologetic tendency makes him acutely sensitive for the rhetorical distortions of his pagan predecessors and he thus questions some of the silent presuppositions of the classical tradition, such as the suitability of rhetorical narrative to represent truly the events. At the same time, his critique on the rhetoric of history is fully rooted in that rhetoric itself. His reliance on *enargeia*, *oratio gravis*, and *pathos* trumps, as it were, previous histories: these rhetorical modes ensure, in his view, that his history possesses a greater verisimilitude than traditional narratives. Orosius believed, just as many of his predecessors, that rhetoric, ultimately, helps to represent the truth.

[109] See, e.g. Pardini 1988; Bessone 2000; Escribaño Paño 2007. Brandt 2010: 122 notes that, for Orosius, history serves as an argument, in contrast with classical history. But does history not serve as an argument in, say, Polybius and Tacitus?

[110] See, e.g. for Ammianus, most forcefully Paschoud 1989 and 1992. Accusations of bias are central to the polemical self-definition of historians: see Luce 1989.

6

A Past for the Present: On Metaphors and Panegyric

Just before the 600[1] made their final charge against Xerxes, Leonidas counselled them to 'eat as you will dine with the gods later'. Orosius comments:

> See, while he promised a better future, they [the contemporary pagans] ascertain that the past is better. Both detest their respective presents, and what can one conclude other than that either the present times are always good but badly appreciated or never better in all respects?[2]

This brief comment shows that Orosius' interest lies not just with the correct depiction of the past (or, for that matter, the future), but that he is concerned with the interpretation and appreciation of the present: both Leonidas, as an exemplum from the past, and contemporary pagans shift attention away from what matters most, the present. This intention is already clear in the general preface, where the pagans are characterized as those who, 'because they do not wish to know the future,[3] forget or ignore the past, and accuse the present' for being worse due to the decline of the pagan cult.[4] Orosius admits that 'to me, having often reflected on it, the disasters of the present times seemed to rage beyond measure'.[5] A more precise inspection of

[1] That is the number given by Orosius.

[2] Orosius 2.11.9: Prandete tamquam apud inferos cenaturi; 2.11.10: ecce cum ille promisit futura meliora, isti adserunt meliora praeterita, quid aliud colligi datur utroque in suis detestante praesentia, nisi aut semper bona esse sed ingrata aut numquam omnino meliora?

[3] i.e. because they refuse to be Christians and know the future life.

[4] Orosius 1.pr.9: qui cum futura non quaerant, praeterita autem aut obliuiscantur aut nesciant, praesenti a tamen tempora ueluti malis extra solitum infestatissima ob hoc solum quod creditur Christus et colitur Deus, idola autem minus coluntur, infamant.

[5] Orosius 1.pr.13: cui plerumque reputanti super modum exaestuauisse praesentium clades temporum uidebantur.

the past, however, proved otherwise. The frequent comparisons between past and present repeatedly remind the reader of Orosius' aim:[6] to get the reader to see the present through the right eyes. This is not an easy task, as Orosius sets out in the preface to book 4: the past is thought to be preferable because it is only present in words and distorted by them; the future is by default deemed superior because absent; present difficulties always seem more difficult because they are present.[7]

The previous chapters have taken a look at the rhetorical toolbox opened by Orosius in order to change the reader's perception of the past, and thus also of the present. The present chapter is concerned with two tools deployed in the *Historiae* to make more direct sense of the present: first, the various models and metaphors of historical development of which the 'four empire theory' is only the most explicit; and second, the use of panegyric in book 7, which elevates contemporary events above those of the past. Whereas the previous chapters focused primarily on the depiction of the past, this one explores how Orosius wishes his readers to understand the present.

I. MODELS FOR THE PRESENT: CYCLES AND LINES

Similarly to what we noticed for the bonfire of rhetoric analysed in the previous chapters, Orosius incorporates many of the metaphors historians and orators had used before him to describe the past: apart from the 'four empire theory' and its *translatio imperii*, he also compares states and historical developments to the human body,[8] illnesses,[9] human relationships,[10] the tidal movements of the sea,[11] and to the germination of seed.[12]

6 e.g. Orosius 3.2.12, 3.7, 5.1–2, 5.5.16, 5.11.6, 5.18.28–9, 5.22, 5.24.9.

7 Orosius 4.pr.2–3.

8 Polybius 1.3.3; Livy 2.32.9–12; Zosimus 4.21.

9 Herodotus 5.28; Livy 22.8.3–5; *Panegyrici latini* 2.3.3; Themistius, *Oratio* 15.186ab.

10 Herodotus 1.56; Tacitus, *Germania* 2.

11 Horace, *Carmina* 3.29; Prudentius, *Contra Symmachum* 2.429; cf. Orosius 6.14.1. For a review of such metaphors, see Demandt 1978 and 1980.

12 Salvianus, *De gubernatione* 7.49; Zosimus 2.34.2.

I have little to add, here, to the 'four empire theory' beyond my analysis in chapter 2,[13] except for one important point. The theory of four empires is explicitly cyclical, and in a very precise way: the empires go through the same stages, after identical intervals.[14] Orosius is unusually precise—as far as I know, no other *translatio imperii* was so specific in temporal terms—but with a definite purpose. As noted by A. Demandt, most cyclical models in Antiquity were not ineluctable or deterministic.[15] Not all individual states, for example, were completely subjected to Polybius' constitutional circle, as set out in his sixth book: Rome's mixed constitution provided a balance that avoided its succumbing to the forces that had captured other states. As one can see from this example, such historical models serve to make a point about the present, and, usually, the exceptional role of that present by showing how certain states do not conform to the expectations raised by the cycle. Polybius' constitutional cycle highlights the unique position of Rome as not going through the stages of the cycle. In Orosius, as we have seen, the 'four empire theory' performs a similar function. Rome is indeed exceptional in escaping the cycle of rise and decline, but only thanks to Christianity. It is here that Orosius' chronological accuracy comes into play: the exact sequence of, and parallelism between, the various empires is presented by Orosius as a proof of God's agency.[16] Only He can be responsible for such a precision. As a consequence, Rome's escape from the cycle must also be due to Christianity, which raised morality and influenced God to overlook his own decrees.

The 'four empire theory' is inextricably bound up with the metaphor of a lifespan to describe the empires.[17] They rise and fall, just as

[13] For earlier usages of the *translatio imperii*, see Dionysius of Halicarnassus, *Antiquities of Rome* 1.2, Sura apud Velleius Paterculus 1.6.6; Tertullian, *Ad nationes* 2.17.18; Minucius Felix 25.12; *Oracula Sibyllina* 3.158–161; Lactantius, *Institutiones* 7.15.13; Sulpicius Severus, *Chronica* 2.3. See Mazza 1999: 1–42. Augustine, *De civitate Dei* 12.14–18 explicitly rejects cyclical interpretations of the cosmos, as they contravene the Christian tenet of the eternity of the world. This critique cannot target the *Historiae*, where the cyclical elements relate to human history. Orosius also explicitly affirms that the world is created (1.1.2). Fear 2010a: 34 sees Orosius as reacting against a cyclical view in this passage, but he actually argues against the idea that the world is eternal.

[14] Cf. Orosius 2.2.10.

[15] Demandt 1978: 239.

[16] Orosius 2.1–3.

[17] This fact does not seem to be fully appreciated: compare Demandt 1978: 43.

a human life waxes and wanes. Just as states grow, they die.[18] As individual states can be described as having a lifespan, the various empires can also be said to be in a family relationship: Babylon and Rome are like an old father and a little son, and in between them stand Carthage and Macedonia as legal guardians.[19] Orosius probably drew his direct inspiration from Florus, whose preface is built around this comparison.[20] The comparison with human bodies that underpins the metaphor of a lifespan is regularly made explicit. Empires are like bodies: they have a head and the constituent parts can be their arms.[21] In Rome the senate is the head and the plebs the body,[22] and, just as all other states, Rome can become ill, suffer fevers, and die.[23] The comparison of a state, and Rome in particular, to a body and lifespan enjoyed considerable popularity in late Antiquity. In our extant literature it surfaces first, in an elaborated form, in (the younger or, more probably, the elder) Seneca,[24] then in Florus. In the fourth century it is picked up by Lactantius[25] and Ammianus, who develop it at length, and is referred to by the *Historia Augusta*,[26] Augustine, Ambrose, and Jerome.[27] Usually four ages are distinguished: childhood, adolescence, adulthood, and old age.

By its very nature, such a comparison conjures up decline: those who use it unavoidably situate themselves in the last phase of old age. It would be too easy, however, to conclude that it is by definition a pessimistic comparison. Whilst it obviously puts the end of Rome on the table, it is making a point about the present. In order to understand this, one has to take into account that a metaphor is a tool, that

[18] Orosius 2.4.15, 2.6.13, 7.2.2.

[19] Orosius 2.1.6; cf. 2.6.13.

[20] Orosius 2.4.15 identifies the early Republic as the *adulta aetas*; Florus, pr.7 calls this the *adulescentia*.

[21] Orosius 2.6.14, 3.12.33, 5.22.7. The metaphor can also be extended to the narrative of these empires, i.e. history: 1.1.13.

[22] Orosius 2.5.5.

[23] Orosius 3.8.2, 5.23.1, 6.12.2–3, 6.14.3, 7, 7.2.2.

[24] But see already Polybius 6.4.11, 28.22; Cicero, *De republica* 1.58, 2.21, 2.3, 3.34. Ps.-Hippodamus in Stobaeus 4.34.71.

[25] Lactantius, *Institutiones* 7.15.14–17 with Freund 2009: 410–44.

[26] Scriptores Historiae Augustae, *Vita Cari* 2–3.

[27] Augustine, *Sermo* 81.8 PL 38.504–5; Ambrose, *Epistula* 18.7; Symmachus, *Relatio* 3.9–10; Jerome, *Vita Malchi* 1. The metaphor of a lifespan is very popular among Church fathers for the ages of the world: see Luneau 1964. Galdi 2009 surveys some of the material. The metaphor can also be used for a spiritual journey (Augustine, *De vera religione* 49–50).

is, it is used for a given purpose in a specific context. As I have already argued for the 'four empire theory,' the *Lebensaltervergleich* is not a theory which makes definite statements about the essence of the past: it tries to make a point for the present. The key point is that the old age in which the author finds his state is established with the aim of overcoming it: the comparison is not a statement but an argument. In late Antiquity, the old age could be overcome in two ways: eschatological or panegyrical. The former attitude is exemplified in Lactantius, who pointedly includes the comparison in the last book of his *Institutiones*. That book discusses the aim of Christian life, namely the *vita beata* in Christ. It therefore also comprises a discussion of the end of time, which Lactantius sees as being close at hand. Indeed, Rome is already in old age: 'what is left, then, besides that death follows old age?'[28] He immediately continues with a detailed description of what the end of time will look like.[29] Roman old age is thus for Lactantius neither lamentable nor a state of distress: it is a fact of life which announces the proximity of the life to come. The panegyrical mode, in turn, is exemplified by the second-century historian Florus, the presumable source of both Ammianus and Orosius. Since Augustus, the empire has been aging and shrivelling. But 'under Trajan, it started to move her muscles and against all expectation, the old age of the empire regains forces as if its youth has returned'.[30] The metaphor thus allows Florus to construct the reign of Trajan as a paradoxical return to youth and vigour. The panegyric rests on the paradox: Trajan is not an emperor who simply continues the work of his predecessors and follows the course of history. He succeeds in doing what is biologically impossible.

These two basic modes can be developed into more complex figures. In Ammianus the comparison is not part of a programmatic passage, but inserted into the famous digression on the vices of Rome.[31] It thus forms part of the explanation why Ammianus can

[28] Lactantius, *Institutiones* 7.15.17: quid restat nisi ut sequatur interitus senectutem?

[29] Lactantius, *Institutiones* 7.15.14–17. See also Augustine, *De civitate Dei* 16.43, 22.30.

[30] Florus, pr.: A Caesare Augusto in saeculum nostrum haud multo minus anni ducenti, quibus inertia Caesarum quasi consenuit atque decoxit, nisi quod sub Traiano principe movit lacertos et praeter spem omnium senectus imperii quasi reddita iuventute reviserit.

[31] Demandt 1965: 14–21; Matthews 1989: 18–28, 185–228.

only talk about seditions, taverns, and vulgarities when discussing Rome. He depicts the current and last phase of Rome's history, the old age, as one of tranquillity after the imperialistic wars of the past. Since it has become an empire, the city has, 'like a thrifty parent, wise and wealthy, entrusted the management of her inheritance to the Caesars, as to her children'. The Roman Empire is depicted as essentially a reign of peace, both in terms of warfare and politics: 'throughout all regions and parts of the world, she is accepted as mistress and queen.'[32] Ammianus deliberately avoids the connotation of decline often associated with old age: rather, it is an age of respect and authority, acquired during the vigour of life. Indeed, whereas in the past the show of force was necessary to impose Rome's rule, now 'the white hair of the senators and their authority are revered and the name of the Roman people is respected and honoured'. Indeed, imperial Rome resembles the gentleman who withdraws to his country estate after years in the hustle and bustle of business and who leaves the daily dealings to his stewards—the emperors. Ammianus is obviously indebted to the panegyrical mode: he even suggests that Rome has returned to the peace of Numa (*Pompiliani securitas temporis*).[33] The noble character of Rome in its old age stands in marked contrast to the moral depravation of the current inhabitants of the capital (sed laeditur hic coetuum magnificus splendor levitate paucorum incondita, 14.6.7). Ammianus' long catalogue of contemporary sins has often been studied and does not need further elaboration here. One striking feature is, however, that it is not further integrated with the *Lebensaltervergleich* and it is left to the reader to draw the conclusions.[34] The stark juxtaposition of Roman vice and the dignity of the Roman Empire in old age clearly dissociates individual moral degeneration from imperial decline. Ammianus here stands in conscious contrast to Seneca and Florus, the latter of whom he surely knew: both explicitly associate the declining age

[32] Ammianus 14.6.5–6: velut frugi parens et prudens et dives Caesaribus tamquam liberis suis regenda patrimonii iura permisit. et olim licet otiosae sint tribus pacataeque centuriae et nulla suffragiorum certamina set Pompiliani redierit securitas temporis, per omnes tamen quotquot sunt partes terrarum, ut domina suscipitur et regina et ubique patrum reverenda cum auctoritate canities populique Romani nomen circumspectum et verecundum. Tr. Rolfe (LCL).

[33] Demandt 1965: 129; Drexler 1974: 155–65; Matthews 1986: 22. Barnes 1998: 142 seems to misinterpret the passage.

[34] Demandt 1965: 129–31.

of Rome with general moral decline. Ammianus, on the contrary, tries to contain the decline and limit it to individuals without conceding that the rot has spread to the fabric of the Roman Empire itself. In that way, he can at once permit himself harsh moral judgments on his contemporaries and harbour an idealistic image of eternal Rome.[35] Indeed, the chapter on the vices of Rome that includes the *Lebensaltervergleich* is very well attuned with the one after the battle of Adrianople, discussed in chapter 3, where Ammianus chides his contemporaries for their lack of culture and morality which induces them to think that Rome is about to fall. Rome is not about to fall, but it would help moral standards if the Romans looked more at the exempla of the past and lived up to the dignity of Rome.

Orosius gives an equally original twist to the metaphor. He is just as panegyrical as Ammianus, but, in contrast to his predecessor, he emphatically affirms the fall of Rome. In chapter 2, we have seen that Orosius consciously conjures up the possibility—and even historical necessity—of Rome's fall by his use of the 'four empire theory'. That this is also the implication of the *Lebensaltervergleich* is made clear in 2.6.13, where Orosius notes, with an authoritative quotation of Cicero, that all that is human will decline and fall.[36] The 'four empire theory' and the metaphor of the ages of man, always intertwined in Orosius, thus point to the same ineluctable conclusion: Rome is due to disappear. Orosius' panegyric therefore is not primarily about Rome. Whom it does regard, is easily found out. Just like Ammianus, Orosius suggests that his own age knows peace, but he explicitly attributes its cause to Christianity. In Orosius, it is not Augustus and his empire which prepares the peace in which Christ could be born: it is the empire which is elected by God to *be prepared* for Christ.[37] This is more than a semantic distinction: as we shall see in greater detail in the last chapter, agency in history is attributed by Orosius exclusively to God and to the Church, which can temper God's wrath. The peace and progress which Rome enjoys since

[35] Demandt 1965: 131 sees the contrast between morality in Rome and the *Lebensaltervergleich* as an 'Inkonsequenz', but I would suggest that it is actually Ammianus' intention to show the contrast. For Ammianus' moralism, see Demandt 1965: 13–98; Rosen 1970: *passim*; Barnes 1998: 143–66.

[36] Cicero, *Pro Marcello* 4.11. Cf. Augustine, *Sermo* 81.9 and 105.8.

[37] See, explicitly, Orosius 6.20.4: hoc autem fideliter commemorasse ideo par fuit, ut per omnia venturi Christi gratia praeparatum Caesaris imperium conprobetur.

Augustus is therefore due to God and not to the empire.[38] The empire is, after all, just a tool for God and his intentions. Orosius thus at once raises the Roman Empire, as a tool of God, and strips it of any real force and impact in history. Secular history is thus devalued in favour of ecclesiastical history. Just as in Florus, therefore, the peace of the present is paradoxical, but now not because of an exceptional emperor who can halt the course of history, but because of God, who, in his all-powerful benevolence, rewards his followers.

That true agency lies with Christianity, and that it is, in a sense, dissociated from Roman history can be sensed in the fact that Orosius prefers another metaphor to describe the rise of Christianity, namely that of sowing and growing.[39] Christianity is also comparable with the pleasant and soft morning light, in contrast with the full heat of noon which stands for all the evils of the world.[40] Whereas Rome is declining, Christianity is at its most fertile beginnings. The future lies with Christianity. The change in agency and perspective is clear in the fact that Orosius calls the present 'the Christian times' (*tempora Christiana*).[41]

Through his original elaboration of the *Lebensaltervergleich*, Orosius inserts himself well in the literature of his age. One notices repeatedly in late fourth-century authors a sense of decline[42] and a regular toying with the idea of Rome's fall.[43] Depictions of Rome in decline are, however, just a rhetorical ploy to highlight, for example, how suddenly Rome's grey hair becomes coloured and shiny again.[44] Orosius deliberately conjures up the same image of decline and

[38] See Orosius 6.1.6. See also Orosius 3.8.8. Orosius can be understood as correcting Vergil's depiction of Augustus as inaugurating a new Golden Age (*Aeneis* 1.289, 6.788–807): it is God, not Augustus, who is responsible for it.

[39] Orosius 6.17.5–8, 6.22.10, 7.2.15, 7.5.3, 7.6.8, 7.9.4. The comparison is also used, negatively, for the consequences of the civil war (6.17.5) or for sins generating war (7.33.9). Note also the comparison of wars with the tides (6.14.1): Demandt 1978: 171.

[40] Orosius 3.8.2, 8.

[41] Orosius 1.6.2, 1.20.6, 2.3.5, 3.8.3, 4.6.35, 5.11.6, 6.23.10, 7.8.4, 7.26.2, 7.33.16, 7.35.6, 7.43.16, 7.43.19: see Schöndorf 1952: 31. See also Augustine, *De civitate Dei* 18.27–36.

[42] Symmachus, *Epistula* 1.4.2; Claudian, *De bello gothic* 571–2, *De consulatu Stilichonis* 2.204–5, 3.106–29, *Panegyricus de sexto consulatu Honorii Augusti* 407–24; Scriptores Historiae Augustae, *Vita Cari* 2.6.

[43] Ammianus 31.13.11; Symmachus, *Relatio* 3.9; Claudian, *De bello Gildonico* 115; Prudentius, *Contra Symmachum* 2.716. Cf. Demandt 1980.

[44] Claudian, *De bello Gildonico* 208; Prudentius, *Contra Symmachum* 2.640–1, 655–7.

possible fall, and thus plays on existing sensibilities. But his answer is not the traditional panegyrical rejuvenation of Rome, found in both pagan and Christian poets of the fourth century, but an affirmation, which can be paralleled in other Christian authors,[45] of the superiority of Christian history over secular events, and thus, ultimately, of the superiority of Christianity. Orosius' originality lies in his defence of the historical necessity of the fall of Rome as a springboard to make an argument for the Christian power of salvation. The deferral of the fall of Rome demonstrates for him that Christianity is the driving force of history and that conversion to the true doctrine generates benefits for the world.[46]

II. PRESENT—NOT FUTURE

All these models—'four empire theory' *Lebensaltervergleich*, and biological metaphors—apply to historical time. This is in itself not remarkable, as they are precisely that: metaphors for history. It has, however, been argued that Orosius' vision extends into the future as well, precisely on the basis of these images. The argument has taken two opposite forms. The first is that Orosius' calculation of the lifespan of Rome and Babylon to 1,400 years implies a millenarian position. Millenarianism refers to the idea that the Second Coming can be precisely calculated. On the assumption that for Orosius Rome is the last empire, the determination of Rome's lifespan to 1,400 years situates the end of time in *ca.* 250 years from his own day. Given the striking absence of any explicit affirmation in that sense, scholars have argued that he was unable or unwilling to assume the implications of his own calculations.[47] The second way of putting this view is

[45] Sulpicius Severus, *Chronica* 2.14.7; Augustine, *De civitate Dei* 18.40; John of Beith-Aphthonia, *Vita Severi* p. 210.7.

[46] Orosius' implicit rejection of the idea of a rejuvenation of Rome, as found, e.g. in Prudentius, is similar to the views of Augustine. It has been argued that Augustine, faced with an aging and declining Rome, does not locate his hopes for rejuvenation in Rome, but in the individual: each individual is spiritually changed and prepared for eternal life, whereas physical life declines unavoidably: see *De vera religione* 26–7 with Häussler 1964: 335–7. For Orosius, the Church is the life-giving force, not secular Rome.

[47] Schöndorf 1952: 16; Corsini 1968: 139–51; Goetz 1980a: 71–80; Arnaud-Lindet 1990–1: i.l; Inglebert 1996: 575.

that Orosius' optimism sprawls into the future: with the Christian empire, the world is effectively becoming pacified, and, as a consequence, the millennium is already realized.[48] This second position has been restated by A. Fear in the form that Orosius is effectively 'post-millenarian', in the sense that he believes in the continuing improvement of the times.[49]

I do not think either position does justice to Orosius. While the former interpretation recognizes that the 'four empire theory' implies the fall of Rome, it does not notice the suspension of the course of history by God in Orosius' perspective. The latter acknowledges Christian optimism, but does not fully take into account that the improvement of the times is conditional on true Christian piety and not a self-evident fact of life.[50] Two basic assumptions of both positions also need to be questioned. First, it is usually stated that, for Orosius, Rome is the last empire that will endure until the Second Coming. Reference is then made to the 'four empire theory,' where Rome indeed assumes the last place. I would suggest this ascribes more to Orosius than he actually says. As I have argued in chapter 2, and earlier in this one, the 'four empire theory' has the very specific aim of making a point about the position of Rome in the present and should not be read as a statement of theology of history. Indeed, as we have just seen, Orosius explicitly indicates that Rome will have an end, without associating it with the end of time.[51] Whereas scholars have been forced to downplay this last remark in order to save the 'four empire theory,' the interpretation proposed in this book does justice to both.

The second assumption is that Orosius' theology of history extends to the end of time: he not only makes a point about the present, but also about the future. This idea ignores Orosius' explicit statements that the end of time is not a part of his history and falls beyond the scope of his work. The point is emphatically made twice, not by accident, in the preface to the first and the last book. The end of the preface to book 1 states that things went badly until the coming of

[48] Paschoud 1967: 283–4; Corsini 1968: 101–2, 154; Marrou 1970: 80: 'millénarisme déjà réalisé'; Brodka 1998: 201–2; Cobet 2009: 73–4. This is a concept first ascribed to Eusebius: see Sirinelli 1961: 483; Farina 1966: 116; Kinzig 1994: 550–3. See also Mir 1978 and Frend 1994.

[49] Fear 2005 and 2010b: 185.

[50] This is further detailed in chapter 8.

[51] Orosius 2.6.13.

Christianity, and that they have started to improve since then. Christianity has indeed chained the forces of evil, 'excepted, obviously, and excluded the last days, at the end of time and at the appearance of the antichrist, or, if one wishes, at the final judgement'. Then the christians will be tried by suffering that matches that of the days before the Incarnation.[52] In 7.3.11, Orosius quotes *Matthew* 24.6–9, where Jesus, in reply to his disciples asking what the end of time will look like, says that there will be wars in the future, but that these are not the end of time. This will be, in fact, much worse than anything they have ever seen. This quote is part of Orosius' argument, that with the Incarnation a great peace will spread across the empire. It allows him at once to fend off a possible counterargument, namely that there were still wars after Christ: Jesus himself predicted this. But by including the reference to the end of time as well, Orosius repeats the argument of the general preface: the end of time will be much worse and stands outside the development he traces in the *Historiae*. The general improvement of times is limited to historical time, in which the end of time is not included. The same point is made again in the famous typological identification of the ten Egyptian plagues with the punishment of the ten persecutors of Christianity. Having linked the ten plagues with specific persecutors, Orosius identifies the passage through the Red Sea with the final judgment. At that moment, all persecutors will be judged and damned. This reading implies that, just as the Egyptians continued to harass the Hebrews after the tenth plague and after having allowed them to leave Egypt, 'the persecution by the pagans will continue for some time' after the Christianization of the empire.[53] Orosius does not identify his own times with full peace; moreover, the end of time is not part of the scope of historical time, whereas the ten plagues and persecutions are. Orosius thus has a very clear conception of what his subject is—historical time—and what is included in it: it runs from Adam to the Antichrist, including the former but excluding the latter. This strict limitation to historical time is not surprising: Orosius explicitly wishes to combat the pagans with their own weapons and not to impose the authority of the Bible. The models he draws on are also taken from classical historiography and the uses to which he puts

[52] Orosius 1.pr.15: exceptis uidelicet semotisque illis diebus nouissimis sub fine saeculi et sub apparitione Antichristi uel etiam sub conclusione iudicii.

[53] Orosius 7.27.15: quandoque persecutio gentilium manet.

them, as we have seen, are similar to those found in Ammianus and earlier authors. There is thus nothing about millenarianism in the *Historiae*, because eschatology lies beyond its scope.

As was argued by R. Herzog, because Orosius writes a history for the present, his presentation of facts is entirely focused on making sense of the present. Given this apologetic aim, the *Historiae* are not prognostic, but at best diagnostic of present woes.[54] They explain how the present is what it is and how it stands in relation to the past, but do not go beyond that. One only looks for statements about the end of time if one defines Orosius in advance as a theologian of history.[55] Yet, as I have argued, this results in a distorted reading of Orosius which lifts the 'theory' out of the text and does not study how metaphors function within the text. That Orosius himself explicitly excludes the end of time from his scope is further support for my contention that we first have to understand him as a historian. Whilst the focus on Orosius' text may force us to rethink some widely held assumptions about his ideas, the preceding argument only makes him more ordinary. Given his emphasis on the omnipotence of God and his free agency in history, Orosius probably held the most traditional view on the end of time: we do not know when it will happen.

III. CONTEMPORARY HISTORY AS A PANEGYRIC OF GOD

The *Historiae* are thus not shaped by eschatological concerns nor do they naively expect the end of all troubles. Nevertheless, it is evident that the tone of the last chapters is very optimistic and should be described as panegyrical. In 7.36.12, Orosius indignantly refutes the idea that he might be lying—itself a panegyrical *topos*[56]—and a few chapters later (7.39.14) he rhetorically asks 'who can proclaim these miracles with suitable praises?'[57] Book 7 also lacks the rhetorical

[54] Herzog 2002: 316. See also Brandt 2009: 128.

[55] Goetz 1980a: 53, followed by Martínez Cavero 2002: 153, 163–4, misinterprets the passages discussed here to argue that the end of time is part of Orosius' history.

[56] See Pliny, *Panegyric* 72.5; Socrates, *Historia ecclesiastica* 7.22.1; Ennodius, *Opuscula* 1.78; Menander Protector fr. 4.6.

[57] Orosius 7.39.14: quis praedicare dignis laudis queat?

cadence of the other books: there is little alternation between descriptive and pathetic passages, with all the rhetoric concentrated in the last third of the book. It is thus clear that Orosius' tone has changed. From the portrait of Theodosius I onwards (7.43), one encounters all the traditional praise of contemporary panegyrics, such as the slaying of tyrants,[58] the suppression of uncouth barbarians,[59] and miraculous and bloodless ends to battles.[60] Concomitant, and equally unoriginal, emphases are on the piety of individual rulers[61] and the civilizing force of Rome and Christianity.[62] The question to be asked is, then, to whom is that panegyric addressed? Is it Rome and the empire as is often asserted?[63] As we shall see, this is only the case when these chapters are superficially read: in fact, they highlight the benefits of Christian virtue, but also serve to flaunt Orosius' close relationship with Augustine and to remind his primary audience, rich Romans having settled in Sicily and Africa, of the privileged position they enjoy thanks to God. It is, then, in the last chapters that the central concerns of the entire *Historiae* surface most explicitly: they aim, as it were, to deliver the final blow to the pagan argument that was already weakened by the preceding books and chapters and to draw its wavering audience finally into the Christian camp.

Before we can understand the crucial last chapters of the *Historiae*, we need to pause briefly in order to reflect on the relationship between panegyric and history. As Orosius' protestations of truthfulness in the context of the miraculous victory over Gildo demonstrate, the use of panegyrical *topoi* in history was pervasive but never self-evident. The relationship between history and panegyric was complex in Antiquity, and should not be reduced to its usual and most obvious formulation, namely that of the opposition of panegyric, the art of flattery, and history, the art of truth. This opposition is indeed part of the usual self-definition of ancient historians, also in late Antiquity,[64] and it has been noted that fourth-century historians often suggest that

[58] Orosius 7.42.1–4, 7.43.17.

[59] Orosius 7.42.6–8, 7.43.4–7.

[60] Orosius 7.35–8, 7.39.1–10.

[61] Orosius 7.42.15–17.

[62] Orosius 7.43. For parallels, see Ambrose, *De obitu Theodosii* 24.8, Claudian, *De sexto consulatu Honorii Augusti* 218–28; *Panegyrici latini* 2.32, 34, 3.18; Prudentius, *Contra Symmachum* 2.815.

[63] In a very radical expression of this view, Martelli 1982: 222–3, 226 calls Orosius a caesaropapist.

[64] Procopius, *Bella* 1.1.4; Agathias, *Historiae* pr. 11–13, 16–17; Menander Protector fr. 4.6.

one can discuss the reign of a dead emperor critically, but that the current ruler could only be praised in a panegyrical way.[65] Yet orators dared to strike back: Themistius derided history for preferring *doxa* over truth, whereas oratory essentially aimed at the latter.[66] Oppositions between panegyric, or more generally rhetoric, and history thus serve in the first place the self-definition of the practitioners of the respective arts: if anything, the intensity of the polemic suggests the closeness of both enterprises.[67] Indeed, Pacatus presents panegyric as a source of history[68] and many historians did indeed use panegyrical sources.[69] Given the social background of most historians in late Antiquity, who belonged to the elite and often served in imperial administration,[70] it is hardly surprising that likes and dislikes were explicitly and implicitly expressed, using tropes from the rhetoric of praise and blame. Protestations to truth and objectivity in histories can then be understood, not as expressing the existence of a rigid separation of rhetoric and history, but as suggesting that the historian, whatever views he has expressed in his work, did not stray beyond the boundaries of his art and remained true to the first duty of the historian.

If panegyric is neither necessarily nor completely alien to history, so was truth to rhetoric. The rhetoric of praise obviously pursues different aims than merely stating the facts, but praise was supposed to be directed at true virtue.[71] Whereas history had to address the complete picture, the rhetoric of praise was allowed to focus on the good aspects.[72] This obviously requires that one reads praise with an eye for its specific function and concomitant distortions. As expressed by R. Rees: 'Through the lens of panegyrical rhetoric, the contingent appears inexorable, what is tentative seems certain, expressions

[65] Eutropius 10.18.3; Jerome, *Chronica* pr.; Festus 30.1; Ammianus 31.16.9 (with Paschoud 2004 and Kelly 2008); Symmachus, *Epistula* 3.47. See in general, Paschoud 2005. Ps.-Aurelius Victor, *Epitome de Caesaribus* ends on a panegyric of Theodosius I.

[66] Themistius, *Oratio* 18.2–3. See also Procopius, *Anecdota* 1.1.5.

[67] See the papers in Whitby 1998.

[68] *Panegyric latini* 2.47.6.

[69] To cite but two examples: Ammianus relied on Julian and Libanius (cf. Sabbah 1978), and Socrates and Sozomen used Libanius, Julian, and Gregory of Nazianzus (Van Nuffelen 2004a).

[70] Harries 1986; Greatrex 2001.

[71] Themistius, *Oratio* 1.46–7.

[72] See, e.g. Plutarch, *Vita Cimonis* 2.2–5; Seneca, *Epistula* 94.39.

of hope give way to confident guarantees of fulfilment.'[73] He demonstrates well that panegyric was, or at least could be, a subtle art: praise could express specific concerns, and in the verbosity typical for the genre silences could be meaningful. Panegyric could be outright and simple flattery, but could also put issues on the table.

If, then, panegyric and history were not mutually exclusive and Orosius' recourse to tropes of the rhetoric or praise is not unique, a different set of questions comes to the fore. Rather than using the presence of panegyric to condemn Orosius as a historian, we should ask why his narrative becomes so panegyrical and what he actually meant by this. The most common explanation is not entirely satisfactory in my opinion. As the culmination of the *Historiae*, it is obvious that the panegyrical passages at the end pretend that the troubles of the present are less important than those of the past. Comparisons with the past are repeated with an intensity unseen in the rest of the work.[74] Noticing this, scholars have suggested that the last book testifies to a triumphant mood: for Orosius, it is argued, the Roman Empire enjoyed full peace, and history has come to an end.[75] While Orosius indeed strikes an optimistic note, such conclusions over-interpret what Orosius actually says: his claim of superiority for the *Christiana tempora* is relative, not absolute, as the following examples show. The typological reading of the ten plagues of Egypt as ten persecutions has often been read as an affirmation that the present is totally free of war and persecution, and then contrasted with Augustine's explicit refutation of such a typological reading and his affirmation that future persecutions are possible as well.[76] But, as we have just seen, Orosius repeatedly affirms that there will be wars after Diocletian, as well as persecutions. He also describes Constantius II, Athanaric, and Valens as persecutors, and Julian as having the ambition to be one.[77] Whilst Augustine may have thought of Orosius when criticizing the typology, Orosius does not pretend that 'the Church will suffer no further persecutions beyond the number she

[73] Rees 2002: 186. See in general Pernot 1993 on panegyric.

[74] Orosius 7.34.2, 5, 7.35.6–8, 20, 7.39.16–18, 7.41.2, 7.42.13, 7.43.16–18.

[75] Corsini 1968; Herzog 2002: 306.

[76] Augustine, *De civitate Dei* 18.52. See Mommsen 1959b: 346; Inglebert 1996: 490–2.

[77] Orosius 7.29.4 (*persecutio*), 7.30.4 (*persecuturus*), 7.32.9 (*persecutus*), 7.33.3 (*persecutionis*). In 7.34.8 Julian is a *persecutor*. Augustine also refers to Julian, Valens, and Athanaric: *De civitate Dei* 18.52.

has already undergone—namely ten—until the time of the Antichrist'.[78] On the contrary, Orosius draws a different conclusion from his typology: after the tenth persecution, Christianity will never be enslaved and forced to worship idols.[79] As the next sentences indicate, this does not mean the end of persecution, but rather a limit to their scope and success. This example shows that the object of Orosius' panegyric is not a naive denial of warfare and suffering in the present. Nor does he minimize the extent of the defeat in Adrianople,[80] and even in the last pages he employs the resources of rhetoric to describe the drama of the usurpations in the West after 410 in terms similar to those employed for periods before the Incarnation.[81] He adds in chapter 41: 'There would be ample occasion for me to talk about events of this kind, were it not that, according to all men, conscience secretly talks to the mind of each and everyone.'[82] Orosius here operates a return to the individual moral conscience of each of his readers. The sufferings of the present are indeed less than those of the past, he ensures his readers, but those that happen are due to the moral failure of each of us.[83] This emphasis on individual morality is repeated at the end of the work, where he states to have described 'the ambitions and punishments of sinful mankind'.[84] Orosius thus makes two, interrelated points: suffering is less now than in the past, and the mechanism is one of punishment for our individual sins.[85] The chapter even suggests that true Christians suffer less: they can go into exile, which is now possible due to the providential unity of the empire, and they can hire the invaders themselves

[78] Augustine, *De civitate Dei* 18.52: quod nonnullis uisum est uel uidetur, non amplius ecclesiam passuram persecutiones usque ad tempus Antichristi, quam quot iam passa est, id est decem.

[79] Orosius 7.27.14: hic numquam postea populus dei ad idolatriam coactus est.

[80] Orosius 7.33.16: Consoletur se, sed in hoc solo, peruicacia miseriaque gentilium, quia temporibus et regibus Christianis tantae simul congestae clades pressam reipublicae onerauere ceruicem: euersae prouinciae, deletus exercitus, imperator incensus. magnum reuera hoc est ad nostrum dolorem magisque miserum quo magis nouum.

[81] Orosius 7.40. He does notice the existence of peace in the East after 387 (7.34.8).

[82] Orosius 7.41.1: Multa nunc mihi de huiuscemodi rebus loquendi facultas foret, si non secundum omnes homines apud unius cuiusque mentem conscientia secreta loqueretur.

[83] Orosius 7.41.2–3.

[84] Orosius 7.43.19: cupiditates et punitiones hominum peccatorum.

[85] See also Orosius 7.33.16–19, where Orosius explicitly admits to his pagan adversaries that the battle of Adrianople was a great disaster. He does not try to diminish its importance, but points out that it is a punishment of Valens.

to serve and help them. Sinners and pagans, in turn, are crushed by the wrath of God.[86] In addition, the invasions lead to the conversion of the barbarians. But even so, 'what loss is there for a Christian, who aspires to life eternal, to be taken away from this age at whatever time and by whatever means?'[87] Pagans, in contrast, can stay a bit longer in this vale of tears as punishment. In chapter 41, the emphasis on man's individual conscience is thus accompanied by a shift away from earthly concerns to what is most important in a Christian's life: the eternal life.[88] Orosius does not suggest anywhere that sins are about to die out, and there is therefore nothing illogical in the fact that he does not try to hide the numerous usurpations and invasions of the early fifth century. The point is not that Christianity has rooted out all evils, but rather that their impact is less than what they would have been on pagan Rome. That difference in degree is due to the identification of the progress of Christianity with a moral improvement: indeed, one can say that true Christian virtue balances out the negative effect of vice. Improvement is not perfection, however: as long as we remain sinful individuals, we shall suffer in this life.

It is clear, then, that Orosius' panegyric does not pretend that times are absolutely good now, or that a reign of perfect peace is announcing itself: his point is that we now suffer less, that we know that our sins are to blame, and that, although Christians can hope for success in this life, the eternal life remains the most important. This is obviously amplified, to show to his adversaries the truth of the link between Christian piety and divine rewards. This is the crucial connection highlighted in the last chapters of the *Historiae* and it is also the central element in the depiction of the Roman emperors. Orosius' portrait of Theodosius, marking the beginning of the panegyrical last section,[89] is a good illustration. Christian emperors before Theodosius are discussed in a remarkably low-key manner: even Constantine does not get special treatment, with Orosius pointing to the emperor's less salubrious side and the murder of Crispus.[90] Theodosius I, on the contrary, is immediately compared with a traditional good emperor, Trajan, with whom he shared 'all human virtues' but whom he

[86] Orosius 7.41.4–7.
[87] Orosius 7.41.9: quid enim damni est Christiano ad uitam aeternam inhianti, huic saeculo quolibet tempore et quoquo pacto abstrahi?
[88] See already earlier Orosius 5.2.6 and 7.3.3.
[89] See Lippold 1976: ii.513.
[90] Orosius 7.28.26.

outshone in faith and devotion.[91] This indicates the line of argument on which the portrait of Theodosius is constructed: he achieves everything a good emperor of the past has achieved, but his human virtue is supported by what truly counts: faith. Although Orosius clearly has drawn on more sources, including the *consularia constantinopolitana* and Rufinus,[92] he also found inspiration in the panegyrical concluding chapter of book 5 of the *City of God*.[93] In line with Augustine, for example, Orosius focuses on Theodosius' suppression of the usurpers Maximus and Eugenius, earthly successes entirely attributed to prayer and supplication: Theodosius humbly puts all his faith only in God.[94] Just as Theodosius is for Augustine the ultimate example of how faith can be rewarded by God in contrast with the belief in idols, Orosius depicts Theodosius' successes as the proof of Christian superiority to which the pagans have no response: 'let them put forward one war since the foundation of Rome which was begun out of such pious necessity, undertaken with such divine felicity, and brought to a close with such benign clemency.'[95] The piety referred to is ancient *pietas*, indicating, among other things, family love: both Maximus and Eugenius were responsible for killing the junior emperors, for which Theodosius had—in the words of Orosius—paternal care.[96] The clemency is the one exercised by Theodosius after his victory, which Orosius does not mention but is included in Augustine.[97] The 'divine felicity' is probably prompted by another passage in Augustine's portrait of Theodosius, where he argues that:

[91] Orosius 7.34.3: cum in omnibus humanae uitae uirtutibus iste par fuerit, in fidei sacramento religionisque cultu sine ulla comparatione praecessit.

[92] Rufinus, *Historia ecclesiastica* 10.8, 10.13, 11.13–14, 17–19, 32–4 (*feliciter gubernato*): see Seeck and Veith 1913: 455; Jülicher 1915; Duval 1966; Courcelle 1969.

[93] Topical links are numerous: Augustine, *De civitate Dei* 5.26 p. 238.29: *paterno custodivit affectu*: Orosius 7.34.10: *paterna piutate susceptus*; Augustine, *De civitate Dei* 5.26 p. 239.11–14: *fide certus* . . . : Orosius 7.35.2: *sola fide maior* . . . ; Augustine, *De civitate Dei* 5.26 p. 239.8–9: Orosius 7.35.5, 10; Augustine, *De civitate Dei* 5.26 p. 239.16–17: Orosius 7.35.12; Augustine, *De civitate Dei* 5.26 p. 239.14–20: Orosius 7.35.18; Augustine, *De civitate Dei* 5.26 p. 239.21–4: Orosius 7.35.21; Augustine, *De civitate Dei* 5.26 p.6: Orosius 7.35.20.

[94] Orosius 7.35.14, 22.

[95] Orosius 7.35.20: unum aliquod ab initio urbis conditae bellum proferant tam pia necessitate susceptum, tam diuina felicitate confectum, tam clementi benignitate sopitum . . .

[96] Orosius 7.34.10.

[97] Augustine, *De civitate Dei* 5.26.

> these deeds, and similar ones which it would take too long to recall, are the good works that Theodosius bore with him from this temporal life, where the greatest of human attainment and exaltation is but smoke. The rewards of these works is eternal felicity (*aeterna felicitas*), which God gives only to those truly godly.[98]

Augustine obviously gives another meaning to the felicity than Orosius: he argues that human achievements count for nothing in the face of eternal salvation. Orosius' 'divine felicity', on the contrary, refers to the divine support Theodosius received in achieving his earthly *felicitas*. This inflection is indicative of Orosius' apologetic and historical focus in the panegyric: against the pagans he emphasizes Theodosius' temporal successes due to his faith.[99] In contrast with the *City of God*, where the example of Theodosius also serves to make a theological point about the primacy of eternal life, the *Historiae* shift the focus to temporal matters.

Theodosius sets an example. The suppression of the rebellion of Gildo by his brother Mascezil is obviously and explicitly calqued on the victories of Theodosius. While going to Africa from Rome, Mascezil stops over at the island of Capraia and gets the spiritual support of the monks there. An apparition of Ambrose of Milan, adapted by Orosius from Paulinus of Milan, indicates to him when and where he should give battle, with obvious miraculous results.[100] Yet Mascezil was not a true Theodosius: he dealt insolently with the Church and was punished by God. Orosius is the only one to report these facts, and their obvious vagueness may indicate a panegyrical amplification of the sudden death of Mascezil and his transformation into a stark reminder of God's power. The examples of Theodosius and Mascezil show that, for most of the last chapters, God is the only agent in the story: he judges, punishes, permits, and blocks human action.[101]

[98] Augustine, *De civitate Dei* 5.26: Haec ille secum et si qua similia, quae commemorare longum est, bona opera tulit ex isto temporali uapore cuiuslibet culminis et sublimitatis humanae; quorum operum merces est aeterna felicitas, cuius dator est Deus solis ueraciter piis. Tr. R.W. Dyson.

[99] Orosius 7.35.6–9. Similar portraits can be found in Prudentius, *Contra Symmachum* 1.410; Rufinus, *Historia ecclesiastica* 11.31–3.

[100] Orosius 7.35.12: sub tantorum miraculorum relatu. The use of Paulinus is another nod at Augustine, who used the life of Ambrose in his portrait of Theodosius: see chapter 4.

[101] An earlier passage shows very well how Orosius sees God as the most prominent agent in his own times. In 2.19 he compares the sack of 387 BC with that of AD 410. In

The engagement with Augustine is pervasive in the last chapters of book 7.[102] Not only is the portrait of Theodosius inspired by him, but Orosius also interprets the invasion of Radagaisus (405) and the sack of Rome by Alaric (410) exactly as Augustine did at the end of book 5 of the *City of God*: the pagan Radagaisus is soundly beaten as a sign that the cult of idols is vain, but God allows the Christian Alaric a bit later to take the city as a punishment for the pagans of Rome. In line with Augustine's argument that human virtue alone cannot achieve full felicity, Orosius demonstrates the inanity of human virtue in the person of Radagaisus, when it is not supported by true piety.[103] Many of Augustine's arguments, namely that Christian piety can be rewarded on earth (as shown by Theodosius), and that God punishes pagans (as shown by Radagaisus), are panegyrically enhanced and stressed by Orosius. Nevertheless, as we have seen, whereas Augustine highlights the ultimate importance of divine felicity, Orosius for panegyrical and apologetic reasons stresses earthly *felicitas*.[104] Yet Orosius operates, just as Augustine does in books 3–5 of the *City of God*, a devaluation of human *virtus*: mankind may achieve something but ultimately fails without divine support. At the same time, just as Augustine, he ends on a panegyric of God's omnipotence.[105] Indeed, with the strong emphasis on the mechanism of sin and punishment, it is hard to read the last chapters as a praise of the eternity of Rome, or even the power of Rome: rather, with God being promoted to the ultimate actor, it is a praise of His benevolence and omnipotence. God rewards piety and punishes blasphemy—not just of emperors, but of all of us. Orosius' description of Theodosius underscores that the emperor knows whom his successes are due to: God who rewards his personal piety. Alaric is depicted as a tool of God, in that his sack is a benign punishment which spares the Christians and is far less bad

the latter, God is the main agent rather than mankind, as shown by the fact that God accomplished what his envoys, Alaric's Goths, could not: a thunder bolt destroyed the pagan images on the forum, which had been spared by the fires of the city (2.19.14–15: in hac clade praesenti plus deum savisse, homines minus).

[102] But it is often not appreciated: see Lacroix 1965: 61; Fainck 1951: 142; Arnaud-Lindet 1990–1: i.298–9; Inglebert 1996: 509, 514, 562. More positive are Corsini 1968: 197; Hingst 1972: 67–9; Lippold 1976: i.xxxv; Goetz 1980a: 26–7; Martínez Cavero 2002: 150–4 although they do not notice the links in the last chapters.

[103] Orosius 7.37.5: indomitamque virtutem.

[104] Orosius 7.42.15, 7.43.16.

[105] I am at present only concerned with the inspiration Orosius found in the *City of God*. Chapter 8 explores the differences that surely exist.

than the fire of Nero or the sack of 387 BC.[106] The sack even has a long-term benefit: Placidia, taken as a hostage and wife by Athaulf 'as if by divine judgment',[107] is depicted in the last chapter as the individual who inspired the barbarian to seek reconciliation with the empire—a policy that was pursued by his successor Vallia.[108] In Orosius' panegyric, human action seems to be eclipsed by divine action. Indeed, after Theodosius, no single individual assumes a historical personality that is more than a tool in God's hands. The closest one gets to an individual who seems to be able to exert influence on history, is the count Constantius, who is depicted as a true actor under the reign of Honorius.[109] The individual disappears in favour of a praise of God. This conclusion is hardly surprising: it fits very well with Orosius' conviction, as we have seen in chapter 2, that Rome survives only because of God's suspension of the course of history out of favour for the piety and probity of the Christians.

We can now see whom Orosius' rhetoric of praise really regards: not divine peace, not eternal Rome, not the emperor, but God. It is His omnipotence, and His rewards for true piety, that the last chapters underscore. Thus, even the panegyric of the last chapters does not do away with the conditionality of current success: as long as we remain true to God's commandments, He will take care of us.

The last chapters fulfil another role too: they allow Orosius to engage in a well-studied attempt at authorial self-presentation. The close engagement with the *City of God* and the adoption of Augustine's interpretation of Theodosius and of the Radagaisus-episode may seem obvious in work commanded by the bishop of Hippo. There is another nod at the *City of God* as well: Orosius praises Marcellinus, the dedicatee of the *City of God*, and narrates his unjust dead and the punishment of the culprit.[110] All of this prepares the concluding statement of the *Historiae*: 'The quality of my little works, you, who have commanded them, will have seen to that. If you publish them, they will have to be attributed to you, if you destroy

[106] Orosius 7.38–9. See Augustine, *De civitate Dei* 1.1, 1.7, 5.23.

[107] Orosius 7.40.2: quasi eam divino iudicio velut speciale pignus obsidem Roma tradiderit.

[108] Orosius 7.43.7–15.

[109] See Orosius 7.42.15. I fail to see how the end of book 7 could be a panegyric of Honorius, as he is only twice referred to and his piety only briefly and vaguely praised (pace Inglebert 1996: 565).

[110] Orosius 7.42.16–17.

them, they will have been judged by you.'[111] Just as in the preface, Orosius hands over authorship to Augustine—as his dependence on the *City of God* had already demonstrated—but also gives a stamp of quality on his own work: any reader that comes across the work will know it has been approved of by Augustine. An astute reader, who has read the *City of God*, will even notice the parallels and contacts.

Orosius not only associates himself with Augustine, but also with that other luminary of early fifth-century Christianity: Jerome. Indeed, in the last chapter he presents himself as eye-witness to a story told by an anonymous Gaul to Jerome about the conversion of Athaulf from an enemy of Rome to its friend.[112] Identifications of this person have been proposed,[113] but the historicity of the story is hardly relevant: the joyful fact of Athaulf's change of heart is guaranteed by the authority of the author and Jerome. The closing chapters of book 7 engage in even more than authorial self-presentation: Orosius, for a last time, implicitly addresses his target audience. The desire of the new Gothic leader, Vallia, to sue for peace with Honorius is attributed explicitly to the fear that the double, and divinely ordained, disaster of the calamitous Gothic attempt to cross to Africa in 415, and the unsuccessful crossing of Alaric to Sicily in 410, inspired.[114] Orosius here reminds his primary audience of rich Romans who had fled to Sicily and Africa, of their privileged position: they are, as it were, divinely protected—maybe not for their own merits, but surely for those of their Christian compatriots, as the preceding demonstration of Christian virtue and divine intervention has amply shown.

The concluding chapters of book 7 are thus a very rich text: it is at once a panegyric of God and the *christiana tempora*, and a reminder of the importance of individual morality, with the latter identified with Christian piety. Rome as a significant historical entity almost disappears in the yawning gap between both: God and the individual human being take control of history, the latter by sinning, the former by punishing. The last chapters are also an engagement with Augustinian themes, with a similar proof of the inanity

[111] Orosius 7.43.20: de qualitate autem opusculorum tu uideris qui praecepisti, tibi adiudicanda si edas, per te iudicata si deleas. Such a transferral of authorship and authority from author to dedicatee can be found elsewhere. See, e.g. Ausonius XIX (*Epigrammata*).1.1.

[112] Orosius 7.43.4–8.

[113] Lippold 1976: ii. 531; Frye 1991 and 1994.

[114] Orosius 7.43.11–12.

of human virtue on its own, but, for panegyrical purposes and genre-conventions, a stronger emphasis on the earthly success that true piety brings than one finds in Augustine. Nevertheless, Orosius does not forget to stress, like Augustine, that the eternal life is the true aim of a Christian. It has, finally, also a socio-literary aim: Orosius reminds the reader of his association with Augustine and Jerome, and thus of the quality of his work. The reminder of the divine safety accorded to Sicily and Africa, where Orosius would have found his primary readership, ties these various strands together: whether his doubting readers like it or not, the historical proof shows that God safeguards these parts of the empire because of the piety of the Christians living there. If they wish to survive as Romans, they should put their trust in God rather than in the historical entity that is Rome.

IV. PANEGYRIC AND HISTORY

As such, the last chapters form a fitting conclusion to the *Historiae*: as we have seen, the whole of the work challenges the traditional perception of the past in order to open the eyes of his audience to the true nature of the present. Earlier books had aimed at destabilizing the view of Roman history as a glorious and exemplary one. Highlighting the benefits of Christianity for Roman society, book 7 builds up towards its final sections, where the alternative view of the present is set out. The message presented there, with its emphasis on God's response to our individual sins and virtues, develops a theme that is persistently present in the entire work. Given the apologetic need to contrast the present with the past, one cannot be surprised that Orosius has recourse to the rhetoric of praise to drive home his point. It may seem an unhistorical way of proceeding to us, but, as I have argued above, the presence of panegyrical tropes in ancient historiography is not unique or uncommon.

In fact, the ways in which Orosius tries to convey his view of the present to his readers are rooted in ancient historiography. None of the metaphors he uses is peculiar to him, nor is the panegyrical end of the *Historiae* an innovation. His exclusion of eschatology from history shows that it was his choice to remain within the limits of the genre and not introduce explicitly theological reflections in his narrative. His history is concerned with historical time, and makes a point about the present, not one about the future. The construction of the narrative is hence the context in which we should understand Orosius. As the previous pages have shown, this does not mean that the *Historiae* do not have a strongly Christian message. The *Lebensaltervergleich* and the concluding panegyric both aim at demonstrating God's omnipotence and the power of Christian virtue. But that message is conveyed through the construction of a historical narrative that explicitly understands itself as such, and not through a theoretical treatise on the meaning of history. The argument of this chapter, and indeed this entire book, is that we must take this self-understanding seriously and read Orosius as he presents himself, namely as a historian.

The clearly moral nature of Orosius' message is obviously not specifically Christian; the prefaces of Sallust, Livy, and Tacitus, for example, are replete with moral assessments of their times and moral injunctions. Yet the gearing of the writing of the past to the apologetic aim of the present, namely showing the pagans that their survival is due to Christianity, does have an original and important consequence. The identification of God and the sins of the individuals as the main agents of history tend to despoil of its significance what the ancients considered the true focus of history: actions by leading individuals. As we noticed above, the end of the *Historiae* is characterized by individual agency fading away in favour of a divine one. The *Historiae* thus downplay the role of the traditional subject of history, not by treating different subjects but by limiting their importance. As Orosius' own insistence on individual morality shows, this is not to be understood as a theoretical affirmation of the overriding power of God's divine plan. Rather, the force of his argument makes Orosius, once more, explore the boundaries of the genre.

The rather dim appreciation of the *Historiae* is to an important degree due to the two narrative tools studied in this chapter. The metaphors have often been interpreted in a theoretical sense and used to reconstruct a theology of history, which is seen as distracting from the correct narration of events. The panegyric towards the end of the work is, in turn, seen as naive. For a historian, the *Historiae* can be a very frustrating work. On the one hand, the sections that focus on the actions of leading individuals and thus conform to our expectations of history, do not offer anything of unique interest, as they derive largely from known sources. On the other, the very end of the work, where Orosius offers information that one finds nowhere else, swamps the facts in a panegyric of God. He is thus unoriginal when informative and uninformative when original. Orosius will always remain a defective source for the confused early decades of the fifth century, but this chapter, and indeed this book, has argued that we should not explain this by a lack of skill on his part. Rather, we should read the *Historiae* in their entirety and interpret specific passages in the context of the entire narrative. The concluding sections are, as I have suggested, a complex tissue of intersecting strands of argument, which defend at once Christianity and Orosius' standing as an author. Moreover, panegyric creeps into many a history in Antiquity. Ultimately, the peaceful vision of his own times presented by Ammianus in the digression on Rome is very similar to Orosius in its disregard for contemporary troubles. Neither ignores these events, but they accord little value to them: for Ammianus, they do not make imperial Rome stray from its eternal civilizing path, whereas Orosius sees them as the consequence of the permanent presence of vice in an imperfect world. Modern scholars usually allow Ammianus to redeem himself by his acute observations of present woes elsewhere in his work. No such indulgence is forthcoming for Orosius, who has had the bad luck of being optimistic just before what we see as the final crash of the empire in the West. I do not wish to claim Ammianus' status for Orosius. But the fact that one can parallel both in many a respect shows that both belong to the same cultural environment, even if they are rarely mentioned in one and the same sentence.

7

Beyond Rome: Universal History and the Barbarian

In the previous chapter I have proposed to understand the last pages of the *Historiae* as a panegyric of God. Barbarian invaders obviously figure prominently in them, being responsible for at least part of the troubles of the empire in the first decades of the fifth century. Scholarship has long sought to establish Orosius' precise views of the barbarians, but interest in this theme seems to have waned in recent years. This is probably due to the dominance of a 'Romanist' paradigm in the study of late Antiquity, which has tended to understand the changes in this period as the result of internal transformations rather than the catastrophic impact of barbarian invasions that is typical for the so-called 'Germanist' position.[1] Orosius' supposed interest in barbarians has not only been explained with reference to the events of his own time. His history is usually characterized as universal, both in space and in time, a view that, in contrast with the discussion of his views of barbarians, is still central to scholarship.[2] This is, at first sight, borne out by Orosius' own statements: the affirmation that he will cover history from the creation of the world to his own time, is followed by a long and famous description of the entire world.[3] For a universal historian, interest in peoples other than the Romans may seem natural.

In this chapter I take issue with both views. Characterizing the *Historiae* as a universal history is misleading, as, in my opinion, his claims to universalism are mainly rhetorical. Rather, as I have

[1] For these positions, see Pohl 2008; Wickham 2004: ch. 1.

[2] See, e.g. these recent studies: Martínez Cavero 2002: 160–1, 199; Allan 2003; Zecchini 2003; Alonso-Núñez 2005; Brandt 2009: 121; Sehlmeyer 2009: 302; Kempshall 2011: 64. I have done so myself in Van Nuffelen 2010: 172.

[3] Orosius 1.1.14 and 1.2.

suggested above, Rome and Roman history lie at the heart of the *Historiae*, even when important chunks of the text deal with Greek and Hellenistic history.[4] The pretension to universalism helps Orosius to challenge the traditional, glorious romanocentric view of the past that was inculcated in the schools of rhetoric across the Roman Empire, but that view remains the core of the *Historiae*. Similarly, the barbarians do not play an independent role in the work. Rather, they are support actors who allow Orosius to foreground the moral relationship of every individual with God. Just as in classical historiography, the barbarian is a malleable figure who usually serves to establish a positive or negative contrast, he helps to bring out the central message of the *Historiae*.

I. WORLDWIDE PERSPECTIVES

Universalism is a slippery concept. For the ancient world, it has been ascribed to historians who cover the history of mankind from the earliest times and for the entire known world.[5] Yet, in a recent collected volume, edited by P. Liddel and A. Fear, a universal intention is attributed to all historians who looked beyond the narrow confines of their own particular region—in fact expanding the concept even to national historians such as the Roman annalists.[6] One senses the difficulty of providing an essential definition for what was, originally, a polemical opposition: in order to emphasize the superiority of his own history, Polybius contrasted the wide scope of his work, including the Hellenistic empires and Rome, with the more limited subject matter of earlier historians.[7] As Liddel and Fear seem to suggest, universalism is more easily pretended to than actually put into practice. Given its vague nature, it is hence imperative to ask what is meant when the label 'universalist' is used. In the context of late antique historiography, it can mean two different things, sometimes at the same time.

First, the term can be taken to suggest that Orosius belongs to a subgenre of ancient historiography.[8] As is well known, especially in

[4] See also Fear 2010a: 20. [5] Alonso-Núñez 2002: 173.

[6] Cornell, Fear, and Liddel 2010. [7] Polybius 1.1–3.

[8] Merrills 2005: 44; Cobet 2009: 62–3. For a similar claim of continuity between Christian chronicle writing and universal history, see Roberto 2006, effectively rebutted by Burgess 2006.

the later Hellenistic period and during the early Roman Empire, many universal histories were composed, at a time when Rome conquered the Mediterranean and the various local histories became intertwined.[9] Examples are Diodorus of Sicily and Pompeius Trogus, of whom an epitome was used by Orosius. This is a problematic view. Universal history never was a subgenre but rather a possible mode of ancient historiography: just as tragic history is not a subgenre but a form historiography could assume depending on the specific aims of the historian, these aims, such as demonstrating the interdependency of Rome and the Hellenistic empires, could lead him to expanding his scope. But, as is shown by the fact that one can ascribe universalism to Herodotus and the Roman annalists alike,[10] there was not one particular form or genre in which it could find expression. Genre presupposes, moreover, some form of direct continuity, that is, Orosius would then be supposed to have found inspiration in the way earlier universal histories were written. Such continuity is hard to establish. Except for the use of Justin's summary of Pompeius Trogus, Orosius has no contacts with the tradition: in fact, his sources are the great classics of Roman historiography and the *breviaria* that were used in schools of rhetoric. In fact, as we have seen, his use of Justin was also conditioned by the fact that the epitome probably was composed for orators. As argued throughout this book, it is in that context that we should situate Orosius.

Second and more commonly, universality is advanced as a defining feature of Christian historiography, on the basis that the Christian view of the world gives a universal outlook to its understanding of history.[11] Two elements in particular are singled out in this respect: the universal intention of God's plan of salvation and the linear development of Christian time from Creation via Incarnation to the Second Coming.[12] God's message, and history as the record of it, is meant for all people of all times. All history written by Christians is thus at least potentially universal, especially chronicles and church

[9] For orientation, see Alonso-Núñez 2002; Yarrow 2006; Marincola 2007, all with references to earlier literature.

[10] Cornell, Fear, and Liddel 2010; Cornell 2010.

[11] See, e.g. Allan 2003: 17: 'The practice of universal history from AD 300 to 1000 reflects basic tenets and wider concerns of Christian belief.'

[12] Dawson 1977: 30–7; Latourelle 1977: 75–7; Luiselli 1980; Goetz 1991: 247; Wallraff 2004 and 2005: 4.

history, the two specifically Christian forms of historiography.[13] In this perspective, Orosius is universal because he is Christian: what is unique, is that he applies Christian universalism to secular history. Such an understanding of Christian universalism reinforces the traditional view of Orosius as a theologian disguised as historian. Indeed, it presupposes that theological considerations determine how a Christian writes history. As a consequence, it is often suggested that there is little difference between a Christian work of history and a Christian theology of history. The ground for this identification is that, although Christians may use different genres, all these are understood as having the same aim: defending the Christian theology of history. Even heresiology has recently been diagnosed as universal history.[14] Such a list could be expanded *ad libidem* given the reasoning behind it. Because the Christian world view is assumed to be universal and to underpin everything a Christian says about the past, present, and future, there does not seem to be a difference between the writing of history and a theology of history. And if the latter is universal by essence, the former must be so as well, at least potentially if not in act. Everything a Christian says about the present and past is thus universal.

I have argued elsewhere that this view is misleading.[15] Christian theology does have some universal aspects, but one should not forget that for much of its early history, Christianity understood itself as a community of the elect. If there was a focus of God's dealings with history, it was that limited community, not the rest of mankind.[16] It is not by accident that an important strand of early Christianity saw itself as a 'third people', besides the Jews and 'pagans'.[17] Thus, rather than harbouring a simple universalism, Christianity was characterized by a tension between, on the one hand, the idea of a universal spread of Christ's message and, on the other, that of a salvation restricted to the adherents of the faith. Moreover, there exists an important contrast between the universalism of Christian historiography as it is assumed on a theological plane and its very limited

[13] den Boer 1961; Goffart 1987: 3–4; Timpe 2001: 108; Wallraff 2004: 153; Ilski 2007.

[14] Schott 2007.

[15] Van Nuffelen 2010.

[16] See the brief remark by Inglebert 2001: 464.

[17] For the example of Eusebius of Caesarea, see now A. Johnson 2006. An emphasis on the universal aspects of Christianity can be found in Schott 2008.

expression in actual histories. Very few works of history actually do what is supposedly the essence of Christian history. Even the so-called universal chronicles are often not very universal at all: the recent events they add tend to focus on provincial matters, whilst the rest is a traditional narrative inherited from their predecessors.[18] Chronicles rarely have a truly universal vision: the heritage of Eusebian apologetic transmitted through genre conventions makes them only look as such.

My criticism does not regard the concept of universalism itself, but rather the essentialism that is attached to it in the two ways it is used: the *Historiae* are not universal because they cannot belong to a subgenre that did not exist, nor are they universal because it is a Christian work of history. In fact, Orosius does not label his own history universal and it is thus misleading for us to do so. Yet, our discussion should not end here. The more fruitful exploration of this issue is, it seems to me, to return to my earlier remark about Polybius and to ask what the function is of the rhetorical claim to universalism in the *Historiae*, as expressed in the geographical chapter that opens the *Historiae*. For, although there is no explicit claim to universalism, that chapter clearly suggests a wider than usual scope for the work. Why does Orosius do so?

The most cogent case for the universalism of Orosius and the role of geography played in it has been made by A. Merrills: 'Perhaps more than any other concept, universality provides the dominant motif within all of Orosius' historical writing, whether spatial or temporal in its emphasis.'[19] He singles out in particular the 'four empire theory', which not only offers an explanation for the course of human history, but also challenges 'Romano-centric models of history',[20] besides the geographical introduction, which was intended as 'an implicit demonstration of the breadth of the Christian world'.[21] Earlier in his introduction, Merrills recognizes the rhetorical function of geographical digressions,[22] and it is that aspect that I wish to emphasize

[18] Goetz 1991 makes the same argument for the medieval 'universal' chronicle.

[19] Merrills 2005: 98. He is followed by Brandt 2009: 123. Earlier discussions of Orosius' universalism include Schöndorf 1952: 73; Corsini 1968: 73–83; Goetz 1980a: 12–13; Chesnut 1992: 698.

[20] Merrills 2005: 50–64 and 98 (quote).

[21] Merrills 2005: 64–97.

[22] Merrills 2005: 11, 48.

over the suggestion that Orosius actually develops universal history to contrast with more traditional approaches to history.

Although Merrills makes a strong case for seeing geographical universalism as the basis on which the *Historiae* rest, it remains a fact that they rhetorically suggest universalism more than actually put it into practice. It has been noticed by Y. Janvier that the geographical digression in 1.2 is not integrated in the rest of the work: numerous place names are in the history but not in the geography (and the other way round), whilst Orosius regularly uses different place names in the geographical chapter and in the history proper.[23] Most regions, however, are hardly ever mentioned again. In fact, the *Historiae* soon mutate into an overview of traditional Greco-Roman history, with, as I have argued in chapter 2, Roman history at its heart, and they leave universalism for what it is. Indeed, if a claim to universalism in contrast with the limited nature of traditional Romanocentric history would be the core of Orosius' enterprise, one would expect the universal perspective to be more prominent throughout the work and especially in book 7, which brings out the message of the *Historiae* most forcefully. In fact, as we have noticed in the previous chapter, book 7 is the narrowest of Roman histories, formally resembling very much the *breviaria* that set out the reigns of the emperors. As this book has argued, Orosius challenges Roman history from within, not by offering the *Historiae* as an alternative set of events: the facts he narrates are those that his audience would have been familiar with from the traditional works of history they had read and, although focused on Roman history, they touched on Near-Eastern, Egyptian, and Greek history too.[24] The suggestion that Orosius' universalism would expand the set of events he narrates is thus not borne out by his actual practice. Moreover, it is hard to see how the 'four empire theory' could challenge romanocentrism, as it had in the past also functioned to emphasize Rome as the last and greatest of the empires. I would therefore argue that the description of the world at the very start of the work, as well as the repeated brief references to the entire world throughout the work,[25] perform a specific rhetorical function: located

[23] Janvier 1982: 139. See also Fear 2010a: 16. On the geographical chapter, see also Klotz 1930 and 1931. In an interesting parallel with Orosius, the sixth-century Syriac historian Pseudo-Zachariah concludes his work with a description of the world (12.7).

[24] See Felmy 2001; Eigler 2003.

[25] Orosius 1.1.14, 1.21.20, 2.5.10, 2.18.4, 3.8.5, 5.1.3, 6.21.19–20.

at the very beginning of the work, the geography serves to remind the reader of the extension of the world and hence of the vastness of past suffering, which can be contrasted with the improvement since Christianity. I have earlier characterized the *Historiae* as a synecdoche of reality: only parts of the horrors of the past are narrated and the reader is expected to consider for himself how much more is left out. The geographical introduction contributes to that as well: it suggests the vastness of the world and hence the vastness of pain and terror. Recurring references to the world keep that impression alive.

I would, thus, concur with Merrills that geographical universalism performs an important rhetorical role in the *Historiae* and that it helps to question the traditional view of the past which was evidently romanocentric. But I think it misleading to put universalism at the heart of one's analysis of the work: the suggestion of worldwide suffering is one of the rhetorical techniques deployed by Orosius to overturn the traditional elite view of the past from within. It comes, admittedly, at the very beginning of the work and hence may make a strong impression on the reader. But it is also evident to the reader that universalism fades away in favour of a focus on mainly traditional Roman history. In fact, although the suggestion of universalism helps to destabilize the glorious narrative that determined the elite view of the past, Orosius' rhetorical universalism does not constitute an alternative to their romanocentric view, for he does not introduce a different selection of facts. The events he narrates remain those the Roman elite had read and studied in the school of rhetoric. Indeed, as I have argued throughout this book, Orosius positions himself on the playing field of his opponents.

II. BARBARIANS IN CONTRAST

Orosius' optimism in the face of the disintegration of the empire has been one of the reasons for his condemnation as a short-sighted historian, not to say *idéologue*. Scholars have indeed often asked whether he believed that the barbarians could be integrated into the empire or if he considered the barbarians a fundamental threat to the future of Rome. The answers have been very diverse. Some scholars have detected a positive view of the barbarians,[26] others a categorically negative one.[27] More subtle analyses have drawn attention to the fact that Orosius seems to appreciate Christian barbarians more than pagan ones, and have hence concluded the existence of a tension between Orosius' Roman identity and his Christian one, albeit that the former is deemed stronger.[28]

As noted earlier in this chapter, the interest for this issue has waned[29] because the scholarly context has changed in favour of an understanding of late Antiquity in which the invasions—if that term is permitted—play a less central role.[30] In fact, there are good reasons for not asking the question in the terms it used to be. Framed as a question about the convictions of Orosius, the entire discussion is based on a reading of the *Historiae* not as a work of history, but as a political pamphlet, justifying the construction of a coherent view out of dispersed remarks. In line with the general approach espoused in this book, I wish to pick up this traditional issue in a different way, that is, by asking what function the barbarians perform in the narrative. Indeed, if my contention is correct that the *Historiae* aim at bringing about a better understanding of the Roman past and present by the Roman elite, and if Orosius indeed refocuses the understanding of history on the relationship between God and the individual, then the barbarians play, at best, an accessory role in the narrative, and one that, moreover, need not be consistent in every aspect. To put it differently: rather than construing a coherent image of 'the' barbarian, Orosius takes part in the habits of ancient historiography of shaping the barbarian in function of the narrative.[31]

In his tenth oration the Constantinopolitan orator Themistius contrasts the barbarians with Rome: the former are driven by their insatiable desires whereas Rome stands for rationality and order.[32] Commenting on this passage, P. Heather has noted the endurance of

[26] Schöndorf 1952: 62–4; Diesner 1963: 102; Brodka 1998: 209.

[27] Paschoud 1967: 287.

[28] Lippold 1952 and 1969; Goetz 1980b. See also Marchetta 1987; Martínez Cavero 2002: 255–78.

[29] Fear 2010a, for example, does not address the issue.

[30] Recently, Ward-Perkins 2005 and Heather 2009 have reacted explicitly against the current rather 'irenic' picture.

[31] Literature on 'the' barbarians is vast. Useful remain Dauge 1981 and, for the fourth century, Chauvot 1998. The latter offers a good *status quaestionis* on pp. 5–12.

[32] Themistius, *Oratio* 10.131bc. Such stark contrasts are common: see, e.g. Prudentius, *Contra Symmachum* 2.807–9.

the classical image of the barbarian, and suggested that education and its focus on exempla explain its perpetuation in late Antiquity.[33] In such exempla, barbarians are figures of contrast: as in the passage of Themistius, they can be the negative counterpoint to the Roman ideal of civilization, or, as happens in Tacitus' *Germania*, they can symbolize what the Romans lack. Given the many, sometimes contrasting, functions that barbarians could fulfil in Roman discourse,[34] asking what Orosius really thought about the barbarians risks to result only in noticing paradoxes and contradictions.[35] If, however, we take the *Historiae* as a Roman history, written from a Roman perspective but to undermine a traditional Roman view of history, then the shifting roles of the barbarian can be understood as performing a specific function within the narrative, namely to question the one-sided glorification of the Roman past.

One way in which Orosius destabilizes the traditional view of Roman history is by reducing, not to say effacing, the distinction between Romans and barbarians. In the third book, he argues against the difference his contemporaries see between glorious wars of conquest and abject wars of destruction. In fact, he suggests, for the Persians, Alexander was a barbarian, just as were the Romans to their enemies. And, Orosius reminds his adversaries, the destructive barbarians of today could be the great kings of a new empire tomorrow.[36] He thus irons out the qualitative differences between barbarians and Romans, justified wars and mere marauding—culminating with the real possibility of Rome's fall, which for later generations would not be fundamentally different from that of Susa or Athens. All history is, ultimately, equal: Roman history is only more prestigious because of the perspective of Roman historians and their culturally determined feeling of superiority.

If this argument is developed explicitly in book 3, it can be traced implicitly in book 5. The preface to book 5 argues that Rome's successes in conquest were matched by the misfortune of those

[33] Heather 1999: 242. On the barbarian as category and its stability into late Antiquity, see Dauge 1981, 305–77; Chauvot 1998: 482 notices a rise in negative views.

[34] Chauvot 1998: 11: 'Mauvais, bons ou différents, promis à la destruction ou à la romanisation, les barbares avaient donc déjà beaucoup été.'

[35] Lippold 1952: 86 and Goetz 1980b: 373 draw attention to the 'ambivalence' of Orosius.

[36] Orosius 3.20.10–13.

conquered.[37] Drawing on the rhetorical contrast between a single city, Rome, and the entire world—one encounters here again the rhetorical function of universalism—Orosius suggests that if Rome's wars of conquest constitute the pinnacle of happiness for Rome, then they must be an abyss of suffering for the rest of the world.[38] Carthage, Spain, and Italy itself are allowed to utter their complaints.[39] The first aim of this argument is to construct a contrast between a world full of suffering then and the relative peace now. It must be obvious by now that Orosius often contrasts the limited impact of current invasions with their devastating effect earlier in history. Now, he asserts, there always is a place of refuge in the united empire and hospitable people whom one can trust to be welcoming—in contrast with a time when various barbarian tribes occupied different parts of the empire, who were even divided by religion.[40] In this preface Orosius espouses rhetorically two, seemingly contradictory, positions. When discussing the Roman conquests of the late Republic, he questions the distinction between Romans and non-Romans and invites his readers to look at the past from a non-Roman perspective. Indeed, several of the descriptions of wars in book 5 show Romans behaving as barbarians.[41] When extolling the improvement of life since the Incarnation, he accepts the benefits of romanization, intensified through Christianity, and the unity it creates in the empire. Both, however, serve the same function, namely that of questioning the traditional romanocentric perspective. This may seem obvious in the first instance, but less so in the second. Yet the second argument is built on the suggestion that an invasion in part of the empire is not a very grave event today, as there are plenty of places in the empire one can flee to. In other words, even if Rome itself is under attack, there are still many locations that temporarily offer shelter. A sack of Rome is thus not very worrying, as it is only one place within the empire.

The two arguments in the preface to book 5 are, thus, only superficially contradictory and only so on the condition that one sees the 'barbarian' as a static category. Yet even in classical Antiquity the borderline between barbarians and Romans was permeable. 'Romanness' could be a form of moral progress, just as Hellenism was not an

[37] Orosius 5.1.3. [38] Orosius 5.1.4. [39] Orosius 5.1.5–9.

[40] Orosius 5.1.14. Cf. Orosius 5.16.9 and 5.22. Compare the sentiments expressed by Ilioneus in Vergil, *Aeneis* 1.539–43.

[41] Orosius 5.19.21–2, 5.21.6.

ethnic but a social marker in the Roman Empire. In late Antiquity, Christianity became another marker of moral progress: conversion of barbarian peoples was often understood as moral progress and, as it were, a taming of their ferocity.[42] As a consequence, numerous permutations of the category of barbarian become possible: Roman-ness and Christianity can become identified, but Christianity can also function independently as a marker of progress.[43] In his study of Victor de Vita's history of the Vandal persecution, T. Howe notes, for example, that the Vandals are judged rather positively when they are Catholic, but that the stereotypes of the barbarian are applied to them when they persecute the Catholics.[44] In the famous last chapters of book 7, Orosius consciously uses different possibilities linking and contrasting Christianity, Roman-ness, and barbarians in order to demonstrate the positive impact of Christianity on history.

Chapter 37 seems to put the history of the late 390s under the sign of engagement with barbarians. There Orosius assimilates the two strong men of East and West, Rufinus and Stilicho, each left in charge of part of the empire after the death of Theodosius I. Both are accused of attempting usurpation and of bringing barbarians into the empire to favour their ends.[45] A threefold *praeteritio* about Alaric's first invasion of Italy in 401–3 then shifts attention to the Goths. The second is, in fact, hardly one: Orosius takes ample time to emphasize that the commander of Roman troops at the battle of Pollentia (402) was Saul, a 'barbarian and pagan leader' who on Easter Day attacked the Goths, who had withdrawn 'out of respect for religion'.[46] God both rewarded and punished the Romans: they won the battle against Alaric, but the Goths were allowed to retreat because the Romans had

[42] See, e.g. Paulinus, *Vita Ambrosii* 36; Rufinus, *Historia ecclesiastica* 10.9–10, 10.11, 11.6; Prudentius, *Contra Symmachum* 1.458–60, 2.578–618; Orosius 7.37.8–9; Victor de Vita 1.36–7. The link between barbarians and bad religion is not typically Christian: see Ammianus 31.2.11 on the bad religion of the Huns. See Chauvot 1998: 429–60 for other Christian authors.

[43] See for Orosius the important remarks of Firpo 1983: 254–63.

[44] Howe 2007: 302.

[45] Orosius 7.37.1: Interea cum a Theodosio imperatore seniore singulis potissimis infantum cura et disciplina utriusque palatii commissa esset, hoc est Rufino orientalis aulae, Stiliconi occidentalis imperii, quid uterque egerit, quidue agere conatus sit, exitus utriusque docuit, cum alius sibi, alius filio suo affectans regale fastigium, ut rebus repente turbatis necessitas reipublicae scelus ambitus tegeret, barbaras gentes ille inmisit, hic fouit.

[46] Orosius 7.37.2: cum barbaro et pagano duci . . . propter religionem.

acted in an irreligious way. A third *praeteritio* then draws attention to subsequent infighting among the barbarians. These opening paragraphs set the tone for the rest of the chapter, which expands the contrast between pagan and Christian barbarians in order to show up God's meekness in relation to the Romans. Indeed, it is not wrong to state that the themes broached here play a role in the rest of book 7.[47]

The remainder of the chapter is built around a comparison of the threat posed to Rome by Radagaisus in 405/6 and the sack of Rome by Alaric, a comparison that was already made by Augustine[48] but is rhetorically elaborated at great length by Orosius. Radagaisus is styled as the greatest and most savage enemy of Rome ever: 'of all ancient and present enemies by far the most ferocious', who vowed, 'as it is custom among such barbarian people', to sacrifice all Romans to his gods.[49] Turning a counterfactual supposition of Augustine into fact, Orosius depicts the inhabitants of Rome bemoaning their coming fate, as they surmise that Radagaisus, supposedly supported by the pagan gods, will win. Just as in the battle of Pollentia, however, God's justice strikes both sides: Radagaisus is resoundingly defeated,[50] but pagan Rome would be punished shortly afterwards by Alaric. Yet Alaric is, as it were, the perfect contrast of Radagaisus: he is a Christian, 'rather more a Roman' whose savagery is mitigated by his fear of God, whereas the latter is a pagan barbarian, a 'true Scythian'.[51] Unsurprisingly, therefore, the sack of Rome, set out two chapters later in 7.39, is a rather civilized event—a fact that again demonstrates the benefits of Christianity to the world. As Orosius himself spells out,[52] the first aim of his presentation of events is religious, namely to demonstrate to the pagan Romans that paganism does not lead to military success, whereas Christianity actually tempers barbarian invasions. Orosius, however, adds to this primary message, which is essentially that of Augustine, an additional one. Indeed, in comparison with Augustine, Orosius emphasizes much

[47] Orosius 7.38 expands the remarks on Stilicho, 7.39 develops the sack of Rome of which the main interpretation is already set out in 7.37.

[48] Augustine, *De civitate Dei* 5.23.

[49] Orosius 7.37.4: Radagaisus, omnium antiquorum praesentiumque hostium longe immanissimus (. . .) ut mos est barbaris huiusmodi gentibus.

[50] Orosius 7.37.12–17.

[51] Orosius 7.37.9: quorum unus Christianus propiorque Romano et, ut res docuit, timore Dei mitis in caede, alius paganus barbarus et uere Scytha.

[52] Orosius 7.37.11.

more the barbarism of Radagaisus and draws attention to the 'quasi-Roman-ness' of Alaric. More consciously than his dedicatee, then, he uses the traditional stock category of the barbarian. The reason for this choice is not difficult to see: just as Orosius used the provincial perspective to question the traditional Roman view of the past, he now uses the distinction paganism/Christianity to that end. As the characterization of Alaric shows, Christianity primarily functions as the bridge between barbarism and civilization: the really dangerous barbarians are the ones who remain pagan. But Christianity has an additional role: it also stops these ferocious barbarians—even the most ferocious ever—from having any real impact. Indeed, picking up again the third *praeteritio* with which he opened the chapter, Orosius notes that Radagaisus was actually defeated by a coalition of Goths and Huns.[53] Thus, the opposition barbarian–Roman is spoiled of its acuity, since Christianity transcends these divisions. The habitual moral divide between barbarians and Romans, inculcated through the study of exempla, should thus not influence how one looks at events of the present. Rather than fearing the barbarians as such, one should ask what their religion is: one will then know what to expect.

Orosius thus aims at destabilizing the traditional perception of his audience, but he does not eliminate it entirely. Whatever his quasi-Roman-ness, Alaric remains an enemy. In chapter 39, Orosius fulfils his promise to show how Alaric sacked Rome. The protracted triple siege of the years 408–10 is reduced in the *Historiae* to a succinct sentence: 'Alaric was present, besieged, shook, and invaded a trembling Rome.'[54] The rest of the long chapter details how they spared the Christian churches and their possessions, and how the Goths avoided, as far as possible, the shedding of blood. As already said, in relation to chapter 37, Orosius makes clear that the sack is God's punishment for the impiety of pagan Romans, not only through an explicit affirmation to this end,[55] but also with explicit and implicit comparisons with the Old Testament, and allusions to apocalyptic passages of the New Testament,[56] thus hinting at the avenging deity

[53] Orosius 7.37.12.
[54] Orosius 7.39.1: adest Alaricus, trepidam Romam obsidet turbat inrumpit.
[55] Orosius 7.37.18.
[56] Orosius 7.37.9: *Matthew* 24.31 and *Revelation* 11.15.

portrayed in these verses.[57] The sack is also, unsurprisingly, compared positively with the destruction wrought by Nero's fire and the Gallic sack of 387 BC.[58] In addition to these statements about the nature and meaning of the sack, Orosius also suggests that the true divisions in mankind are now different from what they used to be. He records the traditional story that a Goth came across a virgin, and asked her 'politely' for her gold and silver (Orosius has eliminated the attempt at rape present in Sozomen's version[59]), she brought out the Church vessels and warned him that he would be punished by God if he would dare to take them. On the orders of Alaric, the vessels were brought in a procession to the Church of St Peter. Romans and barbarians accompanied the procession with a hymn of praise, and many pagans joined it pretending to be Christians so as to be saved. The meaning of this event is spelled out by Orosius: the vessels functioned as the metaphorical sieve of God, who separates corn from straw.[60] Moreover, the fact that the pagans are saved because of Christianity summarizes neatly one of the key messages of the entire *Historiae*.

In his description of the sack of Rome, then, Orosius uses the barbarians in two ways. On the one hand, drawing on the traditional negative stereotype of the barbarian as destructive and dangerous, Orosius depicts them as executing God's punishment of pagan Rome. On the other hand, in stressing their Christian nature and the consequently less horrific nature of the sack, not to mention the protection they offered to Christians, Orosius has the barbarians illustrate the beneficial influence of Christianity on the real world. Orosius again uses two, seemingly contradictory, views of barbarians at the same time, namely that they are Rome's enemies and that Christianization has a positive impact on them. Yet they do not have to be contradictory, although a certain tension exists between both: the former could be characterized as rather negative, the latter as rather positive. In fact, both are held together by Orosius' emphasis on absolute divine agency. Alaric's Goths are the precisely targeted instruments of God's providence: as barbarians, they loot and

[57] Orosius 7.37.2: *Genesis* 19.16; Orosius 7.37.13: *Amos* 9.9.
[58] Orosius 7.37.
[59] Sozomen, *Historia ecclesiastica* 9.11.
[60] Orosius 7.37.11–14.

rampage, but, as Christians, they do so in an urbane way, with special regard for the Christians.

The view argued for here is thus, in some ways, opposite to that set out by Goetz. For him, Orosius' 'ambivalent' concept of the barbarian is rooted not only in the fact that Christian missionary optimism about the barbarians and the classical negative view prevalent among Romans are difficult to reconcile, but first and foremost in the fact that for Orosius, being Roman and being Christian is one and the same thing. Christian barbarians therefore threaten to disrupt this identification and cannot be made to fit into Orosius' categories.[61] As I have argued, it is misleading to read Orosius as making systematic, theoretical propositions about the possibility of barbarian integration: rather, the barbarian has a rhetorical function within a narrative that intends to show the just hand of God at work. Moreover, by questioning the traditional negative role of the barbarian and highlighting how Romans can behave like barbarians and barbarians can be civilized, Orosius destabilizes the Roman self-definition (and self-esteem) through contrast with the barbarians. In this way, Orosius can again show that the traditional perception of past and present, with its clearly defined roles for Romans and barbarians, distorts the true nature of reality, and in particular that Christianity is the true agent in history. Thus, in contrast to Goetz, who thinks that a systematic reflection about the central role of Rome in history underpins Orosius' 'thought', the historian precisely aims at undermining such a romanocentric view and puts the category of the barbarian to use in order to open up the eyes of the pagan for what truly guides history.

God's care for mankind is for a last time made explicit in the last chapter of book 7. The sack of Rome, in fact, even has a long-term benefit: Placidia, the daughter of Theodosius I, taken as a hostage and wife by Athaulf 'as if by divine judgment',[62] is depicted in chapter 43 as the individual who inspired her barbarian husband to seek reconciliation with the empire—a policy that was pursued by his successor Vallia.[63] This marked a change of heart: Athaulf had long desired to eradicate *Romania* and supplant it with a *Gothia*. Yet, he started

[61] Goetz 1980b: 373.

[62] Orosius 7.40.2: quasi eam divino iudicio velut speciale pignus obsidem Roma tradiderit.

[63] Orosius 7.43.7–15.

to realize that the Goths, 'because of their wild barbarism',[64] would be unable to respect laws and to live in a state. Instead of eliminating Rome, he therefore started to seek peace so as to bring about Rome's renewal.[65] The functionality of Orosius' concept of the barbarian is obvious in this passage: Athaulf interiorizes the traditional Roman view of the barbarians as ferocious and wild, and puts himself in the service of Rome, performing one of the key tasks of the later Roman emperor, that is, to restore Rome. Athaulf is at once a true barbarian and a true Roman. The reason that he is transformed from a threat to a saviour is Christianity and God's providence: his peace project was inspired and supported by Galla Placidia, whose Christian credentials are explicitly underlined.[66] If God's providence is not explicitly mentioned in chapter 43, the capture of Galla Placidia had been dubbed providential already in chapter 40.[67] Placidia's story is obviously distorted and idealized: the previous chapter has shown how the last chapters of book 7 are evidently panegyrical. The preceding analysis has again confirmed the conclusions reached there: the panegyric is aimed at God's care for mankind. In line with the overall project of the *Historiae*, attention is implicitly shifted from the punishing action of God towards His providential care. Events are adapted to fit that pattern. One thus has to read the last chapters of book 7 as panegyric and not as theoretical statements on the possibility of the integration of the barbarians into the Roman Empire.

Universalism and the barbarian play thus a similar role in the *Historiae*: they question the traditional perception of history, which was evidently romanocentric. Yet Orosius only suggests that they could constitute the starting points for an alternative history. He does not write an alternative history himself: as I have emphasized before, the scope of his history remains that of the traditional overviews of history. In his narrative, universalism and the barbarian serve to destabilize the habitual perception of the past as glorious and to redirect attention to who truly drives history, that is, God.

[64] Orosius 7.43.6: propter effrenatam barbariem.
[65] Orosius 7.43.6: Romanae restitutionis auctor.
[66] Orosius 7.43.7: feminae sane ingenio acerrimae et religione satis probae.
[67] Orosius 7.40.2.

8

What Difference Does Christianity Make?

In the comment with which we opened the last chapter, Orosius noted that Leonidas' preference for the future and that of the pagans for the past, and their shared contempt for the present, implies 'that the present is always good but badly appreciated or never better in all respects'.[1] Scholars have sometimes detected Orosius' true intentions in the first half of that sentence: Orosius situates all evil in the past, whilst the Christian present is a haven of peace.[2] This turns Orosius into a Pangloss, who, sadly, lacks the sophistication of Leibnitz. Yet, the whole sentence proves otherwise: the present is never fully perfect, even for Orosius. Readers are easily misled by his graphic insistence on the *mala* of the past, but the picture is less black-and-white than his rhetoric might suggest. In the preface to book 4, Orosius readily concedes to his pagan adversaries that grave things (*gravia*) happen in his time; what he refuses to accept is that they are worse (*graviora*). This same passage reveals the truly apologetic nature of his *Historiae*: it is the pagans who establish the negative comparison with the past, a false accusation he has to refute.[3] In the *proemium* to book 5, Orosius even refuses to answer his own rhetorical question: 'Shall I thus call our times happy? We surely think they are happier than the past, we

[1] Orosius 2.11.10: ecce cum ille promisit futura meliora, isti adserunt meliora praeterita, quid aliud colligi datur utroque in suis detestante praesentia, nisi aut semper bona esse sed ingrata aut numquam omnino meliora?

[2] Peterson 1935: 91; Corsini 1968: 88 with the criticism of Fabbrini 1979: 252 and Firpo 1983: 249. Inglebert 1996: 494, 524 argues that Orosius sees the Christian empire as a reign of peace. Herzog 2002: 306 suggests that for Orosius, his history ends in *Ereignislosigkeit*. Arnaud-Lindet 1990–1: i.lx states that, for Orosius, the barbarians are the only problem left for the empire. The series of usurpers of the early fifth century, narrated at the end of book 7, proves otherwise.

[3] Orosius 4.pr.6: sentiendo gravia putent, non tamen conhibeo, ut etiam adserant conparando graviora. The opposition *sentiendo/conparando* picks up the distinction Orosius makes between reality and its distorted perception by a rhetorical culture.

who possess continuously what our ancestors chose at the very end [sc. peace].'[4] Although the rhetorical contrast between past and present as times of war, respectively of peace, consciously suggests otherwise, it is noteworthy that Orosius does not call the present straightforwardly happy. Indeed, the rest of the preface assumes the continued presence of warfare in the present, by developing an argument in favour of the moral and religious unification of the empire. When somebody has to flee from his hometown because of some disturbance in Orosius' days, he can flee to any place in the empire: he does not run the risk of being refused entry for religious or political reasons. In other words, there always will be wars and disturbances, but a Christian empire softens their impact. In another preface, to the seventh book, Orosius quotes Christ's prophecy that there will be wars between his death and the end of times.[5] Numerous other passages could be cited in addition,[6] also from the very end of the work, as we have seen in the previous chapter, and it is noteworthy that Orosius often reiterates in the prefaces the point that full peace is beyond man's reach. His enterprise is comparative, not superlative.

Orosius is thus not as naive as sometimes thought, but the comparative nature of the *Historiae* does raise an important question. Why are the times after the Incarnation only different in degree from earlier history? In other words: What difference does Christianity make? This question leads us to the issues that have been at the forefront of Orosius' research for decades: his relationship with the other leading views on the historical impact of Christianity, namely Eusebius of Caesarea and Augustine. I shall argue that Orosius shares less with Eusebius than usually thought, and more with Augustine than commonly assumed.

I. SIN AND PUNISHMENT

Why are the *christiana tempora*[7] not fully felicitous? The answer is simple: because they are part of historical time which began with

[4] Orosius 5.1.11: igitur nostra tempora uiderim utrum felicia; certe feliciora illis ducimus, qui quod illi ultime delegerunt nos continue possidemus.

[5] Orosius 7.3.11; *Matthew* 24.6–9. See already Lippold 1952: 54.

[6] Orosius 5.5.16, 5.11.6, 5.18.28–9, 5.22, 5.24.9.

[7] On the expression, see Madec 1975.

Adam. Orosius starts his history there because 'we are instructed that with the very first man sin and the punishment of sin started'.[8] Thus, from Adam to his own days, the world burns with evil, 'lighted by the torch of ambition'.[9] Human sinfulness runs through the entire *Historiae*: sins 'are the root of our miseries'.[10] God sends us disasters so that we mend our ways or be punished.[11] If sin is ubiquitous in man's life, how does Orosius explain the difference between the times before and after the Incarnation, on which his case against the contemporary pagans rests? The Christian Church is the answer. Picking up an older apologetic argument,[12] Orosius sees the Church as the only institution capable of placating God. Indeed, when there was 'in the entire world no Church which through the intervention of the prayers of the faithful could temper the deserved punishments of the world and the just judgment of God, by supplicating his clemency',[13] God sent wars and natural disasters. The spread of Christianity is thus of double benefit: not only does it increase the number of Christians who can intervene with God, but Orosius, like all his contemporaries, also associates conversion with moral progress.[14] Indeed, only Christianization completes the process of unification which had started with Augustus: political unity is followed by religious and moral unity, allowing every Roman to settle freely in any part of the empire, without fearing religious persecution as in the past.[15] This argument

[8] Orosius 1.1.11: cum ab ipso primo homine peccatum punitionemque peccati coepisse doceamur.

[9] Orosius 1.1.14: ardentem malis mundum face cupiditatis incensum.

[10] Orosius 2.1.1, 6.1.5, 6.22.11, 7.3.3, 7.5.11, 7.33.9 (*radix miseriarum nostrarum*), 7.41.4–7.

[11] Cf. Schöndorf 1952: 66 ('Heilspedagogie'); Corsini 1968: 126; Goetz 1980a: 49–51; Frend 1989; Inglebert 1996: 568; Martínez Cavero 2002: 209; Kempshall 2011: 72. For Orosius, history is therefore not the ineluctable course of providence, which effectively does away with individual action (as stated by Corsini 1968: 101; Marrou 1970: 80–2; Brandt 2009: 130): Orosius clearly leaves room for it, as does Augustine: see Maier 1955: 171; Firpo 1983: 254. Escribaño Paño 2007: 690 wrongly states that, for Orosius, Christian emperors cause the times to be better.

[12] Tertullian, *Apologeticum* 40.13–15.

[13] Orosius 6.1.27: quando adhuc per uniuersum mundum nulla erat ecclesia, quae interuentu fidelium precum meritas mundi poenas iustumque iudicium Dei exorata ipsius clementia temperaret. See also Orosius 7.5.11, 7.8.5, 7.22.9.

[14] Orosius 7.23.11–13, 7.41.7–8, 7.43.6. See Ambrose, *Epistula* 18.7; Prudentius, *Contra Symmachum* 2.303–15. On the latter's view, and with an overview of other authors, see Buchheit 1985.

[15] Orosius 5.2 and 7.41.4.

is obviously targeted at the Romans who had been able to escape Alaric's Goths and settle peacefully in Sicily and Africa.

Orosius' view of history is thus ecclesiological, in the sense that it attributes the prime role as agent to the Church.[16] It is habitual to assert that the improvement of the times lies in the fact that God has elected the Roman Empire as the chosen vehicle of his message, with reference to the famous synchronism of the Incarnation and the beginning of the *pax romana*. Orosius is then seen as 'sacralizing' the empire. In fact, the synchronism marks the loss of true historical significance for Rome, as Orosius from then on systematically shows that it is the Christian Church that actually drives the course of events. Indeed, his overview of imperial history would seem highly idiosyncratic to the pagan reader. The pattern of war and peace of the empire is strictly correlated with the life of the Church: Tiberius' cruelty is a punishment imposed on the senate for its refusal to publicly recognize the divinity of Jesus,[17] the Jewish campaign of Titus is a vengeance for Christ's Crucifixion,[18] and the violent deaths of many an emperor are a punishment for persecutions of Christians;[19] to name but a few examples of how Rome is punished for sins against the Christians. Significantly, Orosius attributes true influence on Hadrian to the Christian apologists: their instruction is responsible for the end of the Trajanic persecution and Hadrian's felicity.[20] As we have seen in chapter 6, this tendency continues into the contemporary period, when faith alone suffices for Christian emperors to overcome their adversaries.[21] Unsurprisingly, the attribution of paramount historical agency to the Church is accompanied by an upsurge in the critique on pagan historians, who are shown to be less well informed than Josephus and Moses.[22] The ignorance of pagans of what drives history is symbolized in the fact that, whilst Augustus is indeed raised because a series of his actions announce the birth of Christ, he himself is unaware of their significance. Strikingly, Augustus, as a sign in history, ignores his own meaning.[23] The devaluation

[16] Herzog 2002: 308. [17] Orosius 7.4.7. [18] Orosius 7.9.

[19] Orosius 7.7.11, 7.8.2, 7.12.3, 7.15.5, 7.17.5, 7.19.2, 7.20.2, 7.21.5, 7.22.2–3.

[20] Orosius 7.13.2, cf. 7.14.2. See also Orosius 6.1.3, where Christianity is made responsible for 'pagan monotheism'.

[21] Orosius 7.34.5, 7.35.2.

[22] Orosius 7.11.1, 7.10.4, 7.9.7, 7.19.4, 7.27.1.

[23] Orosius 6.20.9: ad contestationem fidei. See also Orosius 6.20.4, where it is specified that the Roman Empire is prepared by God to receive Christ: the empire is

of Roman in favour of ecclesiastical history is also underlined by two significant applications of Vergilian verses to the Church. In 7.4.14, Orosius uses *Georgics* 1.468 (impiaque aeternam timuerunt saecula noctem), which refers to the eclipse at Caesar's death, to describe the darkening of the skies when Jesus breathed his last. Just a few paragraphs later, he quotes the ultimate lines of Jupiter's prophecy about the future of Rome to illustrate the benevolent influence of the budding Christianity on the empire. Significantly, in Vergil these lines predict the end of civil war and the beginning of the Augustan peace.[24] These are not just literary flourishes but ideological statements about what drives history: Jesus, not Caesar; the Church, not Augustus. A few decades later, the Church historian Sozomen will argue explicitly what Orosius suggests: pagan historians fail to grasp the true causes of events, which can only be detected by Church historians.[25] Orosius does not write ecclesiastical history, in that his subject matter is not the Church, but his perspective is that of a Church historian.

Because it is ecclesiological, Orosius' view of history is also moral: the community of Christians and their faith ensure the moral improvement of mankind and intercede with God. As a consequence, there is only one moment of true importance in history since Adam: the Incarnation, which is indeed extensively highlighted by Orosius at the end of his sixth and the beginning of his seventh book with a series of synchronisms. Since Christianity has entered the scene, mankind has become capable of intervening with God. In the community of the faithful, all are, ultimately, equal and important. Orosius obviously recognizes the importance of emperors, but basically treats them as ordinary individuals in their relationship with God. In contrast to Eusebius in his *Ecclesiastical history*, he does not attribute any special position to Constantine. Orosius even underscores that arianism started during his reign and that he murdered his own son Crispus:[26] Constantine is, in the end, a flawed human being. The same holds true for Theodosius, who is, significantly,

a passive instrument. I fail to see how the premonitory role of Augustus turns him into an image of Christ, as stated by Inglebert 1996: 572.

[24] Orosius 7.5.3 and Vergil, *Aeneis* 1.294–6.

[25] Sozomen, *Historia ecclesiastica* 1.1.11, 15. On these and other passages, see Van Nuffelen 2004a: 170–2.

[26] Orosius 7.28.23–6.

not praised for his support to Christianity but adduced as an example of putting one's faith only in God. Emperors, thus, have no special position: they also are punished for their sins, just as ordinary man is.[27] Rome does occupy a special place in this scheme, as Christ, in Orosius' memorable formula, chose to become a Roman citizen.[28] But Christianity completes Rome: the felicity that Rome enjoyed before was due to God's benevolence, but now it enjoys full felicity, on condition that it does not sin.[29] As we have seen, imperial unification is completed by a Christian one. Yet the elevation of Rome as the empire chosen by God for the Incarnation is coupled with a devaluation: the Christian Church visualizes that true agency does not lie with imperial might. Moreover, Roman history is not essentially different from barbarian history[30] or exempt from the universal law that everything human decays. Even less is the completion of Rome by Christianity ever fully achieved: mankind, even when nominally Christian, continues to sin and God therefore continues to punish. In the end, what counts is eternal life, even if Christianity may be of profit here on earth.[31]

II. THE OPTIMISM OF EUSEBIANISM

My emphasis on the ecclesiological nature of Orosius' view of history differs from the dominant view in scholarship which sees the *Historiae* as an enthusiastic espousal of the Christian Roman Empire. In German scholarship, Orosius has been characterized as the culmination of the so-called *Augustustheologie*, which implied that 'the idea of *Roma aeterna* was christianized and the idea of Christianity romanized'.[32] 'Eusebianism' is the term preferred among Italian and French scholars for Orosius' views, referring to the inexorable and providential progress in history that Eusebius saw starting with the

[27] Orosius 7.3.6, 7.33.9. [28] Orosius 6.22.6–8.

[29] Orosius 7.6.11. [30] Orosius 3.20.10–13.

[31] Orosius 7.3.2–3. Cf. Augustine, *Sermo* 111 for a similar idea.

[32] Peterson 1935: 93: 'Die Idee der Roma aeterna wurd christianisiert und die Idee des Christentums romanisiert.' See also Kamlah 1951: 306–10; Maier 1955: 181; Opelt 1961: 44–50; Brodka 1998: 214.

Incarnation and culminating in Constantine.[33] As set out in the introduction, both concepts carry negative connotations, indicating a dangerous approximation of theology and state ideology, to the point that the Church starts to legitimize and sacralise state power. In turn, the Church loses its independence and the possibility to speak out against state abuse. This model has proven extremely powerful for understanding fourth- and fifth-century Christian views of Rome. Yet I do have reservations about its usefulness in interpreting Orosius: it functions as a procrustean bed which severely amputates key nuances in his depiction of the relationship between Church and state and the course of history. Whilst admitting that there are links, this section challenges the idea that Orosius can simply be classified as an 'eusebianist'.

The prime expression of 'Eusebianism' is found at the beginning of the *praeparatio evangelica*, written by Eusebius of Caesarea shortly after 314.[34] This apologetic work, a refutation of primarily pagan errors, starts out with brief affirmations of the reasonableness of Christians for having embraced Christianity. Against the Jews, Eusebius argues that the prophecies of the Old Testament are fulfilled in Christianity, and against the pagans that the rise of Christianity coincides with the spread of peace and morality in the world.[35] The latter argument insists on the 'mysterious' coincidence between the end of 'polyarchy' on earth by the Roman Empire and that of polytheism by Christianity. The apologetic nature of the argument is clear in Eusebius' insistence on the utility of this process: the diffusion of Christian virtues ends all kind of immoral (even in the eyes of the pagans) practices.[36] Against attempts to dissociate Christianity from Roman history,[37] Eusebius firmly roots the former in the latter. This leads—it has been argued—to a devaluation of the traditional eschatological perspective: Eusebius applies prophecies of peace that had been taken to refer to the end of times, to his own age. It has been suggested, therefore, that Eusebius adheres to the idea that the ideal empire promised for the end of times has already been partially

[33] Tanz 1983; Martelli 1982: 234; Chesnut 1992; Inglebert 1996: 507–92; Brodka 1998: 183; Merrills 2005: 58.

[34] Sirinelli and des Places 1974: 8–15.

[35] Eusebius, *Praeparatio Evangelica* 1.3–4.

[36] Eusebius, *Praeparatio Evangelica* 1.4.6–12.

[37] Most famously Hippolytus, *In Danielem* 4.9.

realized in history.[38] Besides a revaluation of secular and in particular Roman history, there are also important political implications to Eusebius' argument: *pax Christi* and *pax romana* are seen as 'two shoots'[39] of the same branch, and imperial monarchy becomes an image of divine monarchy. It is but a small step from this idea to the image of Constantine as the leader of the Church.[40]

Reconstructed in this way, Eusebianism seems a powerful concept. Yet, there are some problems with it as a modern construct. There is, first, the obvious but rarely emphasized fact that the two major expressions of this ideology stem from an apologetic and panegyrical context: there is the passage from the *Praeparatio evangelica*, and another one in the *Praise of Constantine*.[41] It is some time since we stopped reading panegyric as simply an expression of the ideology of either the empire or the speaker:[42] panegyric is now interpreted as the negotiation of a complex relationship between the court, audience, and orator. The argumentative and polemical strategies of apologetic are now better understood too, in particular its situational character: arguments are co-determined by the context in which they are raised and by the ideas they aim at refuting.[43] The argument in the *praeparatio* is a response to the pagan critique that Christianity is a dangerous subversion of the empire, and the *Praise of Constantine* obviously has to tie Constantine as a Christian ruler into the Roman Empire.[44] In both instances, it is only logical that Eusebius gives a more positive role to the Roman Empire. It can be rightly retorted that similar statements return in a different treatise, the *Demonstratio evangelica*,[45] but these achieve coherence by reading them in the light of the more explicit passages in the two other works. Second,

[38] Sirinelli 1961: 483; Farina 1966: 116; Kinzig 1994: 550–3. For further literature, see A. Johnson 2006: 153–4.

[39] Eusebius, *De laudibus Constantini* 16.4.

[40] Girardet 1980.

[41] Eusebius, *De laudibus Constantini* 16. The same holds, as a matter of fact, for some other theologians favourably disposed to the empire: Origen, *Contra Celsum* 2.30 is strongly apologetic.

[42] See Rees 2002.

[43] Edwards, Goodman, Price, and Rowland 1999.

[44] Considerations of genre are absent in most works on Eusebianism: Peterson 1935; Eger 1939; Sirinelli 1961; Paschoud 1967: 178–84; Inglebert 1996. M.J. Hollerich has demonstrated that Eusebius' views in other works, such as his biblical commentaries, tend to be very traditional: see Hollerich 1990 and 1999.

[45] Eusebius, *Demonstratio evangelica* 3.2.37, 3.7.30–6. The *Demonstratio* is also an apologetic work.

as Aaron Johnson has highlighted, there are also several negative judgments on Rome and its empire to be found in Eusebius' works.[46] At the very least, these need to be integrated into our overall understanding of Eusebius' view of Rome, which cannot be said to be unilaterally positive. Indeed, Johnson emphasizes that, whilst Eusebius depicts Rome as less infected by paganism than some other nations, he still sees a clear boundary between Christianity and the Roman traditions.[47] Third, recent scholarship has chipped away at some of the constituent elements of 'Eusebianism'. It has been demonstrated in particular that Eusebius adheres to a traditional view on eschatology and that the notion of a 'realized' eschatology is problematic and not tenable.[48] An important article by M.J. Hollerich has argued that we should take a closer look at Eusebius as a bishop and a scholar, rather than a political theorist and a court flatterer.[49] Crucially, Aaron Johnson has argued that in the famous passage from the *Praeparatio evangelica* the focus is not on Augustus but on Christ: it is Christ alone who brings about the changes in the world. Against the traditional interpretation which emphasizes the providential role of Augustus in the spread of Christianity, he points out that Eusebius actually removes all agency from Augustus, who is at best a tool or a sign of the changes effected by Christ.[50] These arguments point the way to an improved understanding of Eusebius, which does not see him as a herald of the Christianized empire, but rather as a man of the Church, who saw Christ and the Church as the prime movers of history. Whilst a fuller deconstruction of Eusebianism as an ideology and a historical phenomenon would be salutary—be it just as a correction to the too strong an emphasis on ideology in scholarship of the past century—it is more important for our purpose that 'Eusebianism' as it is usually understood cannot adequately describe Orosius' views.

At first sight, one encounters some of the hallmarks of Eusebianism in Orosius. The most prominent one is the synchronism between *pax Christi* and *pax romana*,[51] and the implied choice of God for the Roman Empire. Orosius also has an optimistic view of history since the Incarnation, marked by moral and religious progress, which

[46] Eusebius, *Demonstratio evangelica* 4.9, 7.1: cf. A. Johnson 2006: 180–1.
[47] A. Johnson 2006: 153–97.
[48] Thielman 1987.
[49] Hollerich 1990.
[50] A. Johnson 2006: 185, 196.
[51] Orosius 6.1.7–8.

benefited the empire too. In particular, the Incarnation proves the inanity of the pagan gods and ensures the moral improvement of the world.[52] Nevertheless, the inflection of these ideas is different in Orosius from what one would expect from an Eusebianist. Although he does praise universal peace, it is not presented as putting an end to all warfare and suffering, but as a qualitative improvement: wars are shorter and less dramatic. Unsurprisingly, therefore, Orosius does not pretend the establishment of eschatological peace: the concept of 'realized eschatology' cannot be applied to Orosius,[53] a concept that would, moreover, contradict his own assertion, noticed in chapter 6, that his own history excludes the end of times. Nor does he believe that Rome is so privileged that it is eternal, even in historical time. As we have seen, Rome should have fallen, had it not been for Christian piety. This difference can be understood in the light of the different historical context of Orosius and Eusebius. Eusebius wrote his works at the moment of a renaissance of imperial might, miraculously accompanied by the conversion of Constantine. Orosius' history, on the contrary, was borne out of a crisis, as was rightly seen by R. Herzog.[54] It does not naively hide the serious troubles of the Western empire, but refuses to attribute them any real significance: by integrating them in a historical narrative, they lose much of the calamitous quality pagans attribute to them. Once one has pierced through the panegyrical celebration of the improvement of times due to Christianity, Orosius' judgment on his own times is rather muted and betrays an awareness of the fragility of human existence.

In Eusebianism, Church and empire are two shoots of the same branch, and it hence legitimizes the empire as the result of divine will as much as the Church. While Orosius does emphasize that the empire was chosen to receive Christ, we have also seen that, for him, the empire has lost its historical agency since the Incarnation. Whereas Eusebius seems to leave the causal link between *pax Christiana* and *pax augusta* unspecified,[55] Orosius has no doubts: the

[52] See the long argument in Orosius 6.1, which seems to rely on Augustine, *De civitate Dei*, books 2–3.

[53] Contra Inglebert 1996: 494, 524, 574. He thinks that according to Orosius, the remaining 236 years of Rome's lifespan will be marked by peace, prosperity, and the integration of the barbarians.

[54] Herzog 2002.

[55] Sirinelli 1961: 407–11. A. Johnson 2006: 196 argues in fact that Eusebius also suggests the passivity of Augustus, just like Orosius.

Roman Empire was chosen by God. It is not just the grammar which is passive:[56] the only real actors in the history of the empire are the Church and God. In comparison with Eusebius, Orosius also highlights the Incarnation much more as a watershed in history. Eusebius, as is well known, claimed that the Hebrew patriarchs were proto-Christians, and that Jesus' message is basically a renewal of their old one.[57] Contrary to Eusebius, Orosius sees Christianity as a new phenomenon that entered the world with the Incarnation, allowing, for the first time, a systematic intercession with God. Such a praise of the role of God and the Church leaves little room for a concomitant elevation of the Roman emperor to a key actor on the world historical stage: there is no hint in Orosius that he thought of the emperor as the representative of God, the head of the Church, or the image of God.[58]

The root of Eusebianism is historical optimism: Christianity is seen as contributing a fundamental improvement to history. Orosius no doubt shares such optimism, although I have shown that it is more muted than it seems at first sight: the panegyric of the *christiana tempora* does not obscure the troubles of the early fifth century and Orosius also explicitly admits that his own time is neither fully peaceful nor the best ever in absolute terms. In Eusebianism, however, the historical optimism has a series of political implications, which spring from the attribution of a privileged position to the Roman Empire as a sacralised institution, and raising it, as it were, to the same level as the Church. Orosius, in fact, shares few of the political hallmarks of Eusebianism. The Roman Empire is identified as chosen by God to receive Christ, but this does not lead to a celebration of an eternal, Christian Rome. In marked contrast with Eusebius, Orosius fails to attribute a world-historical significance to Constantine and the conversion of emperor and empire to Christianity. This is hardly surprising given his ecclesiological and moral view of history, which situates the major change at the Incarnation, and attributes to the Church and to individual piety and sins a key role in the movement of history. In fact, as we have seen, even the emperor is

[56] Orosius 6.20.4: hoc autem fideliter commemorasse ideo par fuit, ut per omnia venturi Christi gratia praeparatum Caesaris imperium conprobetur. See also Orosius 6.17.10, 6.20, 6.22.6, 7.1.11.

[57] Ulrich 1999; A. Johnson 2006: 94–125.

[58] That Orosius describes Theodosius and Honorius as intervening in church politics is hardly a sign of Eusebianism (pace Inglebert 1996: 563): in that case, even Augustine would be an Eusebianist.

judged as any individual is, on the basis of his piety and sins.[59] Crucially, as the analysis of historical agency in chapter 6 has shown, 'secular' agents are completely eclipsed by ecclesiastical ones and individual morality in the seventh book: the empire may be chosen by God, but it is the Church that drives history. The equality that Eusebianism attributes to both institutions as willed by God cannot be found in Orosius.

Classifying Orosius as an Eusebianist rightly draws attention to a shared optimism, but has entailed the hasty attribution to him of a naive belief in an earthly reign of peace that announces already the eschatological peace. It has also led to an overestimation of the role played by the Roman Empire in the *Historiae*. Read in his own right, Orosius is less the exponent of an intellectual tradition than a Christian historian who retracts to what are, essentially, traditional positions: an eschatology which is situated in an unknown future and a focus on the Church as the true centre of historical action.

III. AUGUSTINE'S STRAY DOG

The price to pay for situating Orosius in the tradition of Eusebius is usually severing all intellectual ties with Augustine and styling him as the opposite of his dedicatee.[60] The confrontation between both is a *topos* of Orosius research since the Second World War.[61] The key difference is seen to lie in Augustine's radical separation of the *civitas terrena* and *civitas dei*, with the latter understood as an ideal community of true believers which can only be fully realized in eschatology. Human history, be it secular or ecclesiastical, is sidelined in favour of an emphasis on divine grace and the life eternal. History,

[59] Although situating Orosius in the context of Eusebianism, Inglebert 1996: 586–8 also draws attention to some differences with Eusebius. I would, however, insist that these differences make it hard to see Orosius as a political Eusebianist.

[60] See explicitly Inglebert 1996: 514: 'On peut écarter l'hypothèse d'une influence historique d'Augustin sur Orose' (. . .) 'une réponse qui prend le contre-pied d'Augustin.' See also Lacroix 1965: 61, 200; Martínez Cavero 2002: 154–60.

[61] Mommsen 1959b; Paschoud 1967: 276–8; Corsini 1968: ch. 9; Marrou 1970; Lippold 1976: i.xlii; Goetz 1980a: 136–46; Marzullo 1990–1; Inglebert 1996: 485–94; Cobet 2009: 86–7. Diesner 1963: 102 and Fabbrini 1979: 428–9 are the only scholars I know of who, in a polemical subversion of the traditional view, claim a superiority for Orosius over Augustine.

except for sacred history, has no true value: there is no link between true virtue and success in this world. As put by G. O'Daly, 'Augustine's overriding aim is to disassociate Rome's historical destiny from that of Christianity, or any religion'.[62] Augustine thus pointedly refuses to be swayed by Eusebius' enthusiasm for the Roman Empire and urges the true Christian to remain focused on heavenly felicity instead of its earthly variant: the Christian has to achieve inner renewal rather than *regeneratio imperii*. What is earthly is ephemeral; what is truly Christian is eternal. Hence the *City of God* is interpreted as giving the lie to Eusebianism, *Reichstheologie*, and *Augustustheologie*:[63] Augustine has avoided the temptation of identifying state and religion. The contrast with Orosius, interpreted as an Eusebianist, is thus obvious. As a consequence, scholars hear in Augustine's silence about Orosius after the publication of the *Historiae* a damming verdict and some of the later books of the *City of God* are thought to refute some of Orosius' ideas.[64]

Without denying the differences between Augustine and Orosius, which will be discussed below, the stark contrast between both does not do justice to either author. It has led to a strong emphasis on Augustine's originality and his intellectual isolation in his own time,[65] whilst the numerous common points with his contemporaries, including Orosius, are obscured. While it is clear that Orosius had access to the first ten books of the *City of God*, the degree to which Orosius engages with the ideas expressed there is less appreciated. The preceding chapters have repeatedly drawn attention to Orosius' dependency on the *City of God*, and they have already moved out of the way some of the ideas supposedly separating Augustine and Orosius: neither accepts the idea of a 'realized eschatology',[66] nor do they see Rome as the ultimate empire of which it would be unthinkable that it falls in historical time.[67] Augustine's critique on

[62] O'Daly 1999a: 29. See, for a similar but slightly different view, Mommsen 1959a.

[63] Maier 1955: 198.

[64] Mommsen 1959b; Inglebert 1996: 485–94. The silence is relative, as Augustine does seem to have used Orosius repeatedly in the *City of God*, and not always to refute him: Augustine, *De civitate Dei* 18.52 and Orosius 7.32.9 with Grumel 1956: 61 and Courcelle 1969: 127; Augustine, *De civitate Dei* 19.13: cf. Orosius 3.15; Augustine, *De civitate Dei* 21.14: cf. Orosius 1.4.3; Augustine, *De civitate Dei* 18.2 and Orosius 1.4 and 2.1, 6, 10. See Lacroix 1951; Vaz de Carvalho 1955; Hingst 1972: 77–83.

[65] Fuchs 1938: 23–4; Maier 1955: 174.

[66] For Augustine, see Maier 1955: 173.

[67] Augustine, *De civitate Dei* 4.7. For Orosius, see chapter 2.

a typological reading of the ten plagues of Egypt that asserts the end of all persecutions with Diocletian, can only be taken as specifically aimed at Orosius at the price of misinterpreting the latter, as he explicitly does not conclude from the typology that there are no persecutions any more.[68] It is now time to address the key issue that is seen to separate both: Orosius emphasizes the success of Christianity on earth and promotes Christianity as the guarantee of felicity here and now; Augustine's focus is, on the contrary, on eternal felicity. For the former, history thus has a value and Christianity a positive effect on history, whereas Augustine radically devaluates history and denies the mechanical link between Christianity and *felicitas*. I shall argue that while both do indeed have different conceptions, they are closer to one another than often thought.

Augustine's dissociation of terrestrial felicity and Christianity is less straightforward than summaries of the *City of God* suggest. On Augustine's side, there seems to be some hesitation, even in passages such as the end of book 5 that explicitly make that point. There it is argued that God's omnipotence bestows freely success and failure onto empires, wars, and emperors. Even for Christian emperors, true felicity does not lie in temporal success, such as a lengthy reign, a carefree succession, and success in war: true felicity lies in true virtue, which will be rewarded by God with eternal life. 'We say that, for the time being, such Christian emperors are happy in hope and that, in time to come, when that to which we look forward has arrived, they will be so in possession.'[69] Augustine then shows how felicitous Constantine was, but immediately warns that 'no emperor should be a Christian merely in the hope of securing the felicity which Constantine enjoyed': the pious Jovian, for example, had a shorter reign than the persecutor Julian.[70] The equally pious Gratian was killed at a young age by the tyrant Maximus. Augustine then seems to retract part of his argument:

> Gratian's death, however, was far less painful in its circumstances than was that of Pompey the Great, who worshipped the supposed gods of

[68] See pp. 159–60.

[69] Augustine, *De civitate Dei* 5.24: tales christianos imperatores dicimus esse felices interim spe, postea re ipsa futuros, cum id quod expectamus advenerit. Tr. R. W. Dyson.

[70] Augustine, *De civitate Dei* 5.25: sed rursus ne imperator quisquam ideo Christianus esset, ut felicitatem Constantini mereretur.

> Rome. For Pompey could not be avenged by Cato, whom he had, so to speak, left as his heir to the civil war. By contrast (although the minds of the godly do not require such solace), Gratian was avenged by Theodosius, whom he had caused to share in his royal power even though he had a little brother of his own; for Gratian was more eager to secure a faithful colleague than to achieve an excess of power.[71]

The next and final chapter of book 5 is a panegyric of Theodosius I, his achievements and his piety, which we already discussed in chapter 6.

On the one hand, there is the explicit, theoretical argument that there is no link between success in this world and Christianity, which is made explicit in the comment about Constantine: rulers should not embrace Christianity because it brings victory, but out of true, individual piety. On the other, there is the rhetorical suggestion that a link between success and Christianity does exist: the panegyrics of Constantine and Theodosius, proofs of such a link, are only interrupted by brief references to Julian and Jovian. The counterexample of Gratian is even explicitly retracted, by underlining that the young emperor died a less painful death than Pompey and that he was avenged. If Augustine does not claim absolute felicity for Gratian, he suggests a comparative one: Pompey was, all in all, less felicitous than Gratian. Christianity is thus suggested to make a difference, although it is not one of day and night. In more theoretical terms, true, Christian virtue is a necessary but not sufficient condition for felicity and success on earth.[72]

The ambiguity in these pages points to Augustine's difficulty in formulating what is, at least in a polemical context, not a very satisfactory argument. On the one hand, he strongly suggests that there is a link between true (Christian) morality and divine favour. Yet both terms are problematic for him: Augustine is pessimistic about the presence of true Christian morality, even among professed Christians. And God remains omnipotent and cannot be constrained or triggered into rewarding virtue on earth: he may have plans

[71] Augustine, *De civitate Dei* 5.25: Gratianum ferro tyrannico permisit interimi, longe quidem mitius quam magnum Pompeium in colentem uelut Romanos deos. Nam ille uindicari a Catone non potuit, quem ciuilis belli quodam modo heredem reliquerat; iste autem, quamuis piae animae solacia talia non requirant, a Theodosio uindicatus est, quem regni participem fecerat, cum paruulum haberet fratrem auidior fidae societatis quam nimiae potestatis. Tr. R.W. Dyson.

[72] Duval 1964: 141–3; Tornau 2006: 327–8.

unknown to us. In a polemical context, however, Augustine cannot but claim success for Christianity, but in order to avoid that his pagan adversaries could easily point to examples of obvious Christian failure, he has to rely on divine omnipotence and mystery to suggest the link between success and morality.[73]

The argument for a comparative improvement of the times due to Christianity and the emphasis on the benefits of individual morality and piety underpin the entire *Historiae* of Orosius. One cannot, hence, be surprised that the concluding chapters of book 5 of the *City of God* provided much inspiration for Orosius' own accounts of Radagaisus, Alaric, and Theodosius I in the last chapters of the *Historiae.*[74] He capitalizes on Augustine's suggestion of Christian success, but this does not make the views of master and student identical. Indeed, in the last chapters of book 7 of the *Historiae felicitas* usually refers to earthly success, whereas Augustine at the end of book 5, even when praising Theodosius, takes care to add that, for the Christian, only eternal felicity counts. Did Orosius fail to notice the deeper message of the end of book 5 of the *City of God*?

In fact, one can make an argument for Orosius similar to the one I have just made for Augustine: at first sight, Orosius strongly highlights the link between Christian piety and earthly success. When looked at more closely, the *Historiae* do reveal an awareness, often implicit but regularly explicit, that success in this world is not what a Christian is after and that human, in particular Roman, history remains secondary to the aspiration to the life above. As was set out above, Augustine's emphasis on celestial *felicitas* is predicated on the downgrading of human history and the dissociation of the success of Christianity from that of the Roman Empire. Orosius follows, up to a certain point, Augustine. We have discussed above his ecclesiological perspective on history, and how it empties the Roman Empire of any true historical agency at the profit of Church and God: the history of the empire is thus made totally dependent on Christianity. But, as we have seen in the previous chapter, the history of Rome is depreciated in relation not only to ecclesiastical, but also to non-Roman history, for Orosius espouses in the third book momentarily the perspective of the outsider and suggests that, for their enemies, the Romans are the

[73] Scholarship usually prefers the 'theoretical' to the 'rhetorical' Augustine: Maier 1955: 137–8; Paschoud 1967: 263–4; Rist 1994: 227–8; Tornau 2006: 327.

[74] See pp. 156–67.

barbarians.[75] It is only because of the Roman sense of superiority that their history seems more prestigious. The double downgrading of Roman history, in relation to ecclesiastical history and general history, is very much akin to the position developed by Augustine in books 4 and 5 of the *City of God.* Augustine argues that Roman successes of the past are not due to the observation of pagan rites, but the result of divine providence. This does not mean that Rome acquires a privileged place in God's plan for Augustine: Rome is just one player in world history directed by God.[76] Orosius operates a similar 'decentring' of Roman history: although his focus is largely on Roman history, this does not mean that it is qualitatively different from the history of other peoples, which are all equally directed by God's providence. Only church history truly matters.

In Orosius this devaluation of Roman history is related to his attempt to show the Roman aristocracy the true nature of their past, not as one of glory but as one of suffering. The rejection of Roman desire for glory is coupled with a stress on the Christian desire for 'saintly eternity' and true glory.[77] Indeed, Orosius' attachment as a Christian to Rome and humanity, even to Christianity, is only transitory: 'I use temporarily the entire earth as if a fatherland, because the fatherland that is true and the one that I love is not on earth.'[78] There is no love lost between a Christian and the earth, and a Christian can lose nothing where he does not truly love anything. These and various other passages where Orosius rates the ultimate beatitude of eternal life in Christ over temporary success[79] do not seem to fit with his supposed Eusebianist emphasis on success in this world and the realization of eschatological felicity already on earth. As a

[75] Orosius 3.20.10–13.

[76] Augustine, *De civitate Dei* 4.33, 5.11.

[77] See the explicit opposition in Orosius 4.4.41 (beata aeternitas).

[78] Orosius 5.2.6–7: utor temporarie omni terra quasi patria, quia quae uera est et illa quam amo patria in terra penitus non est. nihil perdidi, ubi nihil amaui, totumque habeo, quando quem diligo mecum est, maxime quia et apud omnes idem est, qui me non modo notum omnibus uerum et proximum facit, nec egentem deserit, quia ipsius est terra et plenitudo eius, ex qua omnibus omnia iussit esse communia. Orosius seems to rank attachment to Christianity among the earthly and temporary goods, and to emphasize that only the life in Christ matters. If that is the case, this passage brings him close to Augustine, who, as is well known, ranked the Church also as part of the *civitas terrena*. For similar ideas, see Augustine, *Sermo* 111.

[79] See Orosius 7.3.3, 7.41.9. The latter passage, prominent in the last pages of the work, was discussed in the previous chapter. It is, in fact, a common theme in Christian works: see Prosper Tiro, *De providentia Dei* 908–12.

consequence, they have either been disregarded or credited to Orosius' lack of consistency.[80] A more plausible inference is to detect here an alignment with Augustine's argument in the *City of God* that true, heavenly felicity is the ultimate goal of a Christian life. Augustine indeed develops a contrast between the Roman desire for glory and Christian true virtue which is directed towards life eternal.[81] He relates this to the point that human virtue is, for its success, ultimately dependent on divine grace.[82] As I have argued in the previous two chapters, at the end of book 7 Orosius also emphasizes how human virtue cannot achieve success on its own and needs piety as an absolute precondition.

Orosius and Augustine thus do not unilaterally argue for one side of the debate. Rather, they both show an awareness of the opposite position and, to a degree, even subscribe to it. Although Augustine makes the relationship between Christian virtue and earthly success dependent on the mysteries of divine providence and thus refuses what often seems Orosius' mechanical equation of both, he cannot avoid suggesting a link and, at least, an improvement of the success rate with Christian emperors. It is probably not accidental that this link is rhetorically suggested in the last chapters of book 5 of the *City of God*: these chapters form the peroration of Augustine's argument in books 4 and 5, published together after 415,[83] shortly, that is, before the publication of the *Historiae*. Dissociating completely Christianity and earthly success would hardly sway a pagan in favour of Christianity's merits after the sack of Rome. In that context, it is hardly surprising that Orosius' *Historiae*, as much a rhetorical work as the *City of God*, elaborate much more strongly a connection that even Augustine was not willing to sever completely.[84] Commissioned precisely to question the link between paganism and worldly success, the work does more than defend the opposite connection between Christianity and earthly *felicitas*. Orosius does not simply argue that paganism leads to failure and unhappiness: mankind, even when Christian, remains a captive of sin, and thus has to face again and

80 e.g. Paschoud 1967: 290.

81 e.g. Augustine, *De civitate Dei* 1.24.

82 Augustine, *De civitate Dei* 5.23–6.

83 O'Daly 1999: 34–6.

84 Indeed, our eschatological reading of Augustine's argument is determined by our knowledge of the later books of the *City of God*. Orosius had only books 1–10 available, and thus developed a different response to the work.

again God's wrath. Only the Church, as the intercessor with God, is responsible for appeasing God and thus improving the times, without ever being able to abolish sin. Orosius hence does not support an Eusebianist revaluation of Roman history: history is refocused on universal human suffering, on God and the Church as the only agents, and on our individual morality as an intercession with God or trigger for his punishment, and far less on a celebration of the power of Rome. Throughout, it is shown that all that is earthly is transitory and at the mercy of God; in an Augustinian move, Orosius' readers are repeatedly reminded that what truly counts is the life of virtue which leads to eternal beatitude. But this does not preclude us from worrying about our temporal home and hoping that our prayers will sway God.[85]

The different aims and genres of the *City of God* and the *Historiae* go some way in explaining the differences between both works. The *Historiae*, after all, are a work of history and have a much more limited remit than the *City of God*. Orosius argues against the historical link between paganism and success, and does so, expressly, on the playing field of the pagans: as he says early on, he does not want to use the argument of biblical authority. That Augustine entrusted this task to Orosius shows that this was not his intention in the *City of God*, which, in the first five books, is much more a reflection on the true nature of virtue and felicity; it draws on history, but is not a historical argument. Yet the contrast between Orosius and Augustine, even in the nuanced form I have suggested, cannot be entirely reduced to genre. The contrast revolves, ultimately, around the response to the question 'What difference does Christianity make?' Augustine, in the *City of God*, tends to situate the true importance of Christianity in the individual turn towards God, the individual eschatological perspective, and the hope of divine grace. There is no certainty that one's Christianity improves one's own life, or that Christianity makes the world better. Orosius, on the contrary, does argue that Christianity makes a difference. Although his panegyric has been read to suggest otherwise, the difference is not one of night and day: warfare, famine, and earthquakes still strike mankind, but Christianity succeeds in tempering their harsh effects. Even if the life eternal remains the Christian's ultimate hope and fatherland, one can be certain that

85 Bellen 1990 argues for the relative proximity of Augustine and Orosius. He sees the role of Rome as the stumbling block between both, but I have suggested this is not the case.

Christianity already makes a difference in this life. Both positions are fragile and not without risk. Augustine's is predicated on the ultimate unintelligibility of God and his free gift of grace: an Augustinian Christian is truly at the mercy of God. But, as argued by J. Rist, Augustine cannot properly distinguish divine omnipotence from arbitrariness.[86] One wonders, then, what the necessity, not to say the usefulness, of the Church for wider society can be in Augustine except as the only place where individual salvation can start.[87] Orosius, in turn, is in danger of overestimating the role of the Church and of absorbing secular history into it. For him, Christianity seems to make all the difference at the expense of the complexities of human life.

Both can be understood as responding not just to the external challenges of the times, such as the sack of Rome, but also to internal challenges within the Church: the expansion of the Church in the fourth and fifth centuries was perceived as going hand in hand with a weakening commitment of individual Christians. Many of them only seemed half-heartedly Christian. Questions about what role the Church had to play, and could play, in society and the different answers to these questions, can be understood as arising out of that anxiety.[88] Augustine's vision of eschatological perfection and Orosius' argument for the effectiveness of Christian morality in this life represent two different emphases within the spectrum of answers.

IV. WHAT DIFFERENCE DOES THE CHURCH MAKE?

Christian attitudes to the Roman Empire, one leading scholar has contended, fall into two categories: one assigned the empire 'a sacral significance in terms of the history of salvation', the other embraced the apocalyptic rejection of the empire.[89] Augustine surpasses this dichotomy, as is well known, but Orosius cannot be fitted into it either. It is, in fact, difficult to define precisely Orosius' attitude towards the empire, because of his ecclesiological view of history: all history, Roman and barbarian, is downplayed in favour of the

[86] Rist 1994: 286.
[87] See, on some of Augustine's difficulties, Rist 1994: 229–36.
[88] Markus 1990: ch. 1; Salamito 2005: 165–214.
[89] Markus 1970: 55.

Church. Orosius can thus at once admit that the empire was the vessel chosen by God for Christianity and proclaim repeatedly that Rome will not last. He can admire it as his temporal home and be indifferent to it when thinking of the life eternal. This is not a proof of Orosius' genius or profound originality. Rather, it suggests that the standard categories with which Christian political thought of the fourth and fifth centuries is analysed are too rigid and fail to do justice to the complexities of individual cases. Eusebianism, a rather fragile concept in itself, is not a good description of Orosius' thought: while the term does capture his optimism, it wrongly suggests political ideas about a sacralised, eternal Christian Rome which he did not hold. I wish to make the commonsensical suggestion that one should always return to the texts rather than taking such grand labels for granted. Indeed, many of the confrontations between Orosius, Eusebianism, and Augustine start out from modern reconstructions of these theological systems, and almost seem to forget that Orosius actually read the *City of God* and developed a personal response to it. As I have tried to show throughout this book, Orosius engages much more closely with Augustine than is admitted in scholarship that identifies a great gulf between the master and his dog. My claim is not that Orosius was, after all, a good pupil who just copied his master's thought: whilst they share more than is usually assumed, they also part ways on a different issue than is commonly stated. It is not so much the role of the empire about which both differ as that of the Church. Whereas Augustine's devaluation of human history includes church history,[90] for Orosius, the Church becomes the key agent in history. He believes the Church makes the difference in history; Augustine does not venture that far.

[90] Maier 1955: 181.

Bibliography

Editions

For classical texts, the *Loeb Classical Library* has been consulted. For Latin and Greek patristic texts, the editions in the *Corpus Christianorum* have been used. Exceptions are listed below. Translations are mine, except when indicated otherwise.

Agathias, *Historiae*: Keydell, R. (1967) *Agathiae Myrinaei historiarum libri quinque* (Corpus Fontium Historiae Byzantinae. Series Berolinensis 2). Berlin: Walter de Gruyter.

Ambrose, *De fide*: Faller, O. (1962) *Sancti Ambrosii De fide* (Corpus scriptorum ecclesiasticorum latinorum 78). Vienna: Hoelder, Pichler and Tempsky.

——*Epistulae*: Faller, O. (1968) *Sancti Ambrosii epistulae et acta* (Corpus scriptorum ecclesiasticorum latinorum 82). Vienna: Hoelder, Pichler and Tempsky.

Ambrosius, *De obitu Theodosii*: Faller, O. (1955) *Sancti Ambrosii Explanatio symboli, de sacramentis, de mysteriis, de paenitentia, de excessu fratris, de obitu Valentiniani, de obitu Theodosii* (Corpus scriptorum ecclesiasticorum latinorum 73). Vienna: Hoelder, Pichler and Tempsky.

Augustine, *Epistulae*: Goldbacher, A. (1895–1923) *Sancti Aureli Augustini Hipponiensis episcopi Epistulae* (Corpus scriptorum ecclesiasticorum latinorum 34–58), 5 Vols. Vienna: Hoelder, Pichler and Tempsky; Divjak, J. (1988) *Sancti Aureli Augustini Epistolae ex duobus codicibus nuper in lucem prolatae* (Corpus scriptorum ecclesiasticorum latinorum 88). Vienna: Hoelder, Pichler and Tempsky.

——*Sermones*: Dolbeau, F. (2009) *Saint Augustin. Vingt-six sermons au peuple d'Afrique* (Collection des études augustiniennes. Série Antiquité 147), 2nd edn, Paris: Institut des Etudes augustiniennes.

——*In psalmos enarratio*: Müller, H. (2004) *Sancti Augustini opera. Enarrationes in psalmos 51–100. 1: Enarrationes in psalmos 51–60* (Corpus scriptorum ecclesiasticorum latinorum 94). Vienna: Hoelder, Pichler and Tempsky.

Chronicle of Zuqnin: Harrak, A. (1999) *The chronicle of Zuqnīn parts III and IV: A.D. 488–775* (Mediaeval Sources in Translation 36). Toronto: Pontifical Institute of Medieval Studies.

Consularia constantinopolitana: Burgess, R.W. (1993) *The Chronicle of Hydatius and the Consularia Constantinopolitana. Two Contemporary Accounts of the Final Years of the Roman Empire.* Oxford: Oxford University Press.

De origo gentis romanae: Sehlmeyer, M. (2004) *Origo gentis romanae. Die Ursprünge des römischen Volkes* (Texte zur Forschung 82). Darmstadt: Wissenschaftliche Buchgesellschaft.

De rebus bellicis: Ireland, R. (1984) *Anonymi auctori de rebus bellicis* (Bibliotheca scriptorum graecorum et romanorum teubneriana). Leipzig: Teubner.

De viris illustribus: Gruendel, R. (1970) *Sexti Aurelii Victoris Liber de Caesaribus praecedunt Origo gentis Romanae et Liber de viris illustribus urbis Romae subsequitur Epitome de Caesaribus* (Bibliotheca scriptorum graecorum et romanorum teubneriana). Leipzig: Teubner.

Ennodius: Rohr, C. (1995) *Der Theoderich-Panegyricus des Ennodius* (Monumenta Germaniae historica. Studien und Texte 12). Hannover: Hahnsche Buchhandlung.

Epitome de Caesaribus: Festy, M. (1999) *Pseudo-Aurélius Victor. Abrégé des Césars* (Collection des Universités de France). Paris: Les Belles Lettres.

Eusebius, *Vita Constantini*: Winkelmann, F. (1991) *Eusebius Werke 1.1: Über das Leben des Kaisers Konstantin* (Griechische Christliche Schriftsteller), 2nd edn, Berlin: Akademie Verlag.

——*Historia ecclesiastica:* Schwartz, E. and Mommsen, T. (1909) *Eusebius Werke 2: Die Kirchengeschichte: Vol. 2* (Griechische Christliche Schriftsteller). Leipzig: J.C. Hinrichs.

——*De laudibus Constantini*: Heikel, I.A. (1902) *Eusebius Werke 1: Über das Leben Constantins; Constantins Rede an die heilige Versammlung; Tricennatsrede an Constantin* (Griechische Christliche Schriftsteller 1). Leipzig: J.C. Hinrichs.

——*Praeparatio evangelica*: Mras, K. and des Places, E. (1982–1983) *Eusebius Werke 8: Die Praeparatio evangelica* (Griechische Christliche Schriftsteller 43), 2 Vols., 2nd edn, Berlin: Akademie Verlag.

——*Demonstratio evangelica*: Heikel, I.A. (1913) *Eusebius Werke 6: Die Demonstratio evangelica* (Griechische Christliche Schriftsteller 23). Leipzig: J.C. Hinrichs.

Eutropius: Hellegouarc'h, J. (2001) *Eutrope. Abrégé d'histoire romaine* (Collection des Universités de France). Paris: Les Belles Lettres.

Festus: Arnaud-Lindet, M.-P. (1994) *Festus. Abrégé des hauts faits du peuple romain* (Collection des Universités de France). Paris: Les Belles Lettres.

Gennadius, *De viris illustribus*: PL 58: 1059–120.

Gregory of Nazianzus, *Oratio*: Mossay, J. and Lafontaine, G. (1981) *Grégoire de Nazianze. Discours 24–26* (Sources chrétiennes 284). Paris: Les Belles Lettres.

Hippolytus, *In Danielem*: Bonwetsch, M. and Richard, M. (2000) *Hippolyt Werke. 1.1: Kommentar zu Daniel* (Griechische Christliche Schriftsteller N.F. 7), 2nd edn, Berlin: Akademie Verlag.

Isidorus, *Libellus de arte rhetorica:* Halm, C. (1863) *Rhetores latini minores.* Leipzig: Teubner.

Itinerarium Alexandri: Tabacco, R. (2000) *Itinerarium Alexandri. Testo, apparato critico, introduzione, traduzione e commento.* Turin and Florence: Olschki.

Jerome, *Chronicon*: Helm, R. (1913) *Eusebius Werke 7: Die chronik des Hieronymus* (Griechische Christliche Schriftsteller). Leipzig: J.C. Hinrichs.

——*Epistulae*: Hilberg, I. (1910–18) *Sancti Eusebii Hieronymi Epistulae* (Corpus scriptorum ecclesiasticorum latinorum 54–56), 3 Vols. Vienna: Hoelder, Pichler and Tempsky.

John of Beith-Aphthonia, *Vita Severi:* Kugener, M.-A. (1904) *Vie de Sévère* (Patrologia orientalis 2). Paris: Firmin-Didot.

Julius Victor, *Ars rhetorica:* Halm, C. (1863) *Rhetores latini minores.* Leipzig: J.C. Hinrichs.

Justin: Seel, O. (1972) *M. Iuniani Iustini Epitoma historiarum Philippicarum Pompei Trogi* (Bibliotheca scriptorum Graecorum et Romanorum Teubneriana). Stuttgart: Teubner.

Juvencus, *Evangelia*: Marold, K. (1886) *C. Vetti Aquilini Iuvenci Libri Evangeliorum IIII* (Bibliotheca scriptorum graecorum et romanorum teubneriana). Leipzig: Teubner.

Lactantius, *Institutiones*: Monat, P. (1973–2000) *Lactance. Institutions divines* (Sources chrétiennes 204, 205, 326, 337, 377), 5 vols. Paris: Le Cerf.

——*De mortibus persecutorum*: Städele, A. (2003) *Laktanz. De Mortibus Persecutorum. Die Todesarten der Vervolger* (Fontes Christianae 43). Turnhout: Brepols.

Libanius, *Orationes* and *Epistulae*: Foerster, R. (1903–63) *Libanii opera* (Bibliotheca scriptorum graecorum et romanorum teubneriana), 10 Vols. Leipzig: Teubner.

Menander Protector: Blockley, R.C. (1985) *The History of Menander the Guardsman. Introductory Essay, Text, Translation, and Historiographical Notes.* Liverpool: Liverpool University Press.

Minucius Felix: Kytzler, B. (1965) *Minucius Felix. Octavius.* Munich: Kösel.

Oracula Sibyllina: Kurfess, A. and Gauger, J.-D. (2002) *Sibyllinische Weissagungen* (Sammlung Tusculum), 2nd edn, Düsseldorf and Zürich: Tusculum.

Origines, *Contra Celsum*: Borret, M. (1967–76) *Origène. Contre Celse* (Sources chrétiennes 132, 136, 147, 150, 227), 5 Vols. Paris: Le Cerf.

Orosius, *Commonitorium*: Daur, K.-D. (1985) *Sancti Aurelii Augustini. Contra adversarium legis et prophetarum. Commonitorium Orosii et Sancti Aurelii Augustini contra priscillianistas et origenistas* (Corpus Christianorum. Series latina XV, 3). Turnhout: Brepols.

——*Historiae*: Zangemeister, C. (1882) *Pauli Orosii Historiarum adversum paganos libri VII, accedit eiusdem liber apologeticus* (Corpus scriptorum ecclesiasticorum latinorum 5). Vienna: Hoelder, Pichler and Tempsky;

Arnaud-Lindet, M.-P. (1990–1) *Orose. Histoires* (Collection des Universités de France), 3 Vols. Paris: Les Belles Lettres; A. Lippold and A. Bartalucci (1976) *Orosio. Le storie contro i pagani* (Scrittori greci e latini), 2 Vols. s.l.: Fondazione Lorenzo Valla.

Panegyrici latini: Mynors, R.A.B. (1964) *XII Panegyrici Latini* (Oxford Classical Texts). Oxford: Oxford University Press.

Paulinus, *Vita Ambrosii*: Mohrmann, C., Bastiaensen, A.A.R, Canali, L, and Carena, C. (1975) *Vita di Cipriano. Vita di Ambrogio. Vita di Agostino* (Scrittori greci e latini), s.l.: Fondazione Lorenzo Valla.

Prosper Tiro, *Chronicon:* Mommsen, T. (1892) *Chronica minora*, Vol. 1 (Monumenta Germaniae historica. Auctores antiquissimi 9). Berlin: Hahnsche Buchhandlung.

——*De providentia Dei*: Markovich, M. (1989) *Prosper of Aquitaine. De providentia Dei. Text, Translation and Commentary* (Supplements to Vigiliae Christianae 10). Leiden: Brill.

Rufinus, *De compositione et de metris oratorum*: Halm, C. (1863) *Rhetores latini minores.* Leipzig: Teubner.

—— *Versus*: Halm, C. (1863) *Rhetores latini minores.* Leipzig: Teubner.

Rufinus of Aquileia, *Historia ecclesiastica*, Rufinus of Aquileia: Schwartz, E. and Mommsen, T. (1909) *Eusebius Werke 2: Die Kirchengeschichte: Vol. 2* (Griechische Christliche Schriftsteller). Leipzig: J.C. Hinrichs.

Sallustius, *Historiae*: Maurenbrecher, B. (1891–3) *Sallustius Crispus. Historiarum reliquae*, 2 Vols. Leizpig: Teubner.

Salvianus, *De gubernatione Dei*: Lagarrigue, G. (1975) *Salvien de Marseille. Du gouvernement de Dieu* (Sources chrétiennes 220). Paris: Le Cerf.

Schemata dianoes quae ad rhetores pertinent: Halm, C. (1863) *Rhetores latini minores.* Leipzig: Teubner.

Severus of Minorca: Bradbury, S. (1996) *Severus of Minorca. Letter on the Conversion of the Jews.* Oxford: Oxford University Press.

Socrates: Hansen, G.C. (1995) *Sokrates. Kirchengeschichte* (Griechische Christliche Schriftsteller N.F. 1). Berlin: Akademie Verlag.

Sozomen: Bidez, J. and Hansen, G.C. (1995) *Sozomenos. Kirchengeschichte* (Griechische Christliche Schriftsteller N.F. 4), 2nd edn, Berlin: Akademie Verlag.

Stobaeus: Hense, O. (1894–1909) *Ioannis Stobaei anthologii libri duo posteriores*, 3 Vols. Berlin: Weidmann.

Sulpicius Severus, *Chronica*: de Senneville-Grave, G. (1999) *Sulpice Sévère. Chroniques* (Sources chrétiennes 444). Paris: Le Cerf.

—— *Vita Martini*: Fontaine, J. (1967–9) *Sulpice Sévère. Vie de Saint Martin* (Sources chrétiennes 133–5). Paris: Le Cerf.

Symmachus, *Epistulae* and *Orationes*: Callu, J.-P. (1972–2009) *Symmaque. Lettres. Discours. Rapports* (Collection des Universités de France), 5 Vols. Paris: Les Belles Lettres.

Themistius, *Orationes*: Downey, G. (1965–74) *Themistii Orationes* (Bibliotheca scriptorum graecorum et romanorum teubneriana), 3 Vols. Leipzig: Teubner.

Vegetius, *Epitoma rei militaris*: Lang, C. (1869) *Flavii Vegeti Renati Epitoma rei militaris* (Bibliotheca scriptorum graecorum et romanorum teubneriana). Leipzig: Teubner.

Venantius Fortunatus: Leo, F. (1881) *Venanti Honori Clementiani Fortunati opera poetica* (Monumenta Germaniae historica. Auctores antiquissimi 4.1). Berlin: Hahnsche Buchhandlung.

Victor of Vita: von Halm, K.F. (1879) *Victoris Vitensis Historia persecutionis Africanae provinciae sub Geiserico et Hunrico regibus Wandalorum* (Monumenta Germaniae historica. Auctores antiquissimi 3.1). Berlin: Hahnsche Buchhandlung.

Pseudo-Zachariah: Greatrex, G. (2010) *The Chronicle of Pseudo-Zachariah Rhetor: Church and War in Late Antiquity* (Translated Texts for Historians). Liverpool: Liverpool University Press.

Literature

Allan, M. I. (2003) 'Universal history 300–1000: Origins and western developments', in *Historiography in the Middle Ages*, ed. D.M. Deliyannis. Leiden: Brill: 17–42.

Alonso-Núñez, J.M. (1993) 'Die Auslegung der Geschichte bei Paulus Orosius: die Abfolge der Weltreiche, die Idee der Roma Aeterna und die Goten', *WS* 106: 197–213.

——(2002) *The Idea of Universal History in Greece: From Herodotus to the Age of Augustus*. Amsterdam: Gieben.

——(2005) 'Die Universalgeschichtsschreibung in der Spätantike und die westgotische Historiographie', in *Zwischen Historiographie und Hagiographie*, eds. J. Dummer and M. Vielberg. Stuttgart: Franz Steiner: 9–25.

Arnaud-Lindet, M.-P. (1990–1) *Orose. Histoires* (Collection des Universités de France), 3 Vols. Paris: Les Belles Lettres.

Austin, N.J.E. (1973) 'In support of Ammianus' veracity', *Historia* 22: 331–5.

Avenarius, G. (1956) *Lukians Schrift zur Geschichtsschreibung*. Meisenheim am Glan: Anton Hain.

Ax, W. (1990) 'Die Geschichtsschreibung bei Quintilian', in: *Festschrift für C.J. Classen*. Stuttgart: Franz Steiner: 133–68.

Barnes, T.D. (1998) *Ammianus and the Representation of Historical Reality*. Ithaca: Cornell University Press.

Bartalucci, A. (1976) 'Lingua e stile in Paolo Orosio', *SCO* 25: 213–53.

Beck, G.F.H. (1834) *Dissertatio de Orosii historici fontibus et auctoritate*. Marburg: Hassorum.

Bellen, H. (1990) 'Babylon und Rom—Orosius und Augustin', in *Imperium Romanum. Festschrift (. . .) Karl Christ*, eds. P. Kneissl and V. Losemann. Stuttgart: Franz Steiner: 51–60.

Bennett, C. (1988) 'The conversion of Vergil: The Aeneis in Augustine's "Confessions"', *REAug* 34: 47–69.

Beschorner, A. (1999) 'Das Opusculum des Iulius Exuperantius', *Hermes* 127: 237–53.

Bessone, L. (1982) 'La tradizione epitomaria liviana in età imperiale', *ANRW* II.30.2: 1230–63.

——(1984) 'Le Periochae di Livio', *A&R* 29: 42–55.

——(2000) 'Dalla polemica apologetica al falso storico', *ACD* 36: 137–49.

——(2002–3) '"Consulem ipse se fecit" (Flor. 2, 13, 21): considerazioni sul secondo consolato di Cesare', *ACD* 38–9: 21–36.

Bird, H.W. (1995) 'Some late Roman perspectives on the Republican Period', *AncW* 26: 45–50.

Bleckmann, B. (1997) 'Überlegungen zur Enmannschen Kaisergeschichte und zur Formung historischer Traditionen in tetrarchischer und konstantinischer Zeit', in *Historiae Augustae Colloquium Bonnense*, eds. G. Bonamente and K. Rosen. Bari: Edipuglia: 11–37.

——(2006) *Fiktion als Geschichte: Neue Studien zum Autor der Hellenika Oxyrhynchia und zur Historiographie des vierten vorchristlichen Jahrhunderts*. Göttingen.

——(2007) 'Vom Tsunami von 365 zum Mimas-Orakel: Ammianus Marcellinus als Zeithistoriker und die spätgriechische Tradition', in den Boeft, Drijvers and Teitler: 7–31.

——(2010) 'Tendenziöse Historiographie bei Liberatus von Proterios bis zu Athanasios II', *ZAC* 14: 166–95.

Blockley, R. (2001) 'Ammianus and Cicero on truth in historiography', *AHB* 15: 14–24.

Bonamente, G. (1975) 'Il metus punicus e la decadenza di Roma in Sallustio, Agostino ed Orosio', *GIF* 27: 137–69.

Bosworth, A.B. (2003) 'Plus ça change . . . : ancient historians and their sources', *ClAnt* 22: 167–97.

Bradbury, S. (1996) *Severus of Minorca. Letter on the Conversion of the Jews*. Oxford: Oxford University Press.

Brandt, H. (2009) 'Historia magistra vitae. Orosius und die spätantike Historiographie', in *Jenseits der Grenzen* (Millenium-Studien), eds. A. Golz, H. Leppin, and H. Schlange-Schöningen. Berlin: Walter de Gruyter: 121–33.

Brink, C.O. (1960) 'Tragic history and Aristotle's school', *PCPhS* 6: 14–19.

Brodka, D. (1998) *Die Romideologie in der römischen Literatur der Spätantike*. Frankfurt am Main: Lang.

——(2004) *Die Geschichtsphilosophie in der spätantiken Historiographie*. Frankfurt am Main: Lang.

——(2007) 'Zum Wahrheitsbegriff in den bella des Prokopios von Kaisareia', *Klio* 89: 465–76.

——and Stachyra, M. (eds.) (2007) *Continuity and Change: Studies in Late Antique Historiography* (Electrum. Studies in Ancient History 13). Cracow: Jagiellonian University Press.

Bruggisser, P. (1993) *Symmaque ou le ritual épistolaire de l'amitié littéraire. Recherches sur le premier livre de la correspondence* (Paradosis 35). Fribourg: Editions universitaires.

Buchheit, V. (1985) 'Prudentius über Gesittung durch Eroberung und Bekehrung', *WJA* 11: 189–223.

Burgess, R.W. (1993a) *The Chronicle of Hydatius and the Consularia Constantinopolitana. Two Contemporary Accounts of the Final Years of the Roman Empire*. Oxford: Oxford University Press.

——(1993b) 'Principes cum tyrannis: Two studies on the *Kaisergeschichte* and its tradition', *CQ* 42: 491–500.

——(1995) 'Jerome and the *Kaisergeschichte*', *Historia* 44: 349–69.

——(2005) 'A common source for Jerome, Eutropius, Festus, Ammianus, and the Epitome de Caesaribus between 358 and 378, along with further thoughts on the date and nature of the *Kaisergeschichte*', *CPh* 100: 166–92.

——(2006) 'Apologetic and chronography. The antecedents of Julius Africanus', in Wallraff 2006: 17–42.

Cain, A. (2009) *The Letters of Jerome: Asceticism, Biblical Exegesis, and The Construction of Christian Authority in Late Antiquity* (Oxford Early Christian Studies). Oxford: Oxford University Press.

Calboli, G. (1974) 'La credibilità di Ammiano Marcellino a la sua arte espositiva', *BSL* 4: 67–103.

Callu, J.-P. (1992) 'La preface à l'itinéraire d'Alexandre', in *De Tertullien aux Mozarabes* (Collection des études augustiniennes. Série Antiquité 132), eds. L. Holtz et J.-C. Fredouille. Paris, Institut des Etudes augustiniennes: 429–44.

——(2002) *Symmaque. Lettres. Livres IX–X* (Collection des Universités de France). Paris: Les Belles Lettres.

Cameron, Alan (1970) *Claudian. Poetry and Propaganda at the Court of Honorius*. Oxford: Oxford University Press.

——(2011) *The Last Pagans of Rome*. New York and Oxford: Oxford University Press.

Cameron, Averil (ed.) (1989) *History as Text: The Writing of Ancient History*. London: Duckworth.

Candau Morón, J.M. (2001) 'La historia como espectáculo: sobre algunas tendencias de la historiografía helenística', in *La verdad tamizada:*

cronistas, reporteros e historiadores ante su público, eds. A. Pérez Jiménez and G. Cruz Andreotti. Malaga: Ediciones clásicas: 69–86.

Cesa, M. (2003) 'Le "historiae adversus pagano" di Orosio nel contesto della storiografia tardoantica', in *Forme letterarie nella produzione latina di IV–V secolo con uno sguardo a Bisanzio*, ed. F.E. Consolino. Rome: Herder: 19–31.

Chaplin, J.D. (2000) *Livy's Exemplary History*. Oxford: Oxford University Press.

Chauvot, A. (1998) *Opinions romaines face aux barbares au IVe siècle ap. J.C.* Paris: De Boccard.

Chesnut, S.F. (1992) 'Eusebius, Augustine, Orosius and the Latin patristic and medieval Christian histories', in *Eusebius, Christianity, and Judaism* (Studia post-biblica 42), eds. H.W. Attridge e.a. Leiden: Brill: 687–713.

Clark, G. (2004) 'City of God(s): Virgil and Augustine', *Proceedings of the Vergil Society* 25: 83–94.

——(2005) *Augustine: Confessions*. 2nd edn, Bristol, Bristol Classical Press.

Clausi, B. (1995) 'Storia sacra e strategia retorica: osservazioni sull'uso dell' "exemplum" biblico nell' "Adversus Iovinianum" di Gerolamo', *CrSt* 16: 457–84.

Cobet, J. (2009) 'Orosius' Weltgeschichte: Tradition und Konstruktion', *Hermes* 137: 60–92.

Coffin, H.C. (1936) 'Vergil and Orosius', *CJ* 31: 235–41.

Collingwood, R.G. (1946) *The Idea of History*. Oxford: Oxford University Press.

Consolino, F.E (2004) 'Poetry and politics in Claudian's carmina minora 22 and 50', in Ehlers, Felgentreu, and Wheeler 2004: 142–74.

Conybeare, C. (1999) 'Terrarum orbi documentum: Augustine, Camillus, and learning from history', in Vessey, Pollman, and Fitzgerald 1999: 59–74.

Corbellini, C. (1984) 'Breuitas e ueritas nella storia di Orosio', *MGR* 9: 297–314.

Cornell, T. (2010) 'Universal history and the early Roman historians', in Liddel and Fear 2010: 87–101.

——Fear, A., and Liddel, P. (2010) 'Introduction', in Liddel and Fear 2010: 1–14.

Corsini, E. (1968) *Introduzione alle storie di Orosio*. Turin, G. Giappichelli.

Coskun, A. (2002) 'Die sogenannten "Fasti" und der "Consularis liber" des Ausonius mit einem Exkurs zur Karriere des Proculus Gregorius', *Philologus* 146: 350–9.

——(2006) 'The eucharisticos of Paulinus Pellaeus: Towards a reappraisal of the worldly convert's life and autobiography', *VChr* 60: 285–314.

Courcelle, P. (1963) *Les confessions de Saint Augustin dans la tradition littéraire. Antécédents et postérité* (Etudes augustiniennes. Série Antiquité 15). Paris: Institut des Etudes augustiniennes.

——(1964) *Histoire littéraire des grandes invasions germaniques* (Etudes augustiniennes. Série Antiquité 19), 3rd ed. Paris: Institut des Etudes augustiniennes.

——(1969) 'Jugements de Rufin et de Saint Augustin sur les empereurs du IVe siècle et la défaite suprême du paganisme', *REA* 71: 100–30.

——(1976) 'Les lecteurs de l'Enéide devant les grandes invasions germaniques', *Romanobarbarica* 1: 25–56.

——(1984) *Lecteurs païens et lecteurs chrétiens de l'Enéide. 1. Les témoignages littéraires.* Paris: Institut de France.

Cozzoli, A.-T. (2002) 'Alcuni aspetti della storiografia di Duride di Samo', in *Samo: storia, letteratura, scienza: atti delle giornate di studio, Ravenna 14–16 novembre 2002*, ed. E. Cavallini. Pisa: Istituti Editoriali e Poligrafici Internazionali: 379–98.

Cribiore, R. (2001) *Gymnastics of the Mind. Greek Education in Hellenistic and Roman Egypt.* Princeton: Princeton University Press.

Crosson, F.J. (2003) 'Book Five: The disclosure of hidden providence', in *A Reader's Companion to Augustine's Confessions*, eds. K. Paffenroth and R.P. Kennedy. Louisville and London: Westminster John Knox Press: 71–88.

Dagron, G. (1978) *Vie et miracles de Sainte Thecla* (Subsidia hagiographica 62). Brussels: Société des bollandistes.

Dauge, Y.A. (1981) *Le Barbare. Recherches sur la conception romaine de la barbarie et de la civilisation* (Collection Latomus 176). Brussels: Société des Etudes latines.

David, J.-M. (1998) 'Les enjeux de l'exemplarité à la fin de la République et au début du principat', in David 1998: 9–17.

——(ed.) (1998) *Valeurs et mémoire à Rome. Valère Maxime ou la vertu recomposée.* Paris: De Boccard.

Dawson, C. (1977) 'The Christian View of History', in *God, History, and Historians. An Anthology of Modern Christian Views of History*, ed. C.T. McIntire. New York: Oxford University Press: 28–45.

de Boer, S. (1985) 'Rome, the "translatio imperii" and the early Christian interpretation of Daniel II and VII', *RSLR* 21: 181–218.

De Coninck, L. (1992) 'Orosius and the virtutes of his narrative', *AncSoc* 12: 45–57.

Deferrari, R. (1964) *Orosius. Seven Books of History against the Pagans.* Washington, D.C.: Catholic University of America Press.

De Jonge, P. (1948) *Philological and Historical Commentary on Ammianus Marcellinus XV, 1–5.* Groningen: Wolters.

Demandt, A. (1965) *Zeitkritik und Geschichtsbild im Werk Ammians.* Bonn: Habelt.

——(1978) *Metaphern für Geschichte.* Munich: Beck.

Demandt, A. (1980) 'Das Ende des Altertums in metaphorischer Deutung', *Gymnasium* 87: 178–204.

Demoen, K. (1997) 'A paradigm for the analysis of paradigms: The rhetorical exemplum in ancient and imperial Greek theory,' *Rhetorica* 15: 125–58.

den Boeft, J. (2007) 'Non consolandi gratia, sed probrose monendi (Res gestae 28.1.4). The hazards of (moral) historiography', in den Boeft, Drijvers, and Teitler 2007: 293–309.

——and den Hengst, D. (1992) *Cognitio gestorum. The Historiographic Art of Ammianus Marcellinus*. Amsterdam: North-Holland.

——Drijvers, J.W., and Teitler, H. (eds.) (2007) *Ammianus after Julian. The Reign of Valentinian and Valens in Books 26–31 of the Res gestae* (Mnemosyne Supplements 289). Leiden: Brill.

den Boer, W. (1961) 'Some remarks on the beginnings of christian historiography', *Studia Patristica* 4: 348–62.

Diesner, H.J. (1963) 'Orosius und Augustinus', *AAAHung* 11: 89–102.

Doepp, S. (1980) *Zeitgeschichte in Dichtungen Claudians*. Wiesbaden, Steiner.

Drexler, H. (1974) *Ammianstudien*. Hildesheim: Olms.

Dückers, S. (1999) *Pathos der Distanz. Zur theologischen Physiognomie und geistesgeschichtlichen Stellung Erik Peterson*. Münster: LIT.

Dué, C. (2000) 'Tragic history and barbarian speech in Sallust's Jugurtha', *HSCPh* 100: 311–25.

Duval, Y.-M. (1966) 'L'éloge de Théodose dans la Cité de Dieu (V, 26, 1). Sa place, son sens et ses sources', *RecAug* 4: 135–79.

Dyson, R.W. (1998) *Augustine. The City of God against the Pagans*. Cambridge: Cambridge University Press.

Eck, W. (2000) 'Die Täuschung der Öffentlichkeit oder Die "Unparteilichkeit" des Historikers Tacitus', *A&A* 46: 190–206.

Edwards, M., Goodman, M., Price, S.R.F., and Rowland, C. (eds.) (1999) *Apologetics in the Roman Empire: Pagans, Jews, and Christians*. Oxford: Oxford University Press.

Eger, H. (1939) 'Kaiser und Kirche in der Geschichtstheologie Eusebs von Cäsarea', *ZNTW* 38: 97–115.

Ehlers, W.W., Felgentreu, F., and Wheeler, S.M. (eds.) (2004) *'Aetas Claudianea': eine Tagung an der Freien Universität Berlin vom 28. bis 30. Juni 2002*. Munich: Saur.

Eigler, U. (2003) *Lectiones vetustatis. Römische Literatur und Geschichte in der lateinischen Literatur der Spätantike* (Zetemata 115). Munich.

Enmann, A. (1884) 'Eine verlorene Geschichte der römischen Kaiser und das Buch De viris illustribus urbis Romae', *Philologus Suppl.* 4: 337–501.

Escribaño Paño, V. (1996) 'Tyrannus en los Historiae de Orosio: entre brevitas y adversum paganos', *Augustinianum* 36: 185–214.

——(2007) 'Fortis fide ac viribus semper Hispania: Laus Hispaniae y distorsion historiográfica en Orosio', *Latomus* 66: 690–709.

Fabbrini, F. (1979) *Paolo Orosio. Uno storico*. Rome: Edizioni di storia e letteratura.

Fainck, G. (1951) *Paul Orose et sa conception de l'histoire*. Diss.: Aix-en-Provence.

Farina, R. (1966) *L'impero et l'imperatore cristiano in Eusebio di Cesarea. La prima teologia politica del cristianesimo*. Zurich: Pas Verlag.

Fear, A. (2005) 'The Christian optimism of Paulus Orosius', in *From Orosius to the Historia Silense*, ed. D. Hook. Bristol, HiPLAM: 1–16.

——(2010a) *Orosius. Seven Books of History against the Pagans* (Translated Texts for Historians). Liverpool: Liverpool University Press.

——(2010b) 'Orosius and escaping from the dance of doom', in Liddel and Fear 2010: 176–88.

Feeney, D. (2007) *Caesar's Calendar. Ancient Time and the Beginnings of History* (Sather Classical Lectures 65). Berkeley: University of California Press.

Feldherr, A. (1998) *Spectacle and Society in Livy's History*. Berkeley, University of California Press.

——(ed.) (2009) *The Cambridge Companion to the Roman Historians*. Cambridge: Cambridge University Press.

Felgentreu, F. (1999) *Claudians praefationes. Bedingungen, Beschreibungen und Wirkungen einer poetischen Kleinform* (Beiträge zur Altertumskunde 130). Stuttgart and Leipzig: Teubner.

Felmy, A. (2001) *Die römische Republik im Geschichtsbild der Spätantike. Zum Umgang lateinischer Autoren des 4. und 5. Jahrhundert mit den exempla maiorum*. Diss.: Berlin.

Festy, M. (1999) *Pseudo-Aurélius Victor. Abrégé des Césars* (Collection des Universités de France). Paris: Les Belles Lettres.

Finke, H. (1904) *Ammianus Marcellinus und seine Quellen zur Geschichte der römischen Republik*. Heidelberg: E. Geisendörfer.

Fink-Ferrera, G. (1954) 'San Agustin y Orosio. Esquema para un estudio de los fuentes del "De civitate Dei"', *La Ciudad de Dios* 167: 455–549.

Firpo, G. (1983) 'Osservazioni su temi Orosiani', *Apollinaris* 56: 233–63.

Fornara, C.W. (1983) *The Nature of History in Ancient Greece and Rome*. Berkeley: University of California Press.

Foucher, A. (2000a) 'Nature et formes de l' "histoire tragique" à Rome', *Latomus* 59: 773–801.

——(2000b) *Historia proxima poetis. L'influence de la poésie épique sur le style des historiens latins de Salluste à Ammien Marcellin* (Collection Latomus 255). Brussels: Société des Etudes latines.

Fournet, J.-L. (2003) 'Between literary tradition and cultural change: The poetic and documentary production of Diosorus of Aphrodite', in *Learned*

Antiquity. Scholarship and Society in the Near-East, the Greco-Roman World, and the Early Medieval West, eds. A.A. MacDonald, M. W. Twomey, and G.J. Reinink. Leuven: Peeters: 101–14.

Fowler, D. (1991) 'Narrate and describe: The problem of ekphrasis', *JRS* 81: 25–35.

——(2000) *Roman Constructions: Readings in Postmodern Latin*. Oxford: Oxford University Press.

Fox, M. (1996) *Roman Historical Myths. The Regal Period in Historical Literature*. Oxford: Oxford University Press.

——(2001) 'Dionysius, Lucian, and the prejudice against rhetoric in history', *JRS* 91: 76–93.

Franchet d'Esperey, S. (2010) 'Le statut de l'exemplum historique chez Quintilien', in *Clio sous le regard d'Hermès. L'utilisation de l'histoire dans la rhétorique ancienne de l'époque hellénistique à l'Antiquité tardive*, eds. P.-L. Malosse, M.-P. Noël, and B. Schouler. Alessandria: Edizioni dell'Orso: 65–79.

Fratantuono, L.M. (2006) '"Ut videre Camillam": the nachleben of reckless heroism', *RCCM* 58: 287–308.

Fredouille, J.-C. (1998) 'Les sermons d'Augustin sur la chute de Rome', in *Augustin prédicateur (395–411)* (Collection des études augustiniennes. Série Antiquité 159), ed. G. Madec. Paris: Institut des Etudes augustiniennes: 439–48.

Frend, W.H.C. (1989) 'Augustine and Orosius on the end of the ancient world', *AugStud* 20: 1–38.

——(1994) 'Augustine's reactions to the barbarian invasions of the West, 407–417: some comparisons with his western contemporaries', *Augustinus* 39: 241–55.

Freund, S. (2009) *Laktanz. Divinae Institutiones Buch 7: De vita beata. Einleitung, Text, Übersetzung und Kommentar* (Texte und Kommentare 31). Berlin and New York: Walter de Gruyter.

Fritz, K. von (1958) 'Die Bedeutung des Aristoteles für die Geschichtsschreibung', in *Histoire et historiens dans l'antiquité* (Entretiens Hardt 4). Vandoevres: Fondation Hardt: 83–145.

Frye, D. (1991) 'A mutual friend of Athaulf and Jerome', *Historia* 40: 507–8.

——(1994) 'Rusticus: Ein gemeinsamer Freund von Athaulf und Hieronymus? A Reply', *Historia* 43: 504–6.

Fuchs, H. (1938) *Der geistige Widerstand gegen Rom in der antiken Welt*. Berlin: Walter de Gruyter.

Fugmann, J. (1990–2003) *Königszeit und frühe Republik in der Schrift 'De viris illustribus urbis romae'. Quellenkritische Untersuchungen*, 3 Vols. Frankfurt am Main: Lang.

Galdi, G. (2009) 'Der Lebensaltervergleich: Neue Beobachtungen zu einem alten Bild', *Hermes* 137: 403–24.

Gärtner, H.A. (1996–7) 'Roma redet: Claudianus (In Gildonem 28–127) im Vergleich zu früheren und zeitgenössischen Autoren', *AAntHung* 37: 277–84.

Gemeinhardt, P. (2007) *Das lateinische Christentum und die antike pagane Bildung* (Studien und Texte zu Antike und Christentum 41). Tübingen: Mohr Siebeck.

Gill, C. and Wiseman, T.P. (eds.) (1993) *Lies and Fiction in the Ancient World*. Exeter: Exeter University Press.

Ginzburg, C. (1998) *History, Rhetoric, and Proof. The Menahem Stern Jerusalem Lectures*. Hanover and London: University Press of New England.

Girardet, K.M. (1980) 'Das christliche Priestertum Konstantins d. Gr. Ein Aspekt der Herrscheridee des Eusebius von Caesarea', *Chiron* 10: 569–92.

Glorie, F. (1964) *S. Hieronymi Presbyteri Opera. Pars I. opera exegetica 5: Commentariorum in Danielem Libri III <IV>* (Corpus Christianorum. Series latina 75A). Turnhout: Brepols.

Goetz, H.W. (1980a) *Die Geschichtstheologie des Orosius*. Darmstadt: Wissenschaftliche Buchgesellschaft.

——(1980b) 'Orosius und die Barbaren. Zu den umstrittenen Vorstellungen eines spätantiken Geschichtstheologen', *Historia* 29: 356–76.

——(1991) 'On the universality of universal history', in *L'historiographie médiévale en Europe*. Paris: Editions du Centre national de la recherche scientifique: 247–61.

Goffart, W. (1987) *The Narrators of Barbarian History (A.D. 550–800): Jordanes, Gregory of Tours, Bede and Paul the Deacon*. Princeton: Princeton University Press.

Goldhill, S. (ed.) (2001) *Being Greek under Rome. Cultural Identity, the Second Sophistic, and the Development of Empire*. Cambridge: Cambridge University Press.

Grafton, A. and Williams, M.H. (2006) *Christianity and the Transformation of the Book: Origen, Eusebius, and the Library of Caesarea*. Cambridge, MA: Harvard University Press.

Greatrex, G. (2001) 'Lawyers and historians in late Antiquity', in *Law, Society, and Authority in Late Antiquity*, ed. R. Mathisen. Oxford: Oxford University Press: 148–61.

Green, R.P.H. (1991) *The Works of Ausonius*. Oxford: Oxford University Press.

Griffin, M.T. (1982) 'The Lyons tablet and Tacitean hindsight', *CQ* 32: 404–18.

Grumel, V. (1956) 'Du nombre des persécutions païennes', *REAug* 7: 61–6.

Gunderson, E. (ed.) (2009) *The Cambridge Companion to Ancient Rhetoric*. Cambridge: Cambridge University Press.

Hagendahl, H. (1941) *Orosius und Iustinus. Ein Beitrag zur iustinischen Textgeschichte*. Göteborg: Almqvist & Wiksell.

——(1958) *Latin Fathers and the Classics. A Study on the Apologists, Jerome, and other Christian Writers*. Göteborg: Almqvist & Wiksell.

Hagendahl, H. (1967) *Augustine and the Latin Classics*. Göteborg: Almqvist & Wiksell.

——(1983) *Von Tertullian zu Cassiodor. Die profane literarische Tradition in dem lateinischen christlichen Schrifttum*. Göteborg: Almqvist & Wiksell.

Hamblenne, P. (1996) 'L' "exemplum" formel dans l'œuvre conservé de Jérôme', *Augustinianum* 36: 93–146.

Harries, J. (1986) 'Sozomen and Eusebius: the lawyer as church historian in the fifth century', in *The Inheritance of Historiography 350–900* (Exeter Studies in History 12), eds. C. Holdsworth and T.P. Wiseman. Exeter: Exeter University Press: 45–52.

Häussler, R. (1964) 'Vom Ursprung und Wandels des Lebensaltervergleichs', *Hermes* 92: 313–41.

Heath, M. (1997) 'Invention', in *Handbook of Classical Rhetoric in the Hellenistic Period 330 BC–AD 400*, ed. S. Porter. Leiden: Brill: 89–119.

Heather, P. (1999) 'The barbarian in late Antiquity: image, reality, and transformation', in *Constructing Identities in Late Antiquity*, ed. R. Miles. London and New York: Routledge: 234–58.

——(2009) *Empires and Barbarians: The Fall of Rome and the Birth of Europe*. New York: Oxford University Press.

Hedrick, C.W. (2000) *History and Silence. Purge and Rehabilitation of Memory in Late Antiquity*. Austin: University of Texas Press.

Heinzelmann, M. (2001) *Gregory of Tours. History and Society in the Sixth Century*. Cambridge: Cambridge University Press (German original 1994).

Herzog, R. (2002) 'Orosius oder Die Formulierung eines Fortschrittskonzepts aus der Erfahrung des Niedergangs', in Id., *Spätantike. Studien zur römischen und lateinisch-christlichen Literatur. Herausgegeben von P. Habermehl* (Hypomnemata. Supplement-Reie 3). Göttingen: Vandenhoeck und Ruprecht: 293–320 (= Id. (1980) in *Niedergang. Studien zu einem geschichtlichen Thema*, eds. R. Koselleck and P. Widmer. Manburg: Klett-Cotta: 79–102).

Hingst, G. (1972) *Zu offenen Quellenfragen bei Orosius*. Diss.: Vienna.

Hirschberg, T. (1991) 'Zum gallischen Krieg des Orosius', *Hermes* 119: 84–93.

Hollerich, M.J. (1990) 'Religion and Politics in the Writings of Eusebius: Reassessing the First "Court Theologian"', *Church History* 59: 309–25.

——(1999) *Eusebius of Caesarea's "Commentary on Isaiah": Christian Exegesis in the Age of Constantine*. Oxford: Oxford University Press.

Hose, M. (1994) *Erneuerung der Vergangenheit. Die Historiker im imperium romanum von Florus bis zu Cassius Dio* (Beiträge zur Altertumskunde 45). Stuttgart and Leipzig: Teubner.

Howe, T. (2007) *Vandalen, Barbaren und Arianer bei Victor von Vita* (Studien zur Alten Geschichte 7). Frankfurt: Verlag Antike.

Hünemörder, C. (1998) art. Hund, in *Der Neue Pauly* 5: 755–8.

Ilski, K. (2007) 'Kirchengeschichte als Weltgeschichte', in Brodka and Stachyra 2007: 121–9.

Inglebert, H. (1994) 'Les héros romains, les martyrs et les ascètes. Les virtutes et les préférences politiques chez les auteurs chrétiens latins du 3e au 5e siècle', *REAug* 40: 305–25.

——(1996) *Les romains chrétiens face à leur histoire* (Collection des études augustiniennes. Série Antiquité 145). Paris: Institut des Etudes augustiniennes.

——(2001) *Interpretatio christiana. Les mutations des savoirs (cosmographie, géographie, ethnographie, histoire) dans l'Antiquité chrétienne (30–630 après J.-C.)* (Collection des études augustiniennes. Série Antiquité 166). Paris: Institut des Etudes augustiniennes.

Innocenti, B. (1994) 'Towards a theory of vivid description as practised in Cicero's Verrine Orations', *Rhetorica* 12: 355–81.

Jaffelin, E. (2000) 'Le temps de l'exemple', *RSR* 74: 437–65.

Janiszewski, P. (2006) *The Missing Link. Greek Pagan Historiography in the Second Half of the Third Century and in the Fourth Century AD*. Warsaw, Warsaw University, Faculty of Law and Administration, Chair of Roman and Antique Law.

Janson, T. (1964) *Latin Prose Prefaces. Studies in Literary Conventions*. Stockholm: Almqvist & Wiksell.

Janvier, Y. (1982) *La géographie d'Orose*. Paris: Les Belles Lettres.

Johnson, A. (2006) *Ethnicity and Argument in Eusebius' Praeparatio Evangelica* (Oxford Early Christian Studies). Oxford: Oxford University Press.

Johnson, S.F. (2006) *Greek Literature in Late Antiquity*. Aldershot: Ashgate.

Jülicher, A. (1915) 'Ein Wort zugunsten des Kirchenhistorikers Rufinus', *Klio* 14: 127–8.

Kaldellis, A. (2004) *Procopius of Caesarea. Tyranny, History, and Philosophy at the end of Antiquity*. Philadelphia: University of Pennsylvania Press.

Kamlah, W. (1951) *Christentum und Geschichtlichkeit: Untersuchungen zur Entstehung des Christentums und zu Augustins Bürgerschaft Gottes*. Stuttgart: Kohlhammer.

Kany, R. (2006) 'Vom Umgang des antiken Christentums mit Geschichte', *ZAC* 10: 564–79.

Kaster, R.A (1988) *Guardians of Language: The Grammarian and Society in Late Antiquity*. Berkeley: University of California Press.

Kelly, G. (2004) 'Ammianus and the Great tsunami', *JRS* 94: 141–67.

——(2007) 'The Sphragis and the Closure of the Rest Gestae', in den Boeft, Drijvers and Teitler 2007: 219–41.

——(2008) *Ammianus Marcellinus. The Allusive Historian*. Cambridge: Cambridge University Press.

Kelly, J.N.D. (1975) *Jerome. His Life, Writings, and Controversies*. London: Duckworth.

Kempshall, M. (2011) *Rhetoric and the Writing of History 400–1500*. Manchester: Manchester University Press.

Kinzig, W. (1994) *Novitas christiana. Die Idee des Fortschitts in der Alten Kirche bis Eusebius* (Forschungen zur Kirchen- und Dogmengeschichte 59). Göttingen: Vandenhoeck und Ruprecht.

Klein, R. (1985) 'Das spätantike Romverständnis vor Augustin', *Bonner Jahrbücher* 185: 97–142.

Klotz, A. (1930) 'Beiträge zur Analyse des geographischen Kapitels im Geschichtswerk des Orosius', in *Charisteria Aloïs Rzach zum 80. Geburtstag dargebracht*. Reichenberg, s.n.: 120–30.

——(1931) 'Die geographischen commentarii des Agrippa und ihre Überreste', *Klio* 24: 38–58, 386–466.

Koch-Peters, D. (1984) *Ansichten des Orosius zur Geschichte seiner Zeit*. Frankfurt am Main: Lang.

Kocken, E. (1935) *De theorie van de vier werelrijken en van de overdracht van wereldheerschappij tot op Innocentius III*. Diss.: Nijmegen.

Kraus, C.S. (1994) 'No second Troy: topoi and refoundation in Livy, Book V', *TAPA* 124: 267–89.

Lacroix, B. (1951) 'La date du IIe livre "De Civitate Dei"', *VChr* 5: 121–2.

——(1965) *Orose et ses idées*. Montréal: Institut d'études médiévales.

Laird, A. (1999) *Powers of Expression, Expressions of Power: Speech Presentation and Latin Literature*. Oxford: Oxford University Press.

——(2009) 'The rhetoric of Roman historiography', in Feldherr 2009: 197–213.

Lamirande, E. (1981) 'La datation de la Vita Ambrosii de Paulin de Milan', *REAug* 27: 44–55.

——(1983) *Paulin de Milan et la Vita Ambrosii: aspects de la religion sous le Bas-Empire*. Montréal: Institut d'études médiévales.

Landucci Gattinoni, F. (1997) *Duride di Samo*. Roma: L'Erma di Bretschneider.

Lanéry, C. (2007) 'La vierge au lupanar: réflexions sur l' "exemplum" hagiographique chez Ambroise de Milan (De uirginibus, II, 4, 22–5, 35)', *REL* 85: 168–91.

Latourelle, K.S. (1977) 'The Christian understanding of history,' in *God, History, and Historians. An Anthology of Modern Christian Views of History*, ed. C.T. McIntire. New York: Oxford University Press: 46–67.

Lausberg, H. (1998) *Handbook of Literary Rhetoric*. Leiden: Brill.

Leloir, L. (1992) *Ecrits apocryphes sur les apôtres. Traduction de l'édition arménienne de Venise*, Vol. 2. Turnhout: Brepols.

Lendon, J.E. (2009) 'Historians without history: Against Roman historiography', in Feldherr 2009: 41–61.

Levene, D.S. (1993) *Religion in Livy*. Leiden: Brill.

——(1997) 'Pity, fear and the historical audience: Tacitus on the fall of Vitellius', in *The Passions in Roman Thought and Literature*, eds. S. M. Braund and C. Gill. Cambridge: Cambridge University Press: 128–49.

Liddel, P. and Fear, A. (eds.) (2010) *Historiae mundi. Studies in Universal History*. London: Duckworth.

Lippold, A. (1952) *Rom und die Barbaren in der Beurteilung des Orosius*. Diss.: Erlangen.

——(1969) 'Orosius, christlicher Apologet und römischer Bürger', *Philologus* 113: 92–105.

——and Bartalucci, A. (1976) *Orosio. Le storie contro i pagani* (Scrittori greci e latini), 2 Vols. s.l.: Fondazione Lorenzo Valla.

Loutsch, C. (1998) 'Procédés rhétoriques de la légitimation des exemples chez Valère Maxime', in David 1998: 27–41.

Löwith, K. (1953) *Weltgeschichte und Heilsgeschehen. Die Theologische Voraussetzungen der Geschichtsphilosophie*. Stuttgart: Kohlhammer.

Luce, T.J. (1971) 'Design and structure in Livy, 5.32–55', *TAPhA* 102: 265–302.

——(1989) 'Ancient views on the causes of bias in historical writing', *CPh* 84: 16–31.

Lühken, M. (2002) *Christianorum Maro et Flaccus. Zur Vergil- und Horazrezeption des Prudentius* (Hypomnemata 141). Göttingen: Vandenhoeck und Ruprecht.

Luiselli B. (1980) 'Indirizzo universale e indirizzi nazionali nella storiografia latino-cristiana dei secc. V–VIII', in *La storiografia ecclesiastica nella tarda antichità*. Messina: Centro di studi umanistici: 508–33.

Lumpe, A. (1966) art. Exemplum, in *Reallexicon für Antike und Christentum* 6: 1229–57.

Luneau, A. (1964) *L'histoire du salut chez les Pères de l'Église* (Théologie historique 2). Paris: Beauchesne.

McCaslin, D.E. (1985–6) 'Polybius, Phylarchus, and the Mantineian tragedy of 223 B.C.', *Archaiognosia* 4: 77–102.

MacCormack, S. (1998) *The Shadows of Poetry. Vergil in the Mind of Augustine*. Berkeley: University of California Press.

McLynn, N. (1994) *Ambrose of Milan. Church and Court in a Christian Capital*. Berkeley: University of California Press.

——(1999) 'Augustine's Roman Empire', in Vessey, Pollman, and Fitzgerald 1999: 29–44.

MacMullen, R. (2004) *Les émotions dans l'histoire, ancienne et moderne*. Paris: Les Belles Lettres.

Madec, G. (1975) '"Tempora christiana". Expression du triomphalisme chrétien ou récrimination païenne', in *Scientia augustiniana: Studien über Augustinus, den Augustinismus und den Augustinerorden*, eds. C. P. Mayer and W. Eckermann. Würzburg: Augustinus-Verlag: 112–36.

Mahé-Simon, M. (2006) 'Aspects de l'historiographie hellénistique dans l'œuvre de Tite-Live (livres VIII et IX)', *REL* 84: 168–84.

Maier, F.G. (1955) *Augustin und das antike Rome*. Stuttgart: Kohlhammer.

Maier, H. (2001) 'Erik Peterson und der Nazionalsozialismus', in *Vom Ende der Zeiten. Geschichtstheologie und Eschatologie bei Erik Peterson*, ed. B. Nichtweiss. Münster: Paulusverlag: 240–53.

Mandouze, A. (1999) 'Une théologie de l'histoire inspirée par Saint Augustin', in *De Renan à Marrou. L'historie du christianisme et les progrès de la méthode historique 1863–1968*, ed. Y.-M. Hilaire. Lille: Presses universitaires du Septentrion: 247–59.

——Marrou, H.-I., and Palanque, J.-R. (1982) *Prosopographie de l'Afrique chrétienne 303–533*. Paris: Editions du Centre national de la recherche scientifique.

Marasco, G. (ed.) (2003) *Greek and Roman Historiography in Late Antiquity: Fourth to Sixth Century A.D.* Leiden: Brill.

Marchetta, A. (1987) *Orosio et Ataulfo nell'ideologia dei rapporti romano-barbarici*. Rome: Istituto storico italiano per il Medio Evo.

Marcone, A. (2002) 'Il sacco di Roma del 410 nella riflessione di Agostino e di Orosio', *RSI* 114: 851–67.

Marincola, J. (1997) *Authority and Tradition in Ancient Historiography*. Cambridge: Cambridge University Press.

——(2003) 'Beyond pity and fear: the emotions of history', *AncSoc* 33: 285–315.

——(2007) 'Universal history from Ephorus to Diodorus', in Marincola 2007: 171–9.

——(ed.) (2007) *A Companion to Greek and Latin Historiography*. Oxford: Blackwell.

——(2009) 'Historiography', in *A Companion to Ancient History*, ed. A. Erskine. Oxford: Blackwell: 13–22.

Markus, R. (1970) *Saeculum: History and Society in the Theology of St Augustine*. Cambridge: Cambridge University Press.

——(1990) *The End of Ancient Christianity*. Cambridge: Cambridge University Press.

Marrou, H.-I. (1938) *Saint Augustin et la fin de la culture antique*. Paris: De Boccard.

——(1970) 'Saint Augustin, Orose et l'augustinianisme historique', in: *La storiografia altomedievale. Settimane de studio . . . 17*. Spoleto: Centro Italiano di Studi sull'Alto Medioevo: 59–87.

——(1977) *Décadence romaine ou antiquité tardive? IIIe-VIe siècle*. Paris: Seuil.

Martelli, F. (1982) 'Reazione antiagostiniana nelle historiae di Orosio', *RSA* 12: 217–39.

Martínez Cavero, P. (1994) 'Virgilio y la historia apologética de Orosio', in *VIII congreso español de estudios clásicos.* Madrid: Ediciones clásicas: ii.745–51.

——(2002) *El pensamiento histórico y antropológico de Orosio* (Antigüedad y cristianismo 19). Murcia, Universidad de Murcia: Servicio de Publicaciones.

——Beltrán Corbalán, D., González Fernández, R. (1999) 'El "Commonitorium" de Orosio: traducción y comentario', *Faventia* 21: 65–83.

Marzullo, B. (1990–1991) 'La vita e le opere di Orosio nel contesto delle controversie teologiche ed ereticali del suo tempo', *Miscellanea di studi storici* 8: 49–67.

Maslakov, G. (1984) 'Valerius Maximus and Roman historiography. A study of the exempla tradition', *ANRW* II.32.1: 437–96.

Mastrangelo, M. (2008) *Prudentius. The Roman Self in Late Antiquity.* Baltimore: Johns Hopkins University Press.

Matthews, J. (1986) 'Ammianus and the eternity of Rome', in *The Inheritance of Historiography*, eds. C. Holdsworth and P. Wiseman. Exeter, Exeter: University Press: 17–29.

——(1989) *The Roman Empire of Ammianus.* London: Duckworth.

Mazza, M. (1999) *Il vero e l'immaginato. Profezia, narrativa e storiografia nel mondo romano.* Rome: Jouvence.

Meister, K. (1975) *Historische Kritik bei Polybios.* Wiesbaden: Steiner.

Mellor, R. (1993) *Tacitus.* London: Routledge.

Merrills, A.H. (2005) *History and Geography in Late Antiquity* (Cambridge Studies in Medieval Life and Thought. Series 4, 64). Cambridge: Cambridge University Press.

Mir, J.M. (1978) 'Orosio y los últimos tiempos del imperio', *Helmantica* 19: 383–97.

Moles, J.L. (1993) 'Truth and untruth in Herodotus and Thucydides', in Gill and Wiseman 1993: 88–121.

Mommsen, T. (1959a) 'St. Augustine and the Christian idea of progress: The background of the City of God', in Id., *Medieval and Renaissance studies.* Ithaca: Cornell University Press: 265–98.

——(1959b) 'Orosius and Augustine', in Id., *Medieval and Renaissance studies.* Ithaca: Cornell University Press: 325–48.

Moreschini, C. (2004) '"Paganus pervicacissimus": religione e "filosofia" in Claudiano', in Ehlers, Felgentreu and Wheeler 2004: 57–77.

Morgan, J.R. (1993) 'Make-believe and make believe: The fictionality of the Greek Novels', in Gill and Wiseman 1993: 175–229.

Mörner, T von (1844) *De Orosii vita eiusque historiarum libris septem adversus paganos.* Diss.: Berlin.

Mratschek, S. (2007) 'Et ne quid coturni terribilis fabulae relinquerent intemptatum . . . (Amm. Marc. 28.6.29). Die Göttin der Gerechtigkeit und der Comes Romanus', in den Boeft, Drijvers, and Teitler 2007: 245–70.

Mueller, H.-F. (2005) 'Orosius and the spectacle of roman religious defeat', in *Cynigfiliana. Essays in Classics, Comparative Literature and Philosophy Presented to Professor Roy Arthur Swanson*, ed. C.M. Schroeder. New York: Peter Lang, 122–36.

Mulder, H.A. (1926) *Phaenomenologischphilosophische Studiën over Orosius' Historiae adversus paganos*. Schiedam.

Myers, S. E. (2006) 'Revisiting preliminary issues in the "Acts of Thomas"', *Apocrypha* 17: 95–112.

Nelson, L.H. and Nelson, C. A. S. (1977) 'Orosius' commentary on the fall of Roman Spain', *CF* 31: 85–104.

Nichtweiss, B. (1992) *Erik Peterson. Neue Sicht auf leben und Werk*. Freiburg, Herder.

Nicolai, R. (1992) *La storiografia nell'educazione antica*. Pisa: Giardini.

O'Daly, G. (1999a) *Augustine's City of God. A Reader's Guide*. Oxford: Oxford University Press.

——(1999b) 'Thinking through history. Augustine's method in the City of God and its Ciceronian dimension', in Vessey, Pollman, and Fitzgerald 1999: 4–57.

Oliensis, E. (1998) *Horace and the Rhetoric of Authority*. Cambridge: Cambridge University Press.

Opelt, I. (1961) 'Augustustheologie und Augustustypologie', *JbAC* 4: 44–57.

Pardini, A. (1988) 'Una fonte perduta di Orosio? (Oros. Hist. I,21,1–3)', *Orpheus* 9: 332–7.

Partoens, G. (2000) 'The influence of the historian Florus on Prudentius' *libri contra Symmachum*', *AncSoc* 30: 319–30.

Paschoud, F. (1967) *Roma aeterna. Etudes sur le patriotisme romain dans l'occident latin à l'époque des grandes invasions*. Rome: Institut suisse de Rome.

——(1975) *Cinq études sur Zosime*. Paris: Les Belles Lettres.

——(1980) 'La polemica provvidenzialistica di Orosio', in *La storiografia ecclesiastica nella tarda antichità*. Messina, s.n.: 113–33.

——(1989) 'Se non è vero, è ben trovato: tradition littéraire et vérité chez Ammien Marcellin', *Chiron* 19: 37–54.

——(1992) 'Valentinien travesti, ou: De la malignité d'Ammmien', in den Boeft and den Hengst 1992: 67–84.

——(1995) 'Mendacii splendor: formes d'entrée en matière et protestations de véridicité dans la littérature de fiction', *Latomus* 54: 262–78.

——(1997) 'L' "inventio" dans l' "Histoire Auguste"', *Cassiodorus* 3: 117–30.

——(2004) 'Ammien 31.16.9: une recusatio?', *REL* 82: 238–48.

——(2005) 'Biographie und Panegyrik: wie spricht man vom lebenden Kaiser', in *Biographie und Prosopographie*, ed. K. Voessing. Stuttgart: Steiner: 103–18.

Pédech, P. (1989) *Trois historiens méconnus: Théopompe, Duris, Phylarque.* Paris: Les Belles Lettres.

Pelikan-Pittinger, M.R. (2008) *Contested Triumph. Politics, Pageantry, and Performance in Livy's Republican Rome.* Berkeley: University of California Press.

Pernot, L. (1993) *La rhétorique de l'éloge dans le monde gréco-romain* (Collection des études augustiniennes. Série Antiquité 137–8), 2 Vols. Paris: Institut des Etudes augustiniennes.

Peter: H. (1911) *Wahrheit und Kunst: Geschichtschreibung und Plagiat im klassischen Altertum.* Leipzig: Teubner.

Peterson, E. (1935) *Der Monotheismus als politisches Problem.* Leipzig: Hegner.

Pilhofer, P. (1990) *Presbyteron kreitton: Der Altersbeweis der jüdischen und christlichen Apologeten und seine Vorgeschichte* (Wissenschaftliche Untersuchungen zur Neuen testament. 2. Reihe 39). Tübingen: Mohr Siebeck.

Platnauer, M. (1956) *Claudian. Volume 2* (Loeb Classical Library). Cambridge, MA, and London: Heinemann.

Pohl, W. (2008) 'Rome and the Barbarians in the Fifth Century', *AntTard* 16: 93–101.

Polichetti, A. (2000) *Le 'historiae' di Orosio e la 'storiografia ecclesiastica' occidentale (311–417 d.C.).* Naples: Edizioni scientifiche italiane.

Polleichtner, W. (2003) 'Das "senatus consultum de Cn. Pisone patre" und Tacitus' Bericht vom Prozess gegen Piso', *Philologus* 147: 289–306.

Pomian, K. (1999) *Sur l'histoire.* Paris: Gallimard.

Press, G.A. (1982) *The Development of the Idea of History in Antiquity.* Kingston: McGill-Queen's University Press.

Rábade Navarro, M.A. (1991) 'Historiadores y poetas citados en las Historias de Orosio: Livio y Tácito, Virgilio y Lucano', *Fortunatae* 2: 277–86.

Rebenich, S. (1992) 'Der heilige Hieronymus und die Geschichte: zur Funktion der Exempla in seinen Briefen', *RQA* 87: 29–46.

——(1997) 'Historical prose', in *Handbook of Classical Rhetoric in the Hellenistic Period. 330 BC–AD 400*, ed. S. Porter. Leiden: Brill: 265–337.

Rees, R. (2002) *Layers of Loyalty in Latin Panegyric AD 289–307.* Oxford, Oxford University Press.

——(ed.) (2004) *Romane memento. Vergil in the fourth century.* London: Duckworth.

Riché, P. (2003) *Henri Irénée Marrou, historien engagé.* Paris: Le Cerf.

Riess, W. (2003) 'Die Rede des Claudius über das "ius honorum" der gallischen Notablen: Forschungsstand und Perspektiven', *REA* 105: 211–49.

Rist, J. (1994) *Augustine. Ancient Thought Baptized.* Cambridge: Cambridge University Press.

Roberto, U. (2006) 'Julius Africanus und die Tradition der hellenistischen Universalgeschichte', in Wallraff 2006: 3–16.

Roberts, M. (1989) *The Jeweled Style. Poetry and Poetics in Late Antiquity.* Ithaca: Cornell University Press.

Roberts, M. (2001) 'Rome personified, Rome epitomized: representations of Rome in the poetry of the early fifth century', *AJPh* 122: 533–65.

Rogerson, A. (2002) 'Dazzling likeness: seeing ekphrasis in Aeneid 10', *Ramus* 31: 51–72.

Rohrbacher, D. (2002) *The Historians of Late Antiquity.* London: Routledge.

Rosen, K. (1970) *Studien zur Darstellungskunst und Glaubwürdigkeit des Ammianus Marcellinus.* Bonn: Habelt.

——(1982) *Ammianus Marcellinus.* Darmstadt: Wissenschaftliche Buchgesellschaft.

Russell, D. (1983) *Greek Declamation.* Cambridge: Cambridge University Press.

Sabbah, G. (1978) *La méthode d'Ammien Marcellin. Recherches sur la construction du discours historique dans les* res gestae (Collection d'Études anciennes). Paris: Les Belles Lettres.

Salamito, J.-M. (2005). *Les virtuoses et la multitude. Aspects sociaux de la controverse entre Augustin et les pélagiens.* Grenoble: Millon.

Salvo, D. (2008) 'La Sicilia e la Spagna nelle storie di Paolo Orosio', in *Relaciones interculturales en el mediterráneo antiguo: Sicilia e Iberia*, eds. P. Annello and J. Martínez-Pinna: Málaga and Palermo: Centro de Ediciones de la Diputación de Málaga, Servicio de Publicaciones and Università degli studi di Palermo: 233–43.

Salzman, M.R. (2010) 'Ambrose and the usurpation of Arbogastes and Eugenius: Reflections on pagan-Christian conflict narratives', *JECS* 18: 191–213.

Sanchez, S.J.G. (2009) *Priscillien, un chrétien non-conformiste* (Théologie historique 120). Paris: Beauchesne.

Santini, C. (1978) 'L' "Adversum paganos" di Orosio e la tradizione manoscritta del "breviarium" di Eutropio', *Giornale italiano di filologia* N.S. 9: 79–91.

Santoro L'Hoir, F. (2006) *Tragedy, Rhetoric and the Historiography of Tacitus' Annales.* Ann Arbor: University of Michigan Press.

Scheller, P. (1911) *De hellenistica historiae conscribenda arte.* Diss.: Leipzig.

Schepens, G. (1975) 'ἔμφασις und ἐνάργεια in Polybios' Geschichtstheorie', *RSA* 5: 185–200.

——(1980) 'Polemic and methodology in Polybius' Book XII', in *Purposes of History: Studies in Greek Historiography from the 4th to the 2nd Centuries B.C.: Proceedings of the International Colloquium Leuven, 24–26 May 1988* (Studia hellenistica 30), eds. H. Verdin, G. Schepens, and E. de Keyzer. Leuven, s.n.: 39–61.

Schlumberger, J.A. (1974) *Die Epitome de Caesaribus. Untersuchungen zur heidnischen Geschichtsschreibung des 4. Jahrhunderts n. Chr.* (Vestigia. Beiträge zur Alten Geschichte 18). Munich: Beck.

Schmale, F.-J. (1985) *Funktion und Formen mittelalterlicher Geschichtsschreibung: eine Einführung*. Darmstadt: Wissenschaftliche Buchgesellschaft.

Schmidt, P.L. (1968) *Iulius Obsequens und das Problem der Livius-Epitome: ein Beitrag zur Geschichte der lateinischen Prodigienliteratur*. Wiesbaden: Steiner.

——(1988) 'Zu den Epochen der spätantiken lateinischen Historiographie', *Philologus* 132: 86–100.

——(1989) 'Historiographie', in *Restauration und Erneuerung. Die lateinische Literatur von 284 bis 374 n. Chr.*, ed. R. Herzog. Munich: Beck: 173–211.

Schmitz, T. (1997) *Bildung und Macht: zur sozialen und politischen Funktion der zweiten Sophistik in der griechischen Welt der Kaiserzeit* (Zetemata 97). Munich: Beck.

Schneiderhan, A. (1921) *Die Exempla bei Hieronymus*. Diss.: Munich.

Schöndorf, K.A. (1952) *Die Geschichtstheologie des Orosius*. Munich, s.n.

Schott, J. (2007) 'Heresiology as universal history in Epiphanius' Panarion', *ZAC* 10: 546–63.

——(2008) *Christianity, Empire, and the Making of Religion in Late Antiquity*. Philadelphia: University of Pennsylvania Press.

Schrijvers, P. (1982) 'Invention, imagination, et théorie des émotions chez Cicéron et Quintilien', in *ACTUS. Studies in Honour of H.L.W. Nelson*, eds. J. den Boeft and A.H.M. Kessels. Utrecht: Instituut voor klassieke Talen: 395–408.

Schwartz, E. (1897) 'Die Berichte über die Catilinarische Verschwörung', *Hermes* 32: 554–608.

——(1900) 'Kallisthenes' Hellenika', *Hermes* 35: 107–30.

——(1909) 'Die Zeit des Ephoros', *Hermes* 44: 481–502.

Scourfield, J.H.D. (ed.) (2007) *Texts and Culture in Late Antiquity. Inheritance, Authority, and Change*. Swansea: Classical Press of Wales.

Sebesta, J.L. (1980) 'Claudian's credo. The de salvatore', *CB* 56: 33–6.

Seeck, O. and Veith, G. (1913) 'Die Schlacht am Frigidus', *Klio* 13: 451–67.

Seel, O. (1934) 'Die justinischen Handschriftenklassen und ihr Verhältnis zu Orosius, I', *SIFC* 11: 255–88.

——(1935) 'Die justinische Handschriftenklassen und ihr Verhältnis zu Orosius, II', *SIFC* 12: 5–40.

Sehlmeyer, M. (2004) *Origo gentis romanae* (Texte zur Forschung). Darmstadt: Wissenschaftliche Buchgesellschaft.

——(2009) *Geschichtsbilder für Pagane und Christen. Res Romanae in den spätantiken Breviarien* (Beiträge zur Altertumskunde 272). Berlin and New York: Walter de Gruyter.

Shanzer, D. (1991) 'Arcanum Varronis iter. Licentius's Verse Epistle to Augustine', *REAug* 37: 110–43.

Shumate, N. (1997) 'Compulsary pretense and the "theatricalisation of experience" in Tacitus', in *Studies in Latin Literature and Roman History Vol. 8* (Collection Latomus 239), ed. C. Deroux. Brussels: Société des Etudes latines: 364–403.

Sirinelli, J. (1961) *Les vues historiques d'Eusèbe de Césarée durant la période prénicéenne.* Paris: Macon.

——and des Places, E. (1974) *Eusèbe de Césarée. La préparation évangélique. Introduction générale. Livre I* (Sources chrétiennes 206). Paris: Le Cerf.

Skidmore, C. (1996) *Practical Ethics for Roman Gentlemen. The Work of Valerius Maximus.* Exeter: Exeter University Press.

Sordi, M. (2003) 'Il problema della successione degli imperi tra Pompeo Trogo e Orosio', in *La successione degli imperi e delle egemonie nelle relazioni internazionali*, eds. D. Foraboschi and S.M. Pizzetti. Milan: Unicopli: 77–84.

Spät, E. (1998) 'The Commonitorium of Orosius on the teachings of the Priscillianists', *AAHung* 38: 357–79.

Straub, J. (1972a) 'Christliche Geschichtspologetik in der Krisis des römischen Reiches', in Id., *Regeneratio imperii.* Darmstadt: Wissenschaftliche Buchgesellschaft: 240–71.

——(1972b) 'Augustins Sorge um die Regeneratio imperii', in Id., *Regeneratio imperii.* Darmstadt: Wissenschaftliche Buchgesellschaft: 271–95.

——(1972c) 'Romanus et christianus . . . Die gotische Landnahme im Spiegel der christlichen Geschichtsapologetik', in Id., *Regeneratio imperii.* Darmstadt: Wissenschaftliche Buchgesellschaft: 296–303.

Suerbaum, W. (1997) art. Ennius, in *Der Neue Pauly* 3: 1040–6.

Svennung, J. (1922) *Orosiana. Syntaktische, semasiologische und kritische Studien zu Orosius.* Uppsala: Appelberg.

Swain, B. (2010) 'Jordanes and Vergil: A case study of intertextuality and the Getica', *CQ* 60: 243–9.

Swain, J.W. (1940) 'The theory of four monarchies. Opposition history under the Roman Empire', *CPh* 25: 1–2.

Swain, S. (1996) *Hellenism and Empire. Language, Classicism, and Power in the Greek World, AD 50–250.* Oxford: Oxford University Press.

Swift, L.J. (1986) 'Defining gloria in St Augustine's City of God', in *Diakonia. Studies in Honor of R.T. Meyer*, ed. T. Halton. Washington: Catholic University of America Press: 133–44.

——(1987) 'Pagan and Christian heroes in Augustine's City of God', *Augustinianum* 27: 509–22.

Syme, R. (1988) 'The date of Justin and the discovery of Trogus', *Historia* 37: 358–71.

Szidat, J. (1992) 'Ammian und die historische Realität', in den Boeft and den Hengst 1992: 107–16.

Tabacco, R. (1990) 'L'itinerarium Alexandri. Analisi del proemio', in *La storiografia latina del IV secolo*, ed. L. Lana. Firenze: Olschki: 147–62.

——(2000) *Itinerarium Alexandri. Testo, apparato critico, introduzione, traduzione e commento*. Turin: Gheroni.

Talbert, R. J. A. (1999) 'Tacitus and the senatus consultum de Cn. Pisone Patre', *AJPh* 120: 89–97.

Tanner, R.G. (1989) 'The historical method of Sulpicius Severus', *Studia Patristica* 19: 106–10.

Tanz, S. (1983) 'Orosius im Spannungsfeld zwischen Eusebius von Caesarea und Augustin', *Klio* 65: 337–46.

Thielman, F.S. (1987) 'Another look at the eschatology of Eusebius of Caesarea', *VChr* 41: 226–37.

Timpe, D. (2001) *Römische Geschichte und Heilsgeschichte*. Berlin: Walter de Gruyter.

Tornau, C. (2006) *Zwischen Rhetorik und Philosophie. Augustins Argumentationstechnik in De civitate Dei und ihr Bildungsgeschichtlicher Hintergrund* (Untersuchungen zur antiken Literatur und Geschichte 82). Berlin and New York: Walter de Gruyter.

Torres Rodríguez, C. (1985) *Paulo Orosio, su vida y sus obres*. Santiago: Fundacion 'Pedro Barrie de la Maza Conde de Fenosa'.

Trieber, C. (1892) 'Die Idee der vier Weltreiche', *Hermes* 27: 321–44.

Trout, D. (1994) 'Re-textualizing Lucretia: Cultural subversion in the City of God', *JECS* 1: 53–70.

——(1999) *Paulinus of Nola. Life, Letters, and Poems*. Berkeley: University of California Press.

Ulrich, J. (1999) *Euseb von Caesarea und die Juden. Studien zur Rolle der Juden in der Theologie des Eusebius von Caesarea* (Patristische Texte und Untersuchungen 49). Berlin and New York: Walter de Gruyter.

van Andel, G.K. (1976) *The Christian Concept of History in the Chronicle of Sulpicius Severus*. Amsterdam: Gieben.

Vanderspoel, J. (1986) 'Claudian, Christ and the cult of the saints', *CQ* 36: 244–55.

Van Hoof, L. (2010a) *Plutarch's Practical Ethics. The Social Dynamics of Philosophy*. Oxford: Oxford University Press.

——(2010b) 'Greek Rhetoric and the Later Roman Empire. The "bubble" of the "Third Sophistic"', *AntTard* 18: 211–24.

Van Nuffelen, P. (2004a) *Un héritage de paix et de piété. Étude sur les Histoires ecclésiastiques de Socrate et de Sozomène* (Orientalia lovaniensia analecta 142). Leuven: Peeters.

——(2004b) 'The unstained rule of Theodosius II: A late antique panegyrical topos and moral concern', in *Imago Virtutis* (Collection des Études classiques), eds. T. van Houdt e.a. Leuven: Peeters: 229–56.

Van Nuffelen, P. (2010) 'Theology vs. genre? Tradition as universal historiography in Late Antiquity', in Liddel and Fear 2010: 190–212.

——(forthcoming) 'Olympiodorus of Thebes and eastern triumphalism' in *Theodosius II : The Reformation of the Roman Empire in Late Antiquity*, ed. C. Kelly. Cambridge: Cambridge University Press.

Vaz de Carvalho, C. (1955) 'Dependerá S. Agostinho de Paulo Orosio?', *Revista Portuguese de filosofía* 2: 142–53.

Vessey, M. (1998) 'The Demise of the Christian writer and the remaking of "Late Antiquity": From H.-I. Marrou's Saint Augustine (1938) to Peter Brown's holy man (1983)', JECS 6, 377–411.

——Pollman, K., and Fitzgerald, A.D. (eds.) (1999) *History, Apocalypse, and the Secular Imagination. New Essays on Augustine's City of God*. Bowling Green OH: Villanova University Press.

Veyne, P. (1990) 'La providence stoïcienne intervient-elle dans l'histoire?', *Latomus* 49: 553–74.

Vilella, J. (2000) 'Biografía critica de Orosio', *JbAC* 43: 94–121.

Vitale-Brovarone, A. (1980) 'Persuasione e narrazione. L'exemplum fra due retoriche (VI-XII sec.)', *MEFRM* 92: 87–112.

Vittinghoff, F. (1964) 'Zum geschichtlichen Selbstverstandnis der Spatantike', *HZ* 198: 519–74.

Walbank, F.W. (1943) 'Polybius on the Roman constitution', *CQ 37*: 73–89.

——(1955) 'Tragic history. A reconsideration', *BICS* 2: 4–14.

——(1960) 'History and tragedy', *Historia* 9: 216–34.

——(1962) 'Polemic in Polybius', *JRS* 52: 1–12.

——(2002a) 'Profit or amusement: Some thoughts on the motives of Hellenistic historians', in Id., *Polybius, Rome and the Hellenistic World*. Cambridge: Cambridge University Press: 231–41.

——(2002b) 'A Greek looks at Rome: Polybius VI', in Id., *Polybius, Rome and the Hellenistic World*. Cambridge: Cambridge University Press: 277–92.

Walker, A.D. (1993) 'Enargeia and the spectator in Greek historiography', *TAPhA* 123: 353–77.

Wallraff, M. (2004) 'Protologie und Eschatologie als Horizonte der Kirchengeschichte? Das Erbe christlicher Universalgeschichte', in *Historiographie und Theologie*, eds W. Kinzig e.a. Leipzig: Evangelisches Verlagshaus: 153–67.

——(2005) 'Von der antiken Historie zur mittelalterlichen Chronik', in *Welt-Zeit. Christliche Weltchronistik aus zwei Jahrtausenden in Beständen der Thüringer Universitäts- und Landesbibliothek Jena*, ed. M. Wallraff. Berlin and New York: Walter de Gruyter: 1–16.

——(ed.) (2006) *Julius Africanus und die christliche Weltchronistik* (Texte und Untersuchungen zur Geschichte der altchristlichen Literatur 157). Berlin and New York: Walter de Gruyter.

Walter, U. (2002) 'Geschichte als Lebensmacht im republikanischen Rom', *GWU* 53: 326–39.

Ward-Perkins, B. (2005) *The Fall of Rome and the End of Civilization*. Oxford, Oxford University Press.

Webb, R. (2009) *Ekphrasis, Imagination and Persuasion in Ancient Rhetorical Thought and Practice*. Aldershot: Ashgate.

Werner, K.F. (1987) 'Gott, Herrscher, Historiograph. Der Geschichtsschreiber als Interpret des Wirkens Gottes in der Welt und Ratgeber der Könige (4. Bis 12. Jahrhundert)', in *Deus qui mutat tempora. Menschen und Institutionen im Wandel des Mittelalters. Festschrift Alfons Becker zu seinem fünfundsechzigsten Geburtstag*, eds. E.-D. Hehl, H. Seibert, and F. Staab. Sigmaringen: Thorbecke: 1–31.

Whitby, M. (ed.) (1998) *The Propaganda of Power: The Role of Panegyric in Late Antiquity* (Mnemosyne Supplements 183). Leiden, Brill.

White, H. (1978) *The Content of the Form. Discourse and Historical Representation*. Baltimore: Johns Hopkins University Press.

Whitmarsh, T. (2001) *Greek Literature and the Roman Empire. The Politics of Imitation*. Oxford: Oxford University Press.

Wickham, C. (2004) *Framing the Early Middle Ages: Europe and the Mediterranean 400–800*. Oxford: Oxford University Press.

Winkelmann, F. (1992) 'Grundproblemen christlicher Historiographie in ihrer Frühphase (Eusebios von Kaisareia und Orosius)', *JöByz* 42: 13–28.

Wirth, G. (1997) 'Rome and its Germanic Partners in the Fourth Century', in *Kingdoms of the Empire. The Integration of Barbarians in Late Antiquity* (The Transformation of the Roman World. Volume 1), ed. W. Pohl. Leiden: Brill: 13–55.

Wiseman, T.P. (1979) *Clio's Cosmetics: Three Studies in Greco-Roman Literature*. Leicester: Leicester University Press.

——(1993) 'Lying historians: Seven types of mendacity', in Gill and Wiseman 1993: 122–46.

——(1994) *Historiography and Imagination: Eight Essays on Roman Culture*. Exeter: Exeter University Press.

——(1995) *Remus. A Roman Myth*. Cambridge: Cambridge University Press.

Wittchow, F. (2001) *Exemplarisches Erzählen bei Ammianus Marcellinus: Episode, Exemplum, Anekdote* (Beiträge zur Altertumskunde 144). Munich: Saur.

Wittgenstein, L. (1961) *Tractatus Logico-Philosophicus*. London: Routledge.

Woodman, A.J. (1988) *Rhetoric in Classical Historiography: Four Studies*. London: Croom-Helm.

Woodman, A.J. (1998) *Tacitus Reviewed*. Oxford: Oxford University Press.

Wotke, F. (1939) art. 'Orosius', in RE 19, 1185–95.

Yardley, Y.C. (1994) *Justin. Epitome of the Phillipic History of Pompeius Trogus*. Atlanta: Society for Biblical Studies.

——(2003) *Justin and Pompeius Trogus. A Study of the Language of Justin's Epitome of Trogus*. Toronto: University of Toronto Press.

Yarrow, L. (2006) *Historiography at the End of the Republic. Provincial Perspectives on Roman Rule*. Oxford: Oxford University Press.

Zakai, A. and Mali, A. (1992–3) 'Time, history and eschatology. Ecclesiastical history from Eusebius to Augustine', *Journal of Religious History* 17: 393–417.

Zangara, A. (2004) 'Mettre en images le passé: l'ambiguïté et l'efficacité de l'"enargeia" dans le récit historique', *Métis* 2: 251–72.

Zangemeister, K. (1877) 'Die Chorographie des Orosius', in *Commentationes philologae in honorem Th. Mommseni*. Berlin, s.n.: 715–38.

Zangemeister, C. (1882) *Pauli Orosii Historiarum adversum paganos libri VII, accedit eiusdem liber apologeticus* (Corpus scriptorum ecclesiasticorum latinorum 5). Vienna: Hoelder, Pichler and Tempsky.

Zanker, G. (1981) 'Enargeia in the ancient criticism of poetry', *RhM* 124: 297–311.

Zecchini, G. (2003) 'Latin historiography: Jerome, Orosius, and the Western Chronicles', in Marasco 2003: 317–45.

Index of Sources

Subject Index

DATE DUE
